CRAN
DK 63.3 .
C. 1
SHULMAN,
STALIN'S

D0224030

# STALIN'S
# FOREIGN POLICY
# REAPPRAISED

A Westview Encore Edition

# STALIN'S FOREIGN POLICY REAPPRAISED

*Marshall D. Shulman*

Westview Press / Boulder and London

F K C C. LIBRARY

This is **A Westview Encore Edition** manufactured on our own premises using equipment and methods that allow us to reissue and keep in stock specialized books that have been allowed to go out of print. This book is printed on acid-free paper and bound in softcovers that carry the highest rating of the National Association of State Textbook Administrators (NASTA), in consultation with the Association of American Publishers (AAP) and The Book Manufacturers' Institute (BMI).

All rights reserved. No part of this publication may be reproduced or transmitted in any form or by any means, electronic or mechanical, including photocopy, recording, or any information storage and retrieval system, without permission in writing from the publisher.

Copyright © 1985 by Marshall D. Shulman

Published in 1985 in the United States of America by Westview Press; Frederick A. Praeger, Publisher; 5500 Central Avenue, Boulder, Colorado 80301

First published in 1963 by Harvard University Press

Library of Congress Catalog Card Number: 85-51143
ISBN 0-8133-7098-1

Printed and bound in the United States of America
6    5    4    3    2    1

60-877-101

# ACKNOWLEDGMENTS

It seems to me remarkable how much a study like this represents a community enterprise. I have forgotten how many supporting troops are supposed to be required to keep one soldier in the field, but I am sure the proportions are not less in mounting one scholar at the point of communion with his typewriter. My words of appreciation are intended as a testimony to the public and private generosity which sustains such efforts as these. And by generosity I refer not only to material support but also to the largeness of spirit that is expressed in the sharing of knowledge and in the giving of one's self.

In this sense particularly I welcome an opportunity to express publicly my gratitude to Professor Philip E. Mosely of Columbia University, who has been an inspiring example both as a teacher and a friend.

I am greatly indebted to the Russian Research Center at Harvard University and to its extraordinary series of directors, Clyde Kluckhohn, William L. Langer, and Merle Fainsod, for support and encouragement. To the administrative mainstay of that institution, Mrs. Helen W. Parsons, I am under no less obligation for the transfusions from her New England spirit during the eight years, off and on, in which this book was written. Research abroad was made possible by a Rockefeller Public Service Award and by grants from the Ford Foundation and the Inter-University Committee on Travel Grants. My thanks also to the Centre de Documentation of the Fondation National des Sciences Politiques, Paris, for the use of its files.

During a year's stay with the RAND Corporation, I benefited greatly from the opportunity to carry forward this study in a stimulating environment and from the helpful counsel and criticism of my colleagues, especially Paul Kecskemeti, Alexander L. George,

Alice Langley Hsieh, Allen Whiting, Donald S. Zagoria, Oleg Hoeffding, Nancy Nimitz, Andrew Marshall, Joseph Loftus, and Herbert Dinerstein.

The incomparable resources and helpful spirit of Harvard's Widener Library were indispensable in the preparation of this book, and I express warm thanks to its Director and Associate Director, Paul Buck and Douglas Bryant.

Two old friends, Jacques Katel and Robert Kleiman, contributed practical assistance and long evenings of political discourse, a form of pleasure which I regard as no less practical. Among the many others who gave valued assistance, particularly in the form of interviews, some are listed in the bibliographical note. I also wish to acknowledge the resourceful research assistance of Mrs. Ruth Seidman.

Finally, I have been impressed and touched by the creative contribution of Thomas J. Wilson, Director of Harvard University Press, and deeply appreciative of the intelligent editing provided by Mrs. Joyce Lebowitz.

March 1963                                                          M.D.S.

# CONTENTS

# STALIN'S
# FOREIGN POLICY
# REAPPRAISED

# INTRODUCTION TO THE ARGUMENT

THE prevailing interpretation of recent Soviet foreign policy emphasizes Stalin's death as the great watershed event, from which is charted the shift toward a more flexible policy, broadly known by the term "peaceful coexistence." Although this emphasis properly draws attention to the new departures of the more recent period and to the dynamic character of Soviet policy, it gives insufficient attention to significant changes in outlook and behavior which began to be manifested before the death of Stalin. The issue is not merely one of correctly dating the beginning of a trend; it is, rather, the deepening of our understanding of the forces which shape Soviet foreign policy.

From the end of the Berlin blockade in 1949 to the Nineteenth Congress of the Communist Party of the Soviet Union in October 1952, there were unmistakable signs of a marked evolution in the Soviet strategic outlook toward Western Europe, of a groping toward a more effective adaptation to the new political and technological facts of life. This, in essence, is the argument to which the following pages are addressed.

*Argument*

In looking back at this period now, we have the advantage of more than a decade of historical perspective. This is scarcely enough to increase the pulse rate of diplomatic historians in less arcane fields, perhaps, but, given the nature of our subject, the decade that has passed affords extraordinary retrospective insights. Partly this owes to the rapidity with which the whole character of international politics has been changing in the interval; but our insights have also been greatly enriched by the remembrance of things past of which the Communist world has been unburdening itself.

The point I should like to emphasize is that an analysis of Soviet policy during the closing years of Stalin's life from the perspective of the present calls into question many common assumptions about the character of that policy. If we bring to bear upon this analysis the information now available about the rapidly changing military technology of the period, it becomes clearer to us than it was at the time that the Soviet leadership showed a profound grasp of the nature of the new weapons, that it accepted with some anxiety a period of vulnerability while concentrating its tremendous energies upon the research and development which were intended to produce a favorable shift in the balance of power. This, I believe, was the essential consideration governing Soviet foreign political behavior during the period of our study. Further, if we take into account the rapid economic and social transformations which were beginning to gather momentum in the advanced industrial parts of the world at the time, we are now better able to understand how and why Soviet policy was to become increasingly concerned with power-bloc politics and less with the revolutionary awakening of a proletariat that was busy discovering the joys of the installment plan. To this must be added another fundamental upheaval, the earth-shaking eruption of Asian nationalism, at a time when Africa and other undeveloped areas were also beginning to stir. Although the Russians had predicted this very cataclysm, it came with a speed and in a form for which the Russians were almost as unprepared as we. The consequence, as we shall see, was a somewhat unsteady shifting of attention between Europe and Asia. Finally, as one must never forget in dealing with foreign policy, there was the domestic side of things. In the face of the stirrings in Soviet society and the gear-crunching contradictions between simple theory and complex reality, there is a sense in which it may be said that Stalin unwittingly and probably involuntarily began the tide of revisionism which swept in like a deluge after him. Against the backdrop of these events, the whole pattern of Soviet foreign policy looks somewhat different now from what it did to contemporary observers.

One general characteristic of Soviet policy which becomes more evident when the study is approached in this way is the largely rational responsiveness of Soviet policy to changes in the world environment, and particularly to changes in power relationships. This is a departure from those familiar interpretations of Soviet policy which emphasize enigmatic or occult characteristics or the psychopathology of Soviet leaders. Not that we know all we need to know; compared to the study of diplomatic history, where the materials are relatively more accessible, the gaps in our knowledge here force upon us an unconventional scholarship. Nevertheless, this approach to Soviet behavior as an explicable human phenomenon reveals patterns which bear some resemblance to what we know of human behavior elsewhere in the world.

To anticipate some objections, the word "rational" as I have just used it may require a word or two of further explanation. It does not mean freedom from error, as we know from our own experience. Nor does it mean that Soviet behavior is based upon the same perception or understanding of the world as ours. What it does mean is that, given the distinctive framework of analysis which seems to have shaped Soviet perceptions and anticipations in this period, there is a demonstrably rational relationship between Soviet behavior and changes in the world environment.

Among the practical consequences of this observation, there are two which I should like to mention briefly. The first is related to the chastening experience I have had in reading over the contemporary oracular explanations of the meaning of various developments in the Soviet Union during the period covered by this study, now more than a decade passed. While there is clearly something to be gained from the informed speculations of the Kremlinologists (providing they are expressed with the reservations they require), there is more to the study of Soviet foreign policy than can be derived from the moral or psychological dissection of Stalin and the reading of obscure portents of the goings-on within the Kremlin. Whatever may turn out to be the truth about the irascibility or senility of Stalin, or whatever may have been the shenanigans in the Politburo, the study of the behavior of the Soviet Union within a larger framework suggests a degree of rationality and responsiveness to outside conditions which, though in error at times, is not greatly less than what is found in foreign policy anywhere. Whether this means that Stalin was more lucid than he has been pictured, or whether there were other less-known forces at work in the determination of Soviet foreign policy, is indeed an interesting question.

Another consequence of this general approach is to heighten our awareness of the way in which our own actions have a bearing upon Soviet behavior. Again, this comes from having our attention directed beyond the element of whim in Soviet policy. Specifically, we shall observe how the modulations which begin to appear in Soviet policy in 1949–1952 are clearly related to the developing cohesion and strength of the Western alliance in the immediately preceding period and, conversely, how the potential weaknesses of that alliance invited various forms of militant or manipulative behavior.

There is another general characteristic of Soviet policy which is suggested by this analysis, not altogether novel but not always clearly understood. This has to do with the recurrent pattern of alternation between two marked syndromes of behavior — one essentially militant and direct, the other manipulative, flexible, and longer-term in perspective.[1]

Although the Communists also recognize the presence of these dual modes of behavior and describe them by the terms "Left" and "Right," the designations have become increasingly inadequate for analytical purposes. In the 1920s, Left connoted a revolutionary emphasis and Right meant a breathing spell. With time, the Left syndrome came to be marked typically by an overhanging consciousness of the inevitability of conflict, an emphasis upon those ideological aspects which deal with the class struggle and the necessity for revolutionary advance, a definite militancy of method, and a detachment of the Communist movement abroad from association with other elements of the national or international community. Conversely, the Right phase has come to be associated with "peaceful coexistence," flexibility of tactics, divisive exploitation of "contradictions" abroad, and collaboration with other groups, classes, or nations.

A functional classification of these modes may lead to some confusion, since each has been utilized for offensive and defensive purposes. The militant line of the Left may be used in some circumstances as a mode of revolutionary advance, but, during times when revolutionary opportunities seem distant, it has also been used to conserve Communist forces, to destabilize and undermine the status quo, or to force constraints upon the bourgeoisie. The broad alliances characteristic of the Right behavior have been used defensively, when the Soviet Union has felt itself threatened by hostile trends in the world, or offensively, when the Soviet leadership has thought it opportune to work with auxiliaries to open up avenues to power. During 1949–1952, we shall observe both functions of the broad-alliance policy: as an instrument for weakening the adversaries of the Soviet Union by exploiting their divisive vulnerabilities and as a form of leverage for maximizing Communist influence on the course of international politics.

The prime determinant in selecting the mode to be followed appears to lie in how the Soviet leadership assesses the historical character of the current period, as modified by domestic needs and the exigencies of factional disputes among the party leaders.[2] The operational significance of such terms as Left or Right in Communist usage cannot be assumed without reference to the context of the moment; in fact, both tend to be words of condemnation, since the speaker is by definition a "Centrist" who is likely to reserve his most vigorous denunciation for the tendency which he has in substance adopted. The pure Left position is condemned as unrealistic, adventurist, or sectarian because it tends to maximize risks and minimize opportunities. The pure Right position, on the other hand, is rejected as opportunistic because it leads to compromise, loss of muscularity in the movement, and dissipation of the revolutionary élan. The correct policy is always defined as neither Right nor Left, but as a judicious mixture of both elements, depending on circumstances. One source of confusion arises from the fact that these terms are used in discussing not only Soviet foreign policy, but also Soviet internal affairs and the conduct of the Communist movement abroad; and, although a mood of relaxation in international affairs has on some occasions coincided with a corresponding mood in Soviet domestic life, it has not been thought inconsistent to emphasize "peaceful coexistence" in foreign policy and strict ideological conformity at home. (As we shall see, this was the case at the time of the Nineteenth Congress.) The consistency is to be found in the purposes to which each mode is directed.

At this point it may be useful to add a word of caution about the uses of this analysis of recurrent elements in Soviet behavior. As we have seen, the terms Right and Left have become so overgrown with special meanings in Communist usage over the years, and so dependent upon the particular context in which they are used, that it becomes necessary for the analyst to use them with care and to define with precision the content of each policy he is describing. Further, in characterizing a period of Soviet foreign policy as belonging to one mode or another, there is a danger of being clearer than life itself if one expects to find the archetype of either phase, tidy and simple. Both tendencies have been present in some degree at all times since the beginning. What the analyst seeks to do, but not to overdo, is to identify the dominant tendency at any one time and the shifts in policy emphasis which make for the recurrent pattern in Soviet behavior. Finally, this form of alternation, although it clearly has something to do with the mechanism by which policies get revised in a totalitarian system, is not to be understood as stemming from some internally generated systole and diastole of the Soviet body politic. The analyst, if he happens to be interested in the quantification of human behavior, should not expect to find emerging on his drum chart the regular curves of a pulsing alternation. Since the determination of these choices involves a process of interaction with the events and circumstances of the outside world as these appear to the decision makers in Moscow, one cannot predict the duration or the amplitude or the direction of future cycles. However, this kind of analysis does provide a framework which helps us to interpret isolated data and to distinguish cyclical from evolutionary changes.

The purpose of this general discussion is to make more intelligible the argument that, in responding to a disadvantageous trend in its world power position in 1949–1952, the Soviet Union reintroduced tactical and ideological formulations that had been associated with earlier periods identified as "Right" in Soviet terminology. The first of these periods of "peaceful coexistence" came into being in 1921 in the face of critical domestic and foreign problems, and it was guided by Lenin's classic justification for tactical flexibility: "Left-Wing Communism: An Infantile Disorder," written in April 1920. Again, the period from the end of 1933 to the autumn of 1936 was one in which a broad-front Soviet foreign policy emerged. The central concern of the Soviet government was then with the rise of Nazism as a new form of German, if not international bourgeois, militarism. The militant policy which had been in force since 1928 had left the Soviet Union diplomatically isolated and relatively weak before a potential enemy or alliance of enemies. The need was for a period of intense concentration of resources on Soviet industrial and military capabilities and, at the same time, a collaboration with one section of the "imperialist world" against the other.

Again, after the lapse of the Nazi-Soviet Pact, Soviet policy turned essentially rightward during its wartime collaboration with the Allies. This period was marked by a muting of the revolutionary and sectarian aspects of the ideology and by a commitment to the temporary support of the Western bourgeois governments (a requirement of the defense of the Soviet homeland). After the war, when the militant pressures of Soviet policy in the 1946–1949 period had begun to arouse a remobilization of Western military forces, the Soviet leaders sought once again to return to a policy which would relax international tension and at the same time create opportunities for indirect advances. Thus, in the changes which we shall see emerging experimentally during the period 1949–1952, essentially the same circumstances prevailed as during the rightward shifts of 1921 and 1935 and, to some extent, during the wartime collaboration. In each case, an immediately adverse power relationship, combined with the anticipation of a more favorable prospect in the future, evoked a lengthened time perspective, a policy of indirection, maneuver, expedient alliances, manipulation of Western differences, and peaceful coexistence.

Despite the similarity of the Communist terminology, however, the rightward shift of the early 1950s was not wholly congruent with that of the earlier periods. One reason is that the earlier experiences had left a residual effect not only upon the Communists, but upon the socialists of Western Europe. In striving for a mass base in 1950–1952, the Communists did not repeat the 1935 effort to come to a formal agreement with socialist leaders. In part this may have reflected the unwillingness of the socialists to repeat the experiment after their previous disillusionment and, in part, the Communist desire to avoid the ideological cost of such an agreement. The development of the Peace Movement after 1949 was intended to enable the party to involve people of all classes everywhere in selected foreign-policy objectives, with less dilution of the character and program of the party itself.

Another and more fundamental reason for this evolution of the broad peaceful-coexistence policy was that the Soviet perception of the historical character of the period had begun to change. Significant steps were accordingly taken toward the continuing adaptation of Soviet ideology — Soviet ideas, terms of perception, structure of thought, strategy, and tactics — to an essentially nonrevolutionary reality. Or, to put it more precisely, to a reality in which the revolutionary impulse came from nationalism and from technology, not from the proletariat. As the Soviet leaders began to take the measure of the historical forces of the postwar world, they became aware that the policy which had served for defense, postponement, and consolidation, now appeared to have powerful offensive possibilities. Not proletarian revolutions, but a closer identification of Soviet interests with the historical forces of nationalism and economic, political, and social change — this became the preferred means for the further conversion of the world to socialism, as the Russians use the word, and the further ascendancy of Soviet power and influence.

This evolution was reinforced by the changing strategic relationships of the period. Although at a temporary disadvantage, the Soviet Union had become a leading power, with world-wide involvements and the prospect of great gains as a result of the disintegration of Western ties with the underdeveloped sections of the world. For all these reasons, the Right policy of the 1950s became less a retreat than a maneuver combining a short-term defense with a long-term mode of advance. Particularly in regard to Western Europe, Soviet energies were directed toward the interplay of politics between the power blocs rather than toward the promotion of social change. In the language of the Communist movement, the Soviet leadership began to perceive that "in present historical circumstances the struggle for peace is the key to the ultimate victory of socialism." This perspective was more clearly enunciated by Stalin's successors, but the underlying movement in this direction had become apparent by the time of the Nineteenth Party Congress in October 1952.

To understand the meaning of the formulations that were advanced at the Nineteenth Congress, it is necessary to work back to the events of the immediately preceding years. In Soviet practice it has often been the case that the formal enunciation of a course of action is but the final acknowledgment of the ascendancy of a policy after a period of experimental development, sometimes in contention with alternative policies. (In 1961, Mikoyan disclosed that the line advanced at the Twentieth Congress in 1956 had evolved through two years of thought and action beforehand.) In the case of the Nineteenth Congress, one could conceivably go back thirteen years to the previous congress, or five years to the first public mention of the prospective congress by Malenkov at the founding meeting of the Communist Information Bureau. My study, after a brief review of the earlier period, begins its detailed examination three and a half years before the congress, when the end of the Berlin blockade in the spring of 1949 initiated a new phase of experimentation in Soviet policy.

During these years, from 1949 to 1952, Soviet conduct toward Western Europe, though only a part of the totality of Soviet foreign policy, is for many reasons the most revealing part. It is sometimes argued in the West that, because of a measure of stability in Europe, the decisive theater of international politics has become the underdeveloped areas of Asia, Africa, and Latin America. Perhaps this will be true in time; it is doubtful if it is wholly true today, and it clearly was not the point of view of the Soviet leaders during the period of our inquiry. Soviet attention was directed first and foremost to the advanced industrial areas of the world, for here were to be found the immediately decisive questions of international politics. What was to be the fate of Germany: in which direction would its industrial goods flow? its politics? its military potential? Would the nations of Western Europe continue to develop with the United States a cohesive industrial and military bloc? These were the problems that dictated the central requirement for Soviet foreign policy: to fragment and diminish the power of the Western bloc.

The vast populations and the great resources of the underdeveloped world would of course become of enormous importance, but their chief significance then was found in the extent to which the crucial industrial areas of the world could be weakened by the subtraction of one or another part of the former colonial territories from the Western suzerainty.

The study of Soviet policy toward Western Europe in this period would be incomplete if it did not take account of the auxiliary arms of Communist diplomacy. Many of the doctrinal proclamations from Moscow become clear only when we see how they were applied in specific local situations. Stalin's exhortation to the foreign Communists at the Nineteenth Congress to "raise the banner of nationalism" takes on meaning when one observes the efforts of the French Communists to draw support from French nationalists of the Right for a common fight against West German rearmament. Or the directive force of an editorial in *Pravda* on the priority of the struggle for peace becomes more evident in watching the dilemma of a local Communist official in Western Europe who must decide whether to call a strike for higher wages against a factory owner who happens to be collaborating in the Peace Movement. From time to time, therefore, I shall turn from the account of Soviet diplomacy as such to observe two of the most interesting foreign-policy instrumentalities of this period: the Peace Movement and the French Communist Party.

The organized use of the peace symbol as an auxiliary means of enlisting middle-class and intellectual support for Soviet strategic purposes, for circumscribing the freedom of action of the Western governments and, in time, for developing a broad anti-imperialist coalition, is an essential part of the story of these years, and it has not received the attention it deserves.

Among the European Communists, it was the French who were the most important to the Soviet Union in this period. First of all, France was the keystone of the Western defense arch. From the middle of the war on, and especially in the Franco-Soviet Treaty of

1944, the Soviet Union strove to keep France from becoming the bridgehead of the Western alliance on the continent of Europe.[3] Then, the neuralgic susceptibilities of many Frenchmen to the revival of German power presented the Soviet Union with an opportunity for leverage not to be neglected. The potentialities for Communist action in the African and Southeast Asian territories of the French Union further added to the importance of the French party. Finally, the party consistently drew support during this period from approximately one quarter of the electorate, more than any other party in France; it held a dominant position in the trade-union movement; and its leadership displayed an unwavering if not embarrassing fidelity to Moscow and to Stalin personally. For these reasons, the French Communist Party was a reliable if not always useful instrument of Soviet diplomacy. Fortunately, the proceedings of the party are reasonably accessible to study, and we have the additional benefit of testimony from many former officials who have left the party or been expelled since the time of our concern.

# II

# THE VIEW FROM MOSCOW IN THE SPRING OF 1949

As THE year 1949 began, the Soviet leadership was confronted with one of those situations which it describes as a "shift in the relation of forces in the world." The shift in this case was clearly and massively adverse in its immediate effect. Trends were in motion which would by midyear bring Soviet influence to its lowest ebb in the entire postwar period. A radical change had taken place in the atmosphere of the West since the end of the war, driven by the growing conviction that the Soviet Union possessed both the militant capacity to overrun Western Europe and perhaps the intention of doing so. Speaking on the last day of March 1949, Winston Churchill bluntly laid the responsibility for the changed Western outlook upon the Russians themselves. Three years before, Churchill observed after his Iron Curtain speech at Fulton, Missouri, "many people . . . were startled and even shocked, [but] today there is a very different climate of opinion." [1] Thanks to the "harsh external pressure" of the Russians, he said, "unities and associations are being established by many nations throughout the free world with a speed and a reality which would not have been achieved perhaps for generations." "Why," he asked, "have they deliberately acted for three long years so as to unite the free world against them?"

### Soviet Militancy and the Western Response, 1946–1948

It is possible that the Soviet leadership may have been asking itself the same question. The steps by which this situation had come about show a pattern of action and reaction, challenge and response. It would perhaps require extraordinary detachment to trace the process to its origins, since it is clear that fundamental differences in the perception of the situation were involved. As expressed by Stalin and Zhdanov in 1946, an assumption of the inherent hostility of the West and the inevitability of conflict may have given a defensive quality to the Russians' efforts to consolidate their control as far west as possible.[2] These efforts may have acquired a certain legitimacy in Soviet eyes by an assumed political extension of the wartime agreements regarding spheres of military operations.[3] To those in the West who did not share this perception of inevitable conflict or the same approach to a "sphere of interest" disposition of other people, Soviet actions were baldly expansionist. The formal and public recognition of this conflict of aims did not emerge until 1947, for until that time Russia's efforts to redefine the outer periphery of its interests and control in Europe were constrained in some measure — perhaps concealed would be a better word — by the residual effects of the wartime alliance. By 1947, as the probings became sharper in Central and Eastern Europe and in the eastern Mediterranean area,[4] the Western nations were pricked into an awareness that a new balance of power was in the making, and it was clear that no fundamental stabilization of relations with the Soviet Union was likely to result until the power relationships in Europe had been defined afresh. In the course of the year, Western efforts to strengthen and stabilize the deteriorating situation in Europe by the Greek-Turkish Aid Program and the European Recovery Program, and by braking and then reversing the process of military demobilization, appeared in turn to confirm Soviet expectations of "capitalist hostility" and were followed by a new and more militant phase of Soviet policy. Assessing the Marshall Plan as a threat to its tenuously established position in Eastern Europe and as a device to secure American hegemony in Western Europe, the Soviet Union defined a policy in the fall of 1947 which called for speeding up the consolidation of its controls in Eastern

Europe and for turning the Communist parties of France and Italy from a broad line of national collaboration to a forceful struggle against their governments. This was the essential meaning of Zhdanov's directives at the founding meeting of the Cominform.[5] In the ascendancy from 1946 until midsummer 1948 as an authoritative spokesman for the regime and heir-apparent to Stalin, Zhdanov enforced stringent ideological conformity at home as well as vigorous militancy in foreign policy. At the Cominform session, he proclaimed the revival of the doctrine of the division of the world into two hostile camps, a doctrine last emphasized during an earlier militant period of Soviet policy (1928–1934).

The practical consequences of this doctrine became apparent almost immediately. In Eastern Europe, decisions taken at the Cominform meeting were revealed by the coup in Czechoslovakia and by an acceleration of the process by which non-Communist leaders were eliminated or subjugated in Poland, Hungary, Rumania, Bulgaria, and Albania. Despite strenuous efforts, the Soviet Union was unable to extend political control over Yugoslavia as well, but its miscalculated and heavy-handed attempt to do so produced within a few months the first rupture in the new imperial system. In Western Europe, the Communist parties were obliged to turn away from the parliamentary path to power they had been following since the end of the war. By 1946, the French Communists had developed a theoretical base for a distinctive national path to socialism, by evolution through the stage of "popular democracy."[6] Whatever its ultimate possibilities, the main function of this line had been to support Soviet diplomatic efforts, expressed in the Franco-Soviet Treaty of 1944 and in promises of Soviet support for French interests; the intention was to keep General de Gaulle from allowing France to become a continental bridgehead for a Western bloc.[7] However, after the Council of Foreign Ministers meeting in Moscow in March 1947, at which French hopes for Soviet support on the Ruhr issue were disappointed, France gave up the role as "a bridge between East and West" and turned decisively to the West. The Communists of France, as in Italy, found themselves powerless to prevent this, and by May of that year both parties were excluded from their governments.

At the Cominform meeting in September, the previous strategy of the Western European Communists came under slashing attack as bankrupt and "opportunist," although it had, at least at its beginning in 1944, clearly been directed from Moscow.[8] It is interesting to recall that Milovan Djilas of Yugoslavia and Wladyslaw Gomulka of Poland were among those chosen by Zhdanov to administer the rebuke.[9] The Cominform now inaugurated a period of militancy within the Communist parties of Western Europe, corresponding to a hardening of Soviet policies. The French and Italian Communists were instructed to force a change of national policy by paralyzing the political and economic life of their countries. Zhdanov warned them not to underestimate the strength of the working class in this fight; he called for an intensification of the class struggle, for attacks upon the socialist leadership and upon the bourgeoisie as a class. To strengthen the appeal to the masses, the Communists were told to use the peace symbol and the slogan of national independence from the United States. Within a fortnight, France and Italy were plunged into a series of strikes so violent as to raise the question of whether they expressed an insurrectionary intent. Another wave of strikes followed in the summer and fall of 1948.

The results were not what Zhdanov had anticipated. The strikes did deal a severe blow to the economic recovery of Western Europe, and the class struggle was dramatized by violent clashes between strikers and government forces, but the strikes failed to achieve their political objectives because of the firmness of the government response and the apathy of Communist as well as non-Communist workers. One consequence was that the socialist and Christian trade-union members split off from the Communist-dominated union federations, and the Communists' capacity to use their strength within the labor movement as a political instrument was considerably reduced.[10] More important, this violence contributed to the further isolation of the Communist parties, with the result that the governing coalitions in France and Italy moved farther to the right in domestic affairs and in foreign policy huddled still closer to the Western alliance.

In the atmosphere of heightened international tension which was felt throughout Europe in the autumn of 1948, the Communist parties of France, Britain, and Italy made other ineffective efforts to stop their governments from aligning themselves with the West. For example, a declaration adopted by the politburo of the French Communist Party on September 30, 1948, that "the people of France will not, will never, make war upon the Soviet Union," [11] was echoed by similar declarations from the Communist parties of Great Britain and Italy. But these were unsuccessful attempts to enlist broad working-class resistance to the Western defense alliance.

Before the end of 1948, the hope that the working classes of Western Europe could be mobilized by militant tactics began to run low. Throughout Western Europe it had become clear that the approach laid down by Zhdanov at the Cominform meeting was based upon a misreading of political realities. The profound economic crisis in the West which Zhdanov had predicted had not materialized, although the closing months of 1948 showed some decline in economic activity in the West, particularly in the United States. For the year as a whole, European industrial production had risen by 16 percent and agricultural production by 12 percent.[12] The working classes of Western Europe, whose strength Zhdanov had warned should not be underestimated, turned out to be responsive only to economic appeals and were far from being in a revolutionary temper.

The situation presented the Communists with a number of difficulties. Violent tactics had failed to move the workers to rebellion; instead, they had contributed to the political isolation of the Communist parties. This in turn made it more difficult for the Communists to influence the policies of the governments of their countries, since nowhere in the West did the working classes have the political power to shape governmental policies. Moreover, the isolation of the Communists and their mood of sectarian violence impeded their efforts to utilize the broader appeals of peace and nationalism, as Zhdanov had also urged them to do. These appeals could not be effective so long as the fear of a Soviet military advance across Europe persisted.

Recollecting the events of this period in comparative tranquillity, it is difficult to conjure up the atmosphere of apprehension and imminent war that prevailed in the Western countries by 1948. The rapid process of satellization of Eastern Europe, particularly the seizure of Czechoslovakia; the harshness of the Soviet attack upon Tito and the reports of troop movements on the borders of Yugoslavia; the Soviet blockade of Berlin; the civil war in Greece; the violence then afoot in China, India, Palestine, Indonesia, Malaya, and Burma; the desperate strikes on the continent of Europe; the threats against Iran and Turkey; the successive collapse of instruments intended to conciliate postwar conflicts of interest (the Allied Control Commission in Germany and the Council of Foreign Ministers) — these appeared to many observers at the time as markers on the road to World War III.[13]

These were the "harsh external pressures" responsible for the gathering momentum of Western power and cohesion. In weighing the power balance as of the spring of 1949, however, two aspects held the central place in the Soviet Union's concern: the problem of Germany, and the current and anticipated balance of military capabilities.

The event which most stimulated Western fears of Soviet aggressive intentions was the blockade of Berlin; it had grown from pinprick impediments to travel during the spring of 1948 into a full-fledged stoppage of traffic to the city by the end of June. The blockade was a counterthrust by the Soviet Union to the currency reform in West Berlin and the West's firm denial of Soviet control over the Ruhr; it appeared at the time as the climactic act of this phase of Russia's efforts to establish the outer limits of its new power in Europe. The action and the reaction, the blockade and the airlift, cautiously opposing each other by measures short of war, confirmed the fact that by the end of 1948 the fluidity that had characterized postwar power relationships in Europe had passed. For the time being at least, a provisional line had been drawn across the face of Europe. The failure of the blockade made it evident that the line would be drawn no farther westward than the middle of Germany, which neither side had been able to win in its entirety or could afford to yield.

Just when the Soviet leadership reached the conclusion that it could not immediately extend its control over the whole of Germany is a matter of some dispute. (Djilas quotes Stalin as saying, as early as January 1948, that Germany would remain divided, in contrast with a statement two years earlier that the whole of Germany would become Communist.[14] Whether the Soviet diplomatic note of March 10, 1952, and the New Course in East Germany in May-June 1953 were to be understood as indications of lingering Soviet interest in a reunified Germany are questions still being debated.[15]) To the leaders of the Western nations, it had become apparent by the end of 1947, after the failure of the Moscow and London meetings of the Council of Foreign Ministers, that any agreement with the Soviet Union for the unification of Germany would be possible only on Soviet terms. By early 1948 the United States, Great Britain, and France had reached an accord in principle to unite the three Western zones of Germany under a West German government, which would be encouraged to associate itself with the Western European nations. It was this plan — along with the currency reform of the Western zones in June 1948 which was designed to make it impossible for the Soviet Union to block the independent economic recovery of these areas — that was most directly challenged by the Soviet blockade of Berlin. By the terms it advanced for ending the blockade, the Soviet Union made it clear that its purpose was primarily to force the Western powers to abandon their plans for a West German government or, at the least, to withdraw from Berlin. But, as it worked out, the blockade and the successful airlift response had the effect of accelerating the Western effort to translate the agreement in principle into an agreement in fact. For the French, the blockade had the effect of making them, *nolens volens,* nervous partners in the airlift operation.

Here, as in the case of the militant Cominform counterthrust against the Marshall Plan, the policy of the clenched fist had not only proved ineffective; it had aroused responses in the West which increased Soviet difficulties. By the end of 1948, it was apparent that the Berlin blockade had given a powerful additional stimulus to the gathering of new forces in the West and had added urgency to the question of whether new departures were required in Soviet policies in the early months of 1949.

## The Balance of Military Power

The essential aspect of the Soviet view of the international situation at the beginning of 1949 is to be found in the Soviet appreciation of the balance of military power. Although this perception and judgment can only be reconstructed from the partial evidence available to us, it seems clear in the light of what we now know that Soviet evaluations and decisions in the military field were in fact very different from what the Western world assumed them to be.

At the end of the war, the Soviet Union was left with a large land army and the conviction that it faced a period of extreme vulnerability. In contrast with the devastated Russian economy, American industrial power seemed towering. The United States possessed an uncertain quantity of atomic bombs, a large fleet of long-range aircraft, and an imposing navy. The Soviet Union had virtually no long-range aircraft and little navy.[16]

Some observers in the West were inclined to think that Stalin did not attach much importance to the atomic bomb because of the lack of interest with which he had received news of its development from Truman at Potsdam,[17] his disparagement of the weapon in subsequent interviews[18] — and because not a single article on atomic energy or atomic weapons is known to have appeared in the Soviet military press, open or restricted in circulation, in the period from 1947 through 1953.[19] It is now clear, however, that this outward appearance concealed quite a different evaluation of the importance of nuclear weapons and an intense concentration of resources upon their development at the earliest possible moment. Djilas quotes Stalin as saying of the atomic bomb in January 1948: "That is a powerful thing, pow-er-ful!" Djilas adds: "His expression was full of admiration, so that one was given to understand that he would not rest until he, too, had the 'powerful thing.' But he did not mention that he had it already or that the USSR was working on it." Djilas goes on to say that a month later in Moscow Georgi Dimitrov, the Bulgarian Communist, told Edvard Kardelj and himself in confidence that the Russians had already developed an atomic bomb more powerful than the one exploded at Hiroshima, but that he did not, and still does not, believe it to have been true at the time.[20] It now appears probable that the Soviet Union had a functioning chain reactor by August 1947.[21]

Whether Stalin gave serious weight to the possibility that the United States and its allies might strike against the Soviet Union during this period of weakness is hard to judge, but it does seem obvious that he expected war sooner or later (perhaps within fifteen to twenty years); that he regarded the imbalance of power as a serious political disadvantage; that he felt urgently impelled to overcome this period of vulnerability at a forced-draft pace; and that, finally, in the meantime measures were necessary to deter the "bourgeois imperialists" from any temptation to consider a preventive war.

Stalin's feeling of urgency is evident in his famous pre-election speech of February 9, 1946. There was to be no respite for the weary population of the Soviet Union, no concession to the craving for relaxation and comfort. Instead, he set the painfully high industrial targets to be achieved by the prostrate Soviet economy in the course of three projected five-year plans — that is, by 1961.[22] "Only under such conditions," he warned in language which was all too clear to his audience, "can we consider that our homeland will be guaranteed against all possible accidents." (There is another striking quotation attributed by Djilas to Stalin which bears on this expectation of war. In the course of a dinner in April 1945, Djilas says that Stalin rose from the table, "hitched up his pants as though he was about to wrestle or to box, and cried out almost in a transport, 'The war shall soon be over. We shall recover in fifteen or twenty years, and then we'll have another go at it.' "[23])

One immediate task of Soviet foreign policy was to deter the West from using, or deriving great political advantage from, its nuclear strength before Soviet science could break the Western monopoly. This was to be done in several ways, in the period from 1946 to 1948. First, Soviet disarmament policy during this period, rejecting the Baruch Plan put forward by the United States and its allies for the international control of atomic energy, aroused great public pressure to support the demand that all atomic weapons should be unconditionally abolished, all stocks of atomic weapons destroyed, and the manufacture of additional atomic bombs prohibited. Zhdanov's directive to the Western Communist parties to use the peace symbol was intended to circumscribe the freedom of action of Western governments in making direct or indirect use of their military strength. A later chapter will describe in detail how the Soviet Union made systematic use of the world-wide Peace Movement and specifically aimed it at inhibiting the Western powers from seeking any advantages from their superior nuclear strength. The intended function of the militant Cominform line in the 1947–1948 period was similarly to hold the Western governments in check by aroused action of the masses, to threaten mass resistance in the event of war, and to prevent these governments from forming defense alliances or increasing their military budgets.

Second, the Soviet Union made a short-lived effort to deny the West any surviving military strength in middle Europe — particularly in Germany — in the event that the West should think of aggressive action. This involved borrowing German scientific and technological specialists not only to keep them from the West, but to help in developing Soviet jet aircraft and nuclear and rocket research; it meant dismantling German plants even beyond the ability of the Soviet system to transport and use this material in its own reconstruction; and it included large-scale destruction and post-holing of air facilities in Eastern Germany to keep them out of the hands of the potential enemy (the same air facilities which were rebuilt in such great haste and at great expense during a later phase of Soviet policy).

Third, the Soviet Union sought to get as much deterrent effect as possible out of the one military weapon in which it was strongest — its large army, which was deployed and trained as a direct military threat to Western Europe. A British military specialist describes this effort as follows:

These troops were trained to execute a rapid advance to the Atlantic coast, to sweep forward to occupy every part of Europe from Norway to Portugal. The Soviet leaders recognized that a swift occupation of Western Europe would not damage the United States directly, but they thought that the establishment of Communist regimes throughout Western Europe would strike so severe a blow at American political and economic interests that the United States would not risk preventive war against the Soviet Union.[24]

Fourth, in order to increase the effectiveness of this deterrent, the Soviet Union took a number of immediate measures to modernize its air-defense system, to launch a great naval building program, emphasizing fast and powerful cruisers and long-range submarines, and to build up a long-range bomber force.[25] By August 1947, the Russians produced and displayed the TU-4, a long-range four-engine aircraft (known in the West as the "Bull"), apparently copied from four United States B-29-As which had crash-landed in Siberia in 1944.[26]

The foregoing, however, were no more than stopgap measures to reduce the danger and the political consequences of a period of military disadvantage; the central task was to overcome this disadvantage as soon as possible. This was the major implied burden of Stalin's election speech in February 1946. Buried in that speech were indications, not fully appreciated in the West at the time, that the Fourth Five-Year Plan about to be put into force would concentrate resources heavily upon research and development of modern weapon systems: "special attention will be devoted to . . . the widespread construction of all manner of scientific research institutions that can give science the opportunity to develop its potentialities. I have no doubt that if we give our scientists proper assistance they will be able in the near future not only to overtake but to surpass the achievements of science beyond the boundaries of our country." [27] (*Pravda* indicates that the Moscow audience interrupted the delivery of these sentences with "prolonged and stormy applause," which may perhaps signify that they were understood as having more than perfunctory meaning.) Also, Georgi M. Malenkov, in discussing the Fourth Five-Year Plan at the founding meeting of the Cominform in September 1947, declared: "We have set ourselves the task not only of catching up with scientific achievements abroad, but of surpassing them." [28]

Retrospective studies indicate that Soviet scientists resumed their prewar interests in nuclear research during the last quarter of 1943, that the first chain reactor was built by the spring of 1947 and was in operation by August of that year.[29] This was apparently the basis for Molotov's claim, in his speech celebrating the thirtieth anniversary of the revolution three months later, that the secret of the atomic bomb had "long ago ceased to exist." [30] One study of inferential evidence concludes that the Soviet government increased its budgetary allocations for nuclear research still more heavily following the achievement of this chain reaction in 1947.[31]

In the field of guided missiles, it is now apparent that even before the war ended the Soviet Union was committed to a broad and varied program of research. A leading Soviet specialist in nuclear weapons and long-range missiles, Major General G. I. Pokrovsky, published the first Soviet article on long-range missiles in April 1944.[32] In 1946, A. A. Blagonravov, both an academician and a lieutenant general of artillery, was named President of the Academy of Artillery Sciences, an institute which was to have important responsibilities for the development of rockets and later for space satellites.[33] (In the same year, the United States was deciding, from its observation of German rocket development, to concentrate its energies for the coming decade on manned-bomber delivery systems, in view of the size and weight of nuclear warheads and the undependability of rockets. In 1947 the United States program of research on intercontinental missiles was canceled for budgetary reasons.)

In jet aviation, the Soviet Union committed itself heavily at the end of the war to accelerating the incorporation of jet technology and swept-wing designs into their fighter forces; German scientists and engineers were employed to prepare designs for long-range jet bombers (although the Germans were not permitted to work on the actual jet bombers in the Soviet design bureaus). Stalin is reported as giving personal attention to the development of a modern strategic bombing force immediately after the war, although large-scale procurement and deployment of jet bombers were not evident until after Stalin's death.[34]

In sum, the Soviet leadership appears to have decided, even before the end of the war, to concentrate its resources upon research and development of nuclear weapons, rocket delivery systems, and jet aircraft, and to repair its naval deficiencies. The expectation was that this accelerated development of new weapon systems and the continued emphasis in the Soviet economy upon heavy industry would yield a shift in the balance of power favorable to the Soviet Union. By the spring of 1949, this hope may have seemed neither unreasonable nor distant. It is significant now in retrospect that Soviet physicists figured prominently in the Stalin Prize awards in the spring of 1949.[35] The first Soviet nuclear explosion was four months away; the first Soviet hydrogen explosion, four years; the first intermediate-range missile, six years; the first intercontinental missile, eight years.

There is an element of tragic irony in the way in which Soviet superiority in armed forces and Western superiority in nuclear weapons and long-range aircraft, instead of creating a military equilibrium in this period, led to an interacting spiral of mutual anxiety and rearmament. The unsettling factor in the equation was the Soviet perception of the Western societies as inherently and intractably hostile, with the consequent conviction of the inevitability of conflict. Whatever Stalin's intentions were about the use of force, this opinion about the forces of history was quite enough to produce a situation of rising hostility. The irony is heightened by the fact that the means chosen by the Soviet Union to compensate for its sense of vulnerability stimulated Western military mobilization. The immediate result was to deepen Soviet insecurity and to postpone the desired changes in the balance of power.

During 1948 the consolidation of Soviet control over Eastern Europe and the shadow of Soviet landpower over Western Europe — which, as we have seen, from the Soviet point of view may have been conceived as a counterpoise to Western nuclear striking power — set in motion urgent efforts to build the defenses of Western Europe against an imminent attack. A Western intelligence estimate of the period which found its way into the press said the basic problem was "how to keep the Soviet Union from advancing farther West in Europe," and described the situation in these terms:

The Soviet Union has an estimated 50 to 60 alert and well-equipped divisions poised on the other side of the iron curtain. Against this mountain of troops, the five Western European nations might be able to throw a total of six divisions — three French, recently equipped with surplus United States material, one British, one Belgian and one Dutch. One United States division also is available . . . If the Soviet forces started moving West tomorrow, they could probably sweep to the Channel. En route, the initial 50 to 60 divisions might easily be increased to 150.[36]

Other estimates, then and for some years later, placed the Soviet strength at 175 divisions, between 4 and 5 million men, in contrast with the American ground forces which by 1948–1949 were down to 12 divisions, or about 645,000 men.[37] According to figures released by Khrushchev in 1960, the strength of the Soviet armed forces in 1948 was 2.87 million men, well below the Western estimate.[38] If so, it may nevertheless have suited Russia's purpose at that time to do nothing to dispel the impression that its armies were larger than they in fact were. But this impression, combined with the militancy of Soviet policies, provided a powerful spur to Western rearmament.

From Moscow, the movement of the Western powers toward cohesion and augmented military power must have appeared to be gathering momentum by the spring of 1949. Perhaps the most concrete indication of the trend is to be found in the curve of United States military expenditures, which had dropped from $14.5 billion in fiscal 1947 to $11.7 billion in 1948, but began to rise the following year to $12.9 billion, in 1950 to $13 billion, and from there on climbed year by year to heights unprecedented in peacetime.[39] Since military expenditures usually reflect the appropriations of the previous year and occasionally earlier, the beginning of the rise in military appropriations is related to the political situation as of the spring of 1948. Even these totals, however, do not fully reflect the atmosphere of rising crisis. The original request from the Joint Chiefs of Staff for fiscal 1950 had amounted to $30 billion, which had been cut at the direction of the President to $15.9 before being submitted to Congress.[40] When the President proposed this great amount, the predominant congressional reaction was not one of reluctance, but rather that the sum should have been larger.[41]

The revival of military power in the West was also reflected in the activation of the Western military alliance. In less than a month after the Communists took over full control of Czechoslovakia in February 1948, five nations of Western Europe met at Brussels, in the face of what they declared to be an imminent danger, to form the Western European Union. Within five months, this led to secret staff talks with the United States on the mode of American participation in the alliance. If Stalin had deduced, from his wartime conversations with Franklin Roosevelt, that the United States might withdraw from Europe after the war,[42] the trend of events must have given him little encouragement. Truman's inaugural address in January 1949 signified a substantial step forward in the American reinforcement of the West European power structure, and it was recognized as such by the Russians. The President's pledge of support for renewed economic assistance to Europe resulted in an appropriation of $5.8 billion for foreign aid, of which $4.8 billion was to be used to continue the European program for another fifteen months. (The effect of the previous year's program, aided by the good harvests of 1948, had already begun to be visible in the substantial increase in Western Europe's industrial production and in its growing confidence and political stability.) In providing these funds, Congress made clear the American interest in promoting the integration of Europe, which was read in Moscow as a furthering of American hegemony over Europe. Also, the Point Four plank of the President's inaugural address, calling for technical assistance to underdeveloped areas, was interpreted by the Russians as an effort to strengthen American strategic interests in the Middle East and Southeast Asia.

American military as well as economic involvement in Europe was indicated by the President's declaration of intent to conclude the North Atlantic Treaty, which was at that time in the course of active negotiation, and also by his proposal to provide military advice and equipment for the countries of Western Europe. The result was the Mutual Defense Assistance Program, with a first year's appropriation of $1.5 billion. These measures were stimulated by insistent requests from leaders of the West European countries that the United States increase the size of its forces on the continent.[43]

There were many other indications of the growth of Western power which must have seemed alarming to Moscow. A new peak in the American production of atomic weapons was announced by the Atomic Energy Commission on January 31, 1949. The United States Strategic Air Command had experienced an enormous growth in 1948 and was publicly engaged in a crash program to reach maximum strength by January 1949. An American B-50-A bomber in February successfully completed an around-the-world nonstop flight, dramatizing the possibilities of the new SAC system for refueling planes in flight. In Europe, the British government asked Parliament in February for an increase in military appropriations from £694 million to £759.86 million for the coming fiscal year. In his first quarterly report on the program of American aid to Greece and Turkey, Truman said that the balance was beginning to shift in the Greek civil war. In the Mediterranean, the United States was pointedly staging naval maneuvers. A Russian repatriation mission was ordered out of the United States zone of Germany by the American commander, General Lucius Clay. The Western airlift into Berlin had survived the test of winter weather and in the early spring set a new record of approximately 1,400 flights in one day. The British and American counterblockade of East Germany was being tightened and had already reduced trade with the Soviet zone to a trickle. The movement toward the formation of a West German government was accelerating daily. The rise of international tension had begun to transform Germany as well as Japan from the estate of former culpable aggressors into important potential allies in the new power conflict. Restrictions on German economic activity were gradually lifted, partly for reasons of economy on the part of the United States. Similarly, in the case of Japan, the United States began to seek to strengthen the Japanese economy and to abandon the previous policies of decartelization and demilitarization.

By the early part of 1949, therefore, it had become evident that the militant phase of Soviet policy set forth in 1946 and 1947 had stimulated a trend heavily adverse to Soviet interests. The Soviet Union was confronted with the estrangement of Yugoslavia, the weakening and isolation of its instruments in France and Italy, and the increasing cohesion and military reinforcement of the Western powers around American leadership. On the horizon, the Soviet leadership could perceive an immediate prospect of two further and even more serious developments: the early completion of the negotiation of a North Atlantic Treaty which, in the Soviet view, would strengthen American control over Western Europe; and the creation of a West German state with the addition of West German resources, geographical position, and potential military power to the Western alliance. Whatever may have been its expectations of gains as a result of its concentration of resources on heavy industry and weapons, the Soviet leadership faced a bleak future.

## The Soviet View of American Politics and Economics

Among other factors involved in the Soviet Union's appraisal of the essential character of the current phase of world history — and perhaps central to these calculations — was its estimate of the political mood of the United States and the condition and prospects of the American economy. During the heightening tension of 1947, the American formula of "patience and firmness" in dealing with the Soviet Union as a difficult ally had given way to the official conception of the containment of the Soviet Union as a hostile and expansionist power. In 1948, however, the American presidential campaign apparently raised Soviet hopes for a more pliant course. One encouraging factor was the candidacy of Henry Wallace, which the Soviet press treated as a reflection of a popular movement toward a reconciliation with the Soviet Union. An open letter from Wallace to Stalin in May, proposing terms for ending the cold war, was welcomed by the Soviet leader as "the most important document . . . among recent political documents having as their purpose the consolidation of peace." Stalin sought to encourage overtures by repeating the formula he had used in his interviews with Elliott Roosevelt in December 1946 and with Harold Stassen in April 1947:

The Government of the USSR believes that despite the differences in economic systems and ideologies the coexistence of these systems and the peaceful settlement of differences between the USSR and the USA are not only possible but absolutely necessary in the interests of universal peace.[44]

Another development in the course of the presidential campaign which may have contributed to the Soviet interpretation of the American mood as potentially responsive to "peaceful coexistence" was a series of remarks by President Truman which seemed to indicate a sympathetic personal attitude toward Stalin. On June 11, 1948, at Eugene, Oregon, Truman was reported as saying: "I like Old Joe. He's a decent fellow but he's a prisoner of the Politburo." Again, on December 27, 1948, Truman was quoted as saying that he thought some Russian leaders wanted to be conciliatory toward the United States. During the closing weeks of the campaign, the President mentioned the possibility of sending Chief Justice Fred M. Vinson to Moscow as a personal envoy, presumably in connection with negotiations concerning the lifting of the Berlin blockade. Although this project was promptly dropped following a protest from the Secretary of State, the Russians were obviously fascinated by the possibility and, during the opening weeks of 1949, made many attempts to revive the proposal in a flurry of peaceful-coexistence statements from a number of Communist sources.

Further uncertainty in the Soviet estimate of the American climate may have resulted from the publication in *Life* magazine of a story by a man identified as a former speech writer of Truman's. The article intimated that the President was about to soften his policy toward the Soviet Union.[45] A public storm resulted, despite a personal denial of the story by the President.

Soviet expectations must have been tempered by the violent public reaction to the story and by the President's denial, as well as by the evident lack of support for Henry Wallace in the election. If any such hopes survived, they were surely dispelled by the tone of the President's inaugural address in January 1949. Truman's unequivocal support for the strengthening of American and Western defenses left the Communists "downcast," according to a correspondent in Rome. "Some Communists," he reported, "seem to have been the victims of their own propaganda and really believed that the United States intended, in the future, to adopt a policy of appeasement toward Russia." [46] Whether this belief and the subsequent disillusionment had been prevalent in Moscow can only be conjectured.

There was an equal amount of uncertainty concerning the prospects for the American economy. It is interesting to observe the obvious signs of dispute within the Soviet Union on this question, for it was to have a vital bearing on policy direction. This argument bore a close but still somewhat obscure relationship to a controversy over Soviet domestic economic problems (we shall come to it in a few pages), and both questions were crucially interwoven in Stalin's famous economic essay of 1952 and in the dispute between the "dogmatists" and the "revisionists" long after the death of Stalin.

The focus of discussion of the American economy in the postwar period was a book which had been published in September 1946 by Eugene S. Varga, chief of the Institute of World Economics and World Politics, and one of the most eminent figures in Soviet economics.[47] Although Varga had analyzed the American economy within the framework of orthodox Marxist anticipation of the inevitability of overproduction, he accepted the possibility that the crisis might be deferred for as much as ten years through the increasing intervention of the state in the economic process. He foresaw the possibility of socialist reforms in Europe without revolution and implied that war was not inevitable even while imperialism continued.

In May 1947, at a public discussion in Moscow, Varga's book was severely attacked as being "soft on capitalism." [48] The possibility of even this degree of economic planning under capitalism was rejected by his critics.[49] More important, Varga's analysis implied a nonrevolutionary and less militant policy on the part of the Soviet

Union, anticipating eventual peaceful gains as a result of the break-down of colonialism and evolutionary changes in capitalist societies.[50] Not only was this possibility heatedly rejected, but Varga was also charged with heresy for errors in discussing the economies of the states of Eastern Europe, which had been in a presatellite stage of development at the time of his writing. Apart from the specific issues involved, it was clear that the attack was related to the general hardening of climate which was then being enforced by Zhdanov in many fields of intellectual and artistic activity.

Criticism of Varga, which continued sporadically through late 1947 and early 1948,[51] reached a new intensity in October 1948, at an enlarged session of the Learned Council of the Economic In-stitute of the Academy of Sciences, called to discuss "Shortcomings and Problems of Research in the Field of Economics." [52] Varga continued to hold to the essentials of his position with a remarkable degree of independence of spirit. "I honestly accept a good deal of criticism," he said, "but there are things I cannot accept." [53] Western observers speculatively attributed his survival either to the protection of friends in authority or to uncertainty on the part of the regime about the validity of his argument.

However, in March 1949, matters appeared to come to a head. What appeared to be a fairly thorough recantation was set forth by Varga in an article in *Voprosy ekonomiki* [54] and a letter to the editor of *Pravda*.[55] Denying his previous views, Varga strenuously disavowed any "retreat from Marxism-Leninism to reformism," as had been charged. His recantation was so categorical that it was, perhaps, intended to be understood by his colleagues as a purely formal compliance with the requirements of this period in Soviet life. He promised to correct his errors in a revised edition of his work, which appeared in 1953. He was at particular pains in his letter to *Pravda* to dissociate himself from those in the West who had claimed him as a kindred spirit: "I wish to protest most strongly against the dark hints of the war instigators to the effect that I am a man 'of Western orientation.' Today, in the present historical circumstances, that would mean being a counterrevolutionary, an anti-Soviet traitor to the working class."

What "present historical circumstances" Varga had in mind may be conjectured from the fact that the same issue of *Voprosy ekonomiki* carried a report that the Institute of Economics of the Academy of Sciences had resolved to struggle against "homeless cosmopolitans" in Soviet economics (an intensive campaign around this slogan was raging in other areas of Soviet life). The report listed Varga and seven others as guilty of preaching "bourgeois ideology."

Much of Varga's analysis of capitalism has by now been fully accepted by Soviet officialdom, but for many years following the attack on Varga Soviet writings adhered closely to the classical Marxist conviction that the laws of capital accumulation had led, or were inevitably leading, to a deepening general crisis of capitalism. It so happened that the latter part of 1948 and the first half of 1949 witnessed a recession in the United States, resulting — according to American economists — from the fact that the public demand for goods built up during the war had by this time been fairly well satisfied. The recession was accompanied by a rise in unemployment in the United States from 1.9 million in the second half of 1948 to 3.2 million in the first half of 1949, and to 3.6 million in the second half of 1949. Western Europe felt the strain on its currencies, as a result of the fall in the prices of its exports to the United States, and unemployment in Western Europe was further aggravated by increases in productivity and available manpower.[56] These events were widely treated in the Soviet press as evidence of the correctness of the Soviet analysis and of the imminence of a crisis, as well as proof of the exploitative character of American aid to Europe.[57]

By the latter part of 1949, however, the American economy had recovered, although unemployment in Western Europe and particularly in Italy continued to be a serious problem.[58] The Soviet analysts, unable to share the concept used by American economists of a "short-term inventory crisis," attributed the quick recovery to the vast expenditure under the Marshall Plan and the armament program beginning in 1947. By the summer of 1949, the view had been developed that the Marshall Plan and the huge military expenditures of the West had created an artificial "temporary stabilization of capitalism." In fact, it was argued, these measures, along with the Truman Doctrine and the North Atlantic Treaty, were part of a foreign policy designed to postpone an American economic crisis by providing foreign markets for American surplus production and by maintaining a high level of profits and employment through the stimulation of arms production. This explanation of American motives in promoting cold-war tensions appeared to represent a serious Soviet analytical interpretation, not only a propaganda position.

This was not, of course, a wholly new interpretation: it had been the substance of the Soviet argument ever since Molotov's dismissal of the Marshall Plan in 1947 as a device for postponing the collapse of capitalism. But the point which began to attract Soviet attention was the obverse implication of the argument: that the Peace Movement and other means of damping the tensions of the cold war could help to hasten the collapse of capitalism. A commentary on the international situation in the Cominform newspaper in July 1949 regarded as the most significant feature of that period a correlation between "the growing consolidation of the peace front" and the signs of crisis in the American economy.[59]

The effect of this line of thought added further to the desirability of moderating the "harsh external pressures" that had stimulated — or perhaps, from the Soviet point of view, had been used to justify — the increase in Western armaments. Militant Soviet policies had not only created a disadvantageous strategic trend for the Soviet Union; they were also providing props for the American and West European economies and were preventing capitalism from experiencing the crisis which the Marxist analysis so confidently expected.

## Problems Within the Soviet Orbit

In his tour of the horizon in the spring of 1949, a Soviet policy maker would have been obliged to take into consideration the current state of affairs in the new Soviet empire in Eastern Europe. This was a time of trouble in the new domain, a period of painful and unsettling consolidation, and it was intimately bound up with Soviet relations with the West.

Foremost among the difficulties was the struggle with Yugoslavia. The second meeting of the Cominform in June 1948 had been called for the purpose of expelling the Yugoslavs, who had been showing interest in organizing an East European bloc not altogether subject to control from Moscow. The Yugoslavs had also been resisting the exploitative economic controls which the Soviet Union had been applying elsewhere in Eastern Europe and had stubbornly held to their own ideas about "building socialism." After first trying unsuccessfully to cultivate a Moscow wing among the Yugoslav leaders, Stalin resorted to surgery, apparently confident that this would shock the Yugoslav Communists into scuttling Tito and submitting to the Soviet will.[60] During 1949 the Soviet Union continued to apply the threatening pressure of troop movements toward Yugoslavia's borders, frontier incidents involving Yugoslavia's neighbors, a rigorous economic blockade, and an increasingly bellicose tone in diplomatic notes and propaganda. The effect, however, was the loss to the Soviet Union of an area of both strategic and political importance — and the establishment of a potentially contagious heresy. The draconian measures used by the Soviet Union during this period to pluck out the slightest suspicion of national communism in the other states of Eastern Europe indicated the seriousness with which the Soviet leadership regarded the problem.

Purges had been an intermittent feature of the East European scene ever since the process of satellization was accelerated at Zhdanov's signal in 1947. During the war and particularly after the establishment of Communist control, the ranks of the Communist parties had been greatly enlarged by new members whose party reliability required screening. The particularly heavy incidence of purges in 1949 was associated with an increase of pressure by the Soviet Union for agricultural collectivization and for a faster rate of industrialization. But even more it resulted from the Soviet zeal to cauterize the wound left by the defection of Yugoslavia. Nationalism, the same political force which the Soviet Union found so useful outside its own orbit, became the noxious charge of "national deviationism" in Eastern Europe and "bourgeois nationalism" at home.

In Poland, the arguments over the rate of industrialization and the forced collectivization of agriculture began to rage in the latter part of 1948, when Wladyslaw Gomulka, former secretary general and member of the politburo of the Polish Communist Party, vice premier, and minister of recovered territories, was first demoted and then taken into custody for "rightist and nationalist deviation." The most violent expression of the purges at this time was found in Bulgaria, Hungary, and Czechoslovakia. In Bulgaria, Traicho Kostov, deputy prime minister and member of the politburo, was expelled from the party and his government position in March 1949. Following a trial for treason in December at which Kostov repudiated the confession attributed to him, he was executed. In September, the trial of Laszlo Rajk, Hungarian minister of the interior and member of the politburo, on charges of treason and conspiracy, sent a wave of fear throughout the Communist movement because of the extreme character of the charges and confessions. The major impact of the purge in Czechoslovakia was felt in 1951 and 1952, when Rudolf Slansky, deputy prime minister and former secretary general of the party, and Vladimir Clementis, foreign minister, were tried for conspiracy and executed. In 1949, the first wave of the purge in Czechoslovakia affected officials dealing with foreign affairs and foreign trade, notably Vilem Novy, editor in chief of *Rude pravo* and chairman of the foreign-affairs committee of the National Assembly, who was dropped from these positions in December 1949 and later expelled from the party as a spy. In June of 1949, General Koci Xoxe, former deputy prime minister of Albania, was sentenced to death as a Titoist. It has been estimated that in the course of the following few years, one out of every four members in the satellite Communist parties was purged.[61] No consistent political pattern was discernible among the victims, except the suspicion of Titoism or the interplay of local rivalries. Some, like Gomulka and Clementis, had been known as right-wing moderates; others — Kostov, Rajk, and Slansky — were zealots of the Zhdanov school.[62] Later, Rajk and Kostov were posthumously rehabilitated and their confessions acknowledged to have been extorted by torture.[63]

Nor did this exhaust the list of Communist troubles in Eastern Europe. Economic problems represented another acute source of political tension. The Soviet Union, deeply preoccupied with the restoration of its own economy, was in no position to match the assistance being poured into Western Europe by the United States. In January 1949 the Soviet Union established the Council for Mutual Economic Assistance to counteract the appeal of the Marshall Plan and to encourage the economic development of states in the Soviet orbit; at this stage, however, the council functioned as an instrument of control rather than of cooperation.[64] At the meeting of the Economic Commission for Europe in May 1949, the Soviet delegation displayed evident anxiousness to ease the situation in Eastern Europe by restoring at least some trade with Western Europe.[65]

In sum, by 1949 the Soviet Union was in the early stage in the development of its control mechanism for Eastern Europe. The theory of the Popular Democracy was still being forged in painful practice. The socialization of industry was well advanced, but not industrial output or trade. The collectivization of agriculture was being successfully resisted. In East Germany, the process of satellization was just beginning. Throughout its new dominions, the Soviet Union faced acute and unfinished business. The purges, the poverty, the unsettling fear of war, the battle with the church, and the process of extinguishing all centers of political opposition — all cried out for a period of consolidation and constituted another pressure upon the Soviet leadership for a less adventurous foreign policy.

## The Situation at Home

Within its own borders, the Soviet leadership was deeply involved in a number of thorny problems which had to be taken into account in any calculation of foreign policy. In the four years that had passed since the end of the war, the enormous upsurge of popular feeling, the patriotism, the pride of victory which for the moment shone through exhaustion and tragedy, the relief, the hope — these had all been pricked and deflated. By the spring of 1949, it was a grim, tense, and deeply weary population that stood before the posted newspapers and read of war scares, new arrests, and exhortations to produce, produce, produce. In many different fields — in art, in literature, in economic thought — the war and the cumulative effects of Russia's industrial growth had stirred a faint spirit of innovation; by 1949 these stirrings lay dormant, like spring flowers caught by a late frost.

The high industrial goals, the allocation of vast resources to science and technology, which the Soviet leadership deemed so urgently necessary, meant that there could be no relaxation. On the contrary: to make the iron will of the party leadership prevail upon an "unbuttoned" population meant pressure and more pressure, in all the ways that the party had learned in the 1930s.

But the condition of the party itself required attention, and this too may have argued the need for a period of consolidation in foreign policy. Between the party's great wartime losses and the mass admission of new members during and immediately following the war, about half the party membership by 1947 consisted of unseasoned recruits.[66] In a widespread "party verification," members were subjected to a rigorous screening for ideological and technical competence.[67] A common feature of the press of this period was a substantial volume of self-criticism concerning charges of inefficiency and in some cases corruption on the part of lower party organizations. At the 1947 meeting of the Cominform, Malenkov had indicated that a revision of party statutes was then in process to tighten entrance requirements and ideological discipline, and that a new party program was being prepared by the Central Committee to replace the obsolete 1919 program. (The new party statutes were not presented until the Nineteenth Party Congress in October 1952; the new program was not completed until 1961.)

Another point made by Malenkov at the same time was to lead to widespread confusion in the West. Observing how much party organs had taken on direct operational responsibilities during the war, Malenkov warned that this practice, violating the proper relation between party and government, should now be discontinued. In March 1949, a number of high party officials in the Soviet Union relinquished the governmental administrative duties they had assumed during or immediately before the war. Vyacheslav M. Molotov was relieved of his duties as foreign minister, which he had fulfilled since 1939. He was replaced by his deputy, Andrei Ya. Vyshinsky. At the same time, Anastas I. Mikoyan was replaced as minister of foreign trade by his deputy, Mikhail A. Menshikov. A few days later, Marshal Nikolai A. Bulganin was also replaced by his deputy, Marshal Alexander M. Vasilevsky, as minister of armed forces. Both Molotov and Mikoyan remained as deputy premiers; Molotov was assigned, it was announced, to take charge of an inner defense cabinet responsible for the coordination of the industrial and military resources of Central and Eastern Europe. As always on such occasions, however, a wave of speculation about the significance of these changes swept through the Western capitals. Read in retrospect, this speculation is more instructive in regard to the political climate in these capitals than in assessing the event itself. French officials called this "a vital turning point in international affairs." West Berlin officials thought it marked "the admission of the failure of a policy." From London came the comment that "Molotov's departure coincides with what seems to be an unsuccessful period in Soviet diplomacy . . . [and] reflects perhaps some disagreement about tactics in Moscow." [68] Mayor Ernst Reuter of Berlin was quoted as expressing the conviction that the Western firmness in defeating the Berlin blockade had brought about a change in Soviet policy, of which the removal of Molotov was a symbol.[69] A few days later, after a consultation with its diplomats in Eastern Europe, the Quai d'Orsay was quoted as concluding that the appointment of Vyshinsky immediately after his meeting with Cominform leaders at Karlovy Vary indicated alarming possibilities. The appointment was related, it was felt, to a growing economic crisis in Eastern Europe, a mounting desire among the satellites for increased trade with the West, but also to alarming troop concentrations in southern Rumania and a purge of the "nationalist" rebel leader, General Vafiades Markos in Greece, pointing to the possibility of a coup de main in Greek Macedonia by Bulgaria and a "nerve-wracking war scare" during the coming spring.[70] None of the speculation was unreasonable, and some of the predictions turned out to be sound, but there does not appear to have been any direct relationship between these policy questions and the Russians' administrative rearrangements.

In addition to the internal problems of the party, the Soviet leadership also felt obliged to attend to some postwar reconstruction in the party's relations with other groups in Soviet society. Particularly in the reassertion of party control over intellectuals and artists, international implications were deeply involved. This campaign was launched in August 1946 by Andrei Zhdanov, who, according to Djilas, "was regarded in the Politburo as a great intellectual." [71] Zhdanov's assault on ideological slackness in literature and the arts, in philosophy and other academic fields, was logically related to the heightened militancy in foreign policy which he also spearheaded. Artists and intellectuals were remobilized into the service of the party's goals, and any hint of freedom in form or content was violently attacked as evidence of Western bourgeois influence. Organizations and journals were dissolved or reorganized; distinguished artists and scholars were silenced or banished; and a deadly blight of intimidation drove real creativity into an inner emigration from which it began to emerge only after 1953.

After Zhdanov's death in August 1948, the campaign continued no less virulently, but with a somewhat different inflection. The main target of attack became "homeless cosmopolitanism," a formula which combined elements of anti-Semitism and anti-Americanism. The pejorative use of cosmopolitanism in the Soviet press, particularly in *Pravda,* in *Kultura i zhizn* (Culture and Life), and in *Partiinaya zhizn* (Party Life), the directing organs in this campaign, appeared to be a response to strong but essentially nonpolitical yearnings on the part of Soviet youth and intelligentsia to participate in Western cultural currents — to read new Western books, to get acquainted with new Western art, and, above all, to travel and see the world. Against this appetite, the regime sought to impose a picture of the West, particularly of the United States, as decadent, immoral, rotten; American cultural influences were to be treated as a subtle tool of American political power. "American imperialism strives in every way to establish its world hegemony under the flag of cosmopolitanism," a characteristic *Pravda* editorial of the period warned, going on to explain that cosmopolitanism was to be regarded as the obverse side of bourgeois nationalism, which had become a catchall among the deadly sins.[72]

The charges of homeless cosmopolitanism or national nihilism directed against Soviet writers, historians, and playwrights with particular violence during the first half of 1949 coincided with an increasingly overt anti-Americanism in the Soviet theater and press and with an intensified jamming of Voice of America broadcasts. An American observer recorded that more than a hundred Soviet scholars, writers, and artists were removed from their posts, demoted, or reprimanded during this campaign in the early months of 1949, with a high proportion of Jews among the victims.[73] Jewish names were stressed in Soviet press accounts of these attacks. It is possible that the campaign against the Jewish Anti-Fascist Committee, the Yiddish press and theater, and the Zionist movement involved both domestic and foreign-policy motivations. The rekindling of a latent anti-Semitism was a concomitant of the rise of social tensions; it was also an effort to isolate the Jews as carriers of a Western cultural bacillus and may have been related to the reorientation of Soviet foreign policy from a pro-Israel to a pro-Arab position in the Middle East.

Among the fields of intellectual endeavor, one which drew the withering fire of the party and of Stalin personally was the realm of economic thought. The state of the economy was, of course, one of the major preoccupations of the party leadership, and one which had a most direct bearing upon the country's foreign policy.

By 1949 the Soviet Union was in the fourth year of its Fourth Five-Year Plan and was facing serious problems and decisions. While the economy as a whole had almost reached prewar levels, and in many branches of heavy industry had exceeded them, important deficiencies were being felt in steel, railway transport, grain, livestock, and housing.[74] The extreme seriousness of the grain and livestock shortages in this period were later acknowledged among the post-Stalin disclosures; differences among party leaders (including Khrushchev) over how to overcome the slackness of the collective-farm system and increase agricultural output became a central focus of innerparty conflict and have remained so to the present.[75] Without substantial changes in the pattern of investment, the regime made some efforts in this period to meet public pressures for improved standards of living.[76] Some increase in the availability of consumer goods was indicated by retail-price reductions in February 1949 of from 10 to 30 percent on food, clothing, and other household goods,[77] in line with the policy which was followed until 1955 of using price cuts rather than wage increases to distribute additional supplies of consumer goods.

That "some comrades" among the Communist leadership had been pressing for a shift of emphasis in favor of consumer-goods production was indicated three years later by Stalin's sharp attack on this point of view in his 1952 economic commentary. What made the matter still more intriguing was the subsequent revelation that among the comrades castigated by Stalin was Nikolai A. Voznesensky, deputy prime minister, chairman of the State Planning Commission, and member of the Politburo. Furthermore, we now know that a broad range of economic issues were involved, centering on Voznesensky's advocacy of a greater degree of rationalization in the Soviet economic system.

The Voznesensky case has become partly illuminated by small snippets of information emerging over a ten-year period, a little at a time. Although some important aspects are still obscure, it appears that Voznesensky, like Varga, was in some respects a precursor of the revisionist trend in present-day Soviet economics.[78] His case also illustrates the inextricable involvement of innerparty politics with questions of domestic and foreign policy.

Also like Varga, Voznesensky had the misfortune to have written a book.[79] He gave a detailed account of the growth of the Soviet economy during the war and set forth an enthusiastic perspective of the reconstruction and further growth of the Soviet economy from the point of view of a professional economic planner. First published in 1947, the book received a Stalin Prize in May 1948, was serialized in *Pravda,* published by the Russians in the English language, and highly praised in the Soviet and the world Communist press. Voznesensky was among the most promising of the younger men at the top of the hierarchy. He had become deputy prime minister in 1939 as a result of the purges of older men during the preceding years,[80] and in that post had been in charge of defense industries. According to Khrushchev, he was very close to Stalin.[81] Djilas describes a dinner at Stalin's villa in January 1948 at which Voznesensky was one of five Soviet leaders in attendance.[82] According to the description, Voznesensky conducted himself as a junior among seniors (he was then about forty-five years old), being questioned directly by Stalin only about the feasibility of building the Volga-

Don canal (Stalin thought it would be valuable in case of war, as a means of evacuating the Black Sea fleet). Djilas concludes the episode: "Voznesensky agreed that the means could be found, took out a little notebook and made a note of it."

Suddenly on March 13, 1949, without any elaboration, *Pravda* reported that Voznesensky had been relieved of his various positions at a meeting of the Supreme Soviet a few days before. Although rumors concerning his disappearance circulated widely, nothing further was known until three and a half years later when, on December 24, 1952, Mikhail A. Suslov, a secretary of the Central Committee of the party, revealed a hitherto secret decree of the Central Committee concerning Voznesensky. In a *Pravda* article, Suslov was attacking a former editor of the magazine *Bolshevik*, P. N. Fedoseyev, for having failed to acknowledge in a recent series of articles that he had mistakenly praised the Voznesensky book back in 1948. In the course of his articles Suslov's primary purpose became apparent: to disclose a decree of the Central Committee on July 13, 1949, reprimanding and removing the editorial board of *Bolshevik* for their "sycophantic praise" of Voznesensky. This revelation in 1952, which coincided with a wave of public meetings at which economists, historians, administrators, and others were called upon to admit their error in having praised Voznesensky some four years earlier, plus the fact that Stalin's 1952 essay was still refuting ideas advanced in Voznesensky's book — all testify to the persistence of Voznesensky's influence.

What the precise content of this influence may have been can be surmised from the book itself and from a study of Stalin's refutation in his last article (which is the subject of a later chapter). In brief, Voznesensky appears to have been arguing, in guarded language, for a greater degree of rationality in the administration of the economy, for taking account of real costs in assigning prices to producer goods,[83] and for reapportioning the balance of the economy between light and heavy industry, presumably with some additional emphasis on consumer goods. Although Voznesensky had been among those who had led the attack on Varga in 1948, and had argued in his book against Varga's belief that capitalist states could engage in planning, there is no necessary inconsistency between Varga's analysis of capitalism and Voznesensky's prescriptions for the Soviet economy. If one had accepted the possibility of a temporary stabilization of capitalism, a lower estimate of the probability of war, and a long-term perspective on the competition between the two systems, as Varga had advocated, then Voznesensky's redistribution of emphasis between heavy and light industry and the rationalization of the planning process in the Soviet economy would have been a wholly compatible policy. Indeed, in some degree these elements have been accepted by the present Soviet administration. Voznesensky's condemnation of Varga may have had political motivations, of course, unrelated to the substance of the argument.

This possibility seems credible because it is still uncertain to what extent Voznesensky's fall resulted from differences over policy and to what extent he was caught in a factional fight within the second tier of party leaders. In his de-Stalinization speech of 1956, Khrushchev named Voznesensky as one of the innocent victims of the Leningrad Case.[84]

In concluding this account of the domestic factors which had a bearing on Soviet foreign-policy calculations, it is instructive to consider briefly some aspects of the intriguing mystery which has become known as the Leningrad Case, for they suggest the possibility that a factional struggle between rival claimants for power may also have had some bearing on foreign policy.

Looking back over the shifting fortunes of Stalin's immediate subordinates from the end of the war until the spring of 1949, one is led to speculate that Stalin deliberately may have allowed his principal officers to contend with one another as they carried forward main policy responsibilities under his guidance. This arrangement would have had several advantages: Stalin could more easily disengage himself from policies which proved ineffective; the interplay of conflicting opinions in his immediate circle would help him to examine alternative courses of action; and subordinates who were played off against each other would be less able to combine forces to threaten Stalin's own command. This possibility is suggested by the signs of contention between Zhdanov and Malenkov in the period from 1946 to 1948 and, posthumously on the part of Zhdanov, into 1949.[85]

From 1946 on, Zhdanov was in the ascendancy, while Malenkov ceased to be listed as a secretary of the Central Committee. Zhdanov's approach to politics was narrow, dogmatic, and militant. He drove hard for an ideologically stringent line at home. In foreign policy, his actions were predicated upon an assumption of unalloyed hostility, and they involved the aggressive use of the foreign Communists, mass action by the proletariat, the rapid satellization of Eastern Europe, the blockade of Berlin. By the summer of 1948, the effectiveness of this policy seemed at best questionable. The estrangement of Yugoslavia; the failure of potentialities in Germany, France, and Italy to materialize; the unhappy involvement in the Berlin blockade; and, above all, the stimulus which Soviet militancy had provided to the mobilization and cohesion of the Western powers — these represented seriously adverse trends for the Soviet power position. In July 1948, Malenkov returned to the Secretariat. Zhdanov died on the last day of August, at the age of 52.[86]

Zhdanov's stronghold had been Leningrad where, as first secretary of the party, he had guided the heroic defense of the city against the German siege. Early in 1945, he had returned to a post in the Secretariat of the Central Committee in Moscow, and by the following year had emerged as the most powerful figure in the party next to Stalin.[87] Within five months after his death, a systematic purge of his followers and former associates in Leningrad began, including virtually all of the top figures in the party and the government. Some disappeared, some were demoted, and some — including Voznesensky — were executed. In December 1954 it was announced that Victor S. Abakumov, who had been minister of state security from 1947 to 1951, and several of his close colleagues were executed for their part in fabricating the Leningrad Case, but the names of the victims were not given and no details beyond the suggestion that Lavrenti Beria had been deeply implicated. That Stalin had also been involved was charged by Khrushchev in his secret speech at the Twentieth Congress in February 1956, and then Khrushchev for the first time gave the names of some of the victims of the affair. In addition to Voznesenky, an uncertain number of prominent Leningrad party and state officials had perished, including A. A. Kuznetsov, secretary of the Central Committee, Piotr S. Popkov, secretary of the Leningrad Provincial Committee, and Mikhail I. Rodionov, chairman of the Council of Ministers of the Russian Republic. In July 1957, one month after his fight with the so-called antiparty group had come to a climax in the Central Committee, Khrushchev made a speech at a Leningrad factory in which he identified Malenkov as "one of the chief organizers" of the Leningrad affair.[88] In view of the tense factional dispute then in progress, this charge cannot be taken as conclusive evidence of Malenkov's responsibility for the liquidation of Zhdanov's associates, although careful studies of the career lines of the men substituted for the victims suggest that they had been closely associated with Malenkov.

It has been argued that the Leningrad affair may have had significant international implications, in two direct ways. One is a possible tie between Tito and the Leningrad party group, which is charged by Stalin in one of his letters of indictment against the Yugoslavs in which he accuses Djilas of having collected intelligence from the Leningrad organization during a visit to the city in January 1948.[89] Although the charge as stated has the appearance of gross inflation, it is difficult to dismiss the linkage altogether in view of the fact that the nature of the relationship between Zhdanov and Tito has never been clear; the possibility remains that the overt attack on Tito did bear some connection to the collapse of Zhdanov's position and the attack on his followers.

The other and related speculation is that the purge of Zhdanov's associates also extended into the Communist international movement and had something to do with the arrests of Traicho Kostov in March 1949, of Laszlo Rajk in June 1949, and subsequently of Rudolf Slansky in November 1951.[90] These three, who were executed with a number of others on charges of Titoism and other capital offenses, were, with the exception of Slansky, posthumously rehabilitated in 1956.

To come back to Voznesensky — the mystery remains about whether his policies or his politics were his undoing. He has been listed among the victims of the Leningrad Case, and his removal from office coincides with that of the other associates of Zhdanov. But Stalin was involved in important differences of policy with Voznesensky,[91] and was still fighting these issues in his last article. Moreover, Voznesensky is listed in Soviet official sources as having been shot in October 1950, whereas the other Leningrad victims are said to have died in 1949.[92] Perhaps time will reveal that both causes were involved in his downfall, or conceivably still other factors will come to light.

We must remind ourselves that to associate men and events in Soviet policy is to tread upon very uncertain ground. The case for Zhdanov's identification with the "harsh external pressures" which stimulated the Western mobilization seems fairly strong, but it is not conclusive. It would be surprising if there were not some differences of emphasis among the various leaders of the Soviet Union, whether from temperament, experience, age, area of predominant interest, or as an incidental aspect of personal rivalries. Whether this is so or not and, if so, which men are identified with which political tendencies in which period — these for the most part still remain in the realm of speculation. In a field with so many hidden reaches, responsible speculation performs a valuable function. It suggests hypotheses and sharpens perceptions. The danger lies in forgetting what it is we think we know and what we think may be so.

In the present case, it is sufficient to remind ourselves that these shifts in policies may have been accompanied and complicated by rivalries within the party leadership. However this may be, the view from Moscow in the spring of 1949 would have looked out upon adverse trends in Europe and North America, an unconsolidated control position in Eastern Europe, and, above all, a domestic base which needed time before it would be strong enough to bring about a more favorable balance of forces in the world.

# III

# PEACEFUL COEXISTENCE, SWEET
# AND SOUR

THE period in Soviet foreign policy from the beginning of 1949 to the autumn of that year is dominated by two climactic waves of effort, one directed against the signing of the North Atlantic Treaty and the other against the formation of a West German government. With the failure of these efforts, Soviet fortunes reached their lowest point in the postwar years.

As in Aesop's fable of the wind and the sun, the Soviet Union sought to improve its situation alternatively by intimidation and by conciliation. These conflicting tendencies give the period a feeling of groping experimentation. But one advantage of such contradictions is that a shift in emphasis is sufficient to achieve a change of course. The elements of the new course had been present during the previous period as a subordinate peace theme, like a piccolo accompanying the tympani.

Reiterations of belief in the possibility of "peaceful coexistence" had been a consistent feature of Soviet pronouncements, even during the most militant phases of Soviet policy. Stalin's interviews during 1946 with Associated Press correspondent Eddy Gilmore and Elliott Roosevelt, and in 1947 with Harold E. Stassen,[1] all repeated the formula that peaceful coexistence was possible between states having different economic systems, provided the capitalist states wished to collaborate and were willing to abide by wartime and postwar agreements. The implication of this formula was that the responsibility for breaking the Yalta and Potsdam agreements

regarding Central and Eastern Europe rested with Great Britain
and the United States. Even at the founding meeting of the Cominform in 1947, the declarations of Zhdanov and Malenkov included
a passing reference to peaceful coexistence, although the context,
particularly of the uncompromisingly militant Zhdanov speech,
suggested that the Soviet leaders saw the current situation as one
of conflict so long as the West resisted Soviet terms of settlement
for Europe.[2]

During the latter part of 1948, when the Soviet Union was shifting
the main brunt of its attack from the Marshall Plan to the North
Atlantic Treaty, it continued for a long while to put its main reliance upon a policy of thundering intimidation, with occasional
interspersions of conciliatory statements to selected audiences in
the West, such as the exchange of correspondence between Stalin
and Henry Wallace in May 1948. At this stage, these sporadic efforts were relatively ineffective, first because they were drowned
out by the Berlin blockade and other militant actions and, second,
because they lacked the systematic and organized character of subsequent Soviet efforts to manipulate public opinion in the Western
countries. There are signs during this period of the dawning Soviet
awareness of the possibilities for such manipulative action and a bit
of trial-and-error experimentation in this direction.

At the end of October 1948, for example, Stalin published an
interview in *Pravda* in which he drew a lesson from the defeat of
Churchill at the polls and called upon "the social forces standing
for peace" to deal a similar fate to "all the other warmongers" in
the West.[3] This paragraph was generally understood in the Communist movement as a directive toward political action to unseat
the leaders in the West who supported the North Atlantic Treaty
and other measures intended to strengthen the Western position
against the Soviet Union. It was often quoted as such by the French
and Italian Communist parties in the following months, and it was
also used in the Peace Movement, as we shall see in the next
chapter.

The same kind of experimental probing was suggested in the annual speech on the anniversary of the revolution, delivered in November 1948 by Foreign Minister Molotov. The tone of Molotov's address was essentially defensive. Taking note of the increase in the United States military budget, the creation of American military bases in various parts of the world, the stationing of American troops abroad, the continued functioning of the Anglo-American military staff in Washington, and "the creation of all sorts of 'alliances' and 'blocs' of Western states," Molotov diagnosed these symptoms as indications that "changes have taken place in the policy of the ruling circles of the United States and Great Britain."[4] (This analysis was formalized as the basic assumption of Soviet policy in this period, as indicated in a statement of the Ministry of Foreign Affairs on the North Atlantic Pact in January which began: "The Soviet Union is compelled to take into consideration the fact that the ruling circles of the United States and Great Britain have gone over to a frankly aggressive political course . . ."[5] In characterizing this policy of the West, however, Molotov made a small but important distinction. "Among the ruling circles of these countries," he said, "there are many hankering to realize their predatory plans, plans aimed at establishing the world domination of the Anglo-American bloc." The difference between a situation in which an entire ruling class is committed to aggression and one in which some leaders are not so committed seemed to him to offer some small footing for maneuver. The implication was plain that leverage remained for political and diplomatic action with those who were opposed to the prevailing Western policy. Like Zhdanov in his 1947 Cominform speech, Molotov saw the existence in the world of two hostile camps, but the division between them appeared to him as a dotted line running through the middle of the Western societies.

Molotov cited the opposition of scientists and others in Great Britain and the United States to their governments' rejection of the Soviet demand for a ban on atomic bombs. He also banked heavily on the opposition to this policy by the Progressive Party in the United States (the election which demonstrated its small following had occurred only two days before Molotov's speech). Molotov expressed his reliance upon world public opinion, including the people of the Western countries, to isolate and restrain the "aggressive elements."

## The Failure of a Peace Offensive

The first efforts of the Soviet leadership to check the adverse trend in international affairs were directed toward creating an atmosphere of détente, or relaxation of tension, by measures which, without involving any substantive alteration of Soviet policy, might diminish public support for the Western mobilization.

In following the course of Soviet policy, it is often necessary to make a careful distinction between efforts to reduce the atmosphere of international tension and measures which actually deal with the issues responsible for tension. There is of course a large subjective element in the shifting moods of public opinion in democratic countries, susceptible to change under the influence of symbolic propaganda — a smiling photograph of the Soviet leader, an exchange of visits by heads of state, an amiable interview, or, in the other direction, by a public display of anger and rudeness. The effect of such symbolic acts is magnified by Western mass media to the point where, as an observer once described it, a second helping of ice cream by Molotov in San Francisco launches a new "peace offensive."

This kind of atmospheric change was evident, for example, in the *Information Bulletin* issued by the Soviet Embassy in Washington in January 1949. It departed from its previous pattern of denunciation of American warmongers and imperialists and carried instead a conciliatory article by the *Pravda* correspondent at the United Nations, wishing the people of the United States a Happy New Year and expressing the conviction that "there are no barriers to the goodwill of peoples aspiring toward a common aim."

The first step in what was to be a short-lived experiment with a peace offensive in Europe was taken by the French Communist Party on January 11, 1949. The veteran French Communist, Marcel Cachin, as dean of the French National Assembly, used the opening of its sessions to declaim, in terms of surprising mildness, on the possibilities of peaceful coexistence. Remembering Cachin's violent discourse on the same occasion the year before, the deputies and journalists present looked at each other with astonishment as Cachin, avoiding direct criticism of the United States or the Marshall Plan, spoke of the possibility of the peaceful settlement of problems between East and West, the desirability of a meeting between Stalin and Truman, and the noninevitability of war. It was understood that this utterance had meaning beyond the walls of the Chamber, and the deputies asked themselves: "Is this a new peace offensive launched by the Soviet Union?" [6] Astonishment deepened as the Communist deputies accepted with good grace two secondary vice presidencies of the Assembly instead of the first vice presidency, in contrast with their undisguised resentment over the same issue twelve months before.

The impression that Cachin had been designated to signal a change in tone, at least, of Communist deportment was strengthened when, three days later, he flew to Italy; his arrival was followed by an immediate cessation of a Communist "campaign of noncollaboration" with the government and a series of speeches on peaceful coexistence by Palmiro Togliatti, leader of the Italian Communist Party. Both Cachin and Togliatti endeavored to breathe life into the abandoned project of President Truman to send a personal representative to talk with Stalin.

What was necessary to solve world problems peacefully, said Togliatti, was a "complete collaboration between the Great Powers in strict compliance with the agreements reached after the War, which have been unilaterally violated." [7] The experience of the Italian Communist Party with militant tactics had paralleled that of the French party: strikes, riots, and demonstrations in the parliament had reduced Communist influence and had pushed the government toward the right. Now Togliatti announced that the Communists were ready to discuss all Italian social problems with the adversaries of Communism, that the new course was devoted to peaceful methods. "We are profoundly convinced," he said, "that within this generation socialism will win at least in all European countries. But it will win by peaceful methods."

A theoretical underpinning for this position was provided by Victor Michaut, a leading member of the French Communist Party in the January issue of the organ of the Central Committee of the party. At no time, he said, had either Lenin or Stalin "seen war as a means of fructifying humanity or hastening the victory of social- ism . . . Socialism, to triumph finally in the world, has no need of a monstrous apocalypse; its best ally is not war but peace."[8] The article recalled the various interviews with Americans in which Stalin had advanced the position that it was possible for different systems to coexist and even collaborate peacefully. This showed, he said, that "on the Soviet side, there exists no reason of principle for excluding the possibility of cooperation with the capitalist states, this cooperation on the contrary being judged useful and desirable in the interests of the people and in the interest of Peace."

A major policy declaration by the Soviet leadership soon con- firmed peaceful coexistence as the order of the day, but it illustrated the difficulty which the Soviet Union had in freeing itself from the narrow constraints and contradictions of this period. This was delivered on January 21, 1949, the twenty-fifth anniversary of Lenin's death, by Piotr N. Pospelov, editor of *Pravda,* before an audience which included the entire Politburo. Pospelov recalled, as was ap- propriate to the occasion, how Lenin had appealed to the peoples of the West over the heads of their governments during periods of Soviet weakness. Although he advanced the standard argument about the inevitable decline of the capitalist world and expressed confidence that Communism would emerge triumphant, the im- mediate defensive function of the peaceful-coexistence line, he emphasized, was to hold in check the "forces of aggression and incendiaries of a new war." [9]

The question was, how to do this? From the practical point of view, who could be regarded as the "social forces standing for peace," whom Stalin had urged the Communists to cultivate, and what was to be the basis of cooperation? The narrowness of Pospelov's answer is evident in this key sentence: "The working class is drawing to its side wide strata of the peasantry and progressive intelligentsia, rallying them for the struggle for a lasting peace, for democracy, for the vital interests of the working people, for national independence." This directive meant that the preferred cooperation was to stop short of the middle classes; that it was to include only the peasants and left-wing intellectuals; and that the program of cooperation went no further than the Cominform line of peace, proletarian class interests, and national independence from the United States. There was not much room here for the foreign Communists to achieve the political action they were called upon to perform in their countries. Particularly, as Pospelov recognized, the issue of nationalism was a dangerous two-edged sword. While appealing to the nationalism of the peoples of the West, as an antibody to the spread of American hegemony, he decried any manifestation of the same phenomenon within the Soviet orbit. "Nationalism, as the ideology of the bourgeoisie, is the enemy of Marxism," he declared. "Today the imperialists are striving to use nationalism to weaken the democratic, anti-imperialist camp."

This dialectical argument reflects one of the embarrassments under which Soviet policy was laboring at this moment. Against the supranational appeal of Western policy expressed in the Marshall Plan, the NATO proposal, and various unification schemes then in the air, Soviet policy was seeking to arouse nationalist sentiments within the Western European countries. At this very time, however, the systematic campaign against national deviationism in Eastern Europe as a result of the Titoist heresy was reaching a fever pitch, and at home the attack against homeless cosmopolitanism was just then being mounted. The Writers' Union was in the same month beginning its campaign against servility to the West among Soviet writers and critics; *Pravda* and *Kultura i zhizn* were launching a series of exposés of Soviet intellectuals and artists charged with "antipatriotic" sentiments. The virulence of this campaign, with its narrow chauvinism and its undisguised attacks upon Jews, Catholics, and Americans as the culprits who were trying to undermine the "national roots" of the Soviet people, was a practical as well as logical contradiction to the internationalist pretensions of the Communist movement. The effect of this contradiction is most vividly seen in an explosive episode which brought the peace offensive to an abrupt halt.

### The Attack on Nationalism

On February 22, 1949, at a meeting of the Central Committee of the French Communist Party in Paris, its general secretary, Maurice Thorez, advanced a new formula to define the party's relationship to the Soviet Union. Up to this time, the governing statement on this point had been formulated by the Politburo of the French party on September 30, 1948, as: "The people of France will not, will never, fight against the Soviet Union."[10] Now Thorez apparently felt it necessary to go further. In response to the question, "What would you do if the Red Army occupied Paris?" which he propounded rhetorically as one that the "enemies of the people" had been putting to the French Communist Party, he replied with a declaration of all-out support for the Red Army, even if it should enter upon the territory of France.[11]

Although Thorez sought to keep the flag of French nationalism in his grasp by attacking the government for following a "treacherous antinational" policy of "surrender to the American monopolists," this new line actually marked the extreme antinational position of the party and of the world Communist movement. The Thorez statement was reproduced in the pages of the *Cominform Bulletin*, and within ten days it had been copied almost verbatim by Communist parties throughout the world.

The repercussions in France were intense and immediate. Within a day, it was announced that the National Assembly would debate the matter. Reacting defiantly, *L'Humanité,* the daily newspaper of the French party, declared editorially that Thorez had opened "a new phase of the fundamental and decisive battle for peace." [12]

When the National Assembly opened its debate on February 24, Thorez was confronted with a direct question posed by an MRP (Catholic moderate left) deputy: "Are you or are you not the chief of a party at the orders of a foreign government?" Thorez repeated his original declaration word for word, and then for forty minutes developed his argument that the French government had associated itself with the imperialist governments of Britain and the United States which were preparing for war. The outraged Assembly demanded Thorez' prosecution for treason, the outlawing of the French Communist Party, the lifting of the parliamentary immunity of its leaders, and a full investigation. However, the rhetorical and hypothetical phrasing of Thorez' declaration offered no grounds for prosecution, and the Assembly faced a dilemma: if Thorez' parliamentary immunity were to be lifted for treason, the sentence would have to be death, or — and this was more likely — the matter would end in an acquittal. After stormy fulminations the Assembly passed a resolution, 386 to 182, condemning the Thorez declaration and calling upon the government to defend national independence and apply the law. [13]

This dramatic confrontation was followed by police raids upon Communist publishing centers and the CGT (Communist-dominated labor federation) headquarters in Paris, and seizures of party documents. A number of people were held for interrogation, eight of whom were eventually threatened with prosecution for divulging military information to diplomatic attachés of an Eastern European state or for possessing national security information. These prosecutions dragged on ineffectually for several months, while the government was shaken by the impotent anger of the other parties, most notably that of General de Gaulle, who declared at an emergency session of the executive committee of his party that the state must be reorganized "to wrest from the Communists their power over part of the people" and to save France from a Soviet invasion.[14] In the tense atmosphere of the following weeks, the police reported the finding of bombs of the Molotov cocktail type in coal pits in the north and of a severed electric cable in another mine, implying sabotage, and announced that street demonstrations would be banned and that persons distributing handbills calling for demonstrations would be arrested.

Perhaps the obvious impotence of the government reinforced the strong public feeling that Thorez had gone too far. Even among those who had no sympathy for the government's policy, this challenge to French patriotism was received with aversion. It is reported that among party cadres the extreme antinationalism of the Thorez position caused doubts and resignations.[15] This extreme declaration of fealty to the Soviet Union was bound to weaken the party's support from the French people for the current antiwar platform. Why, then, did Thorez feel it necessary to go so far?

Was this a measured utterance, planned in advance, or an outburst in the heat of argument? The fact that it was delivered in the Central Committee, not in public debate, suggests that the declaration did not arise in response to the heckling of the opposition. The immediate public dissemination of the statement by the Communist press and the echoing response of the other Communist parties suggest strongly that it was a deliberate maneuver. At the same time, the party had arranged a large public meeting of "Homage to the Soviet Army in Honor of Its Thirty-First Anniversary," and on this occasion the Central Committee issued a "Salute to the Soviet Army" declaring that "the people of France . . . put themselves resolutely and in all circumstances in the camp where the Soviet Union and its heroic Army is naturally to be found, the world camp of democracy and peace." If Thorez' declaration was part of a deliberate pattern, why did he go beyond the previous declaration of the politburo that the people of France would not go to war against the Soviet Union?

By this action, the French Communist Party and the other parties following in its wake demonstrated in an unmistakable way their freedom from any taint of nationalism, any suspicion of Titoist heresy. The Soviet campaign against Tito and bourgeois nationalism was in full tide, and the parties of Eastern Europe, as we have seen, were in the midst of a purge of deviationists. In throwing away the patriotic reputation that the French party had painfully regained since its policy of revolutionary defeatism during the period of the Nazi-Soviet Pact, Thorez was making a grand gesture of absolute loyalty to the Motherland of the Revolution. It could not have been regarded as necessary or useful within the French context alone.[16]

On the plane of international politics, the action can be understood as a reinforcement of the desperate Soviet effort to block the signing of the North Atlantic Treaty by measures of extreme militancy, playing upon the deeply rooted fear of war in Western Europe. Repeating the strategy of revolutionary defeatism which had characterized the foreign Communist parties during the Nazi-Soviet Pact, these new declarations, coordinated with strikes which were at the moment particularly violent in Italy, clearly implied the threat of invasion, sabotage, and civil war if the North Atlantic Treaty were to come into force. The French party at this time was organizing a clandestine network to carry out sabotage in the event of war or, in any case, to block the delivery of military supplies under the North Atlantic Treaty. In Italy, after brief but violent Communist demonstrations in the parliament and a one-hour general strike in Rome against the treaty, the Communist labor federation was obliged to drop its plans for a nation-wide general strike because of the non-Communist unions' refusal to join in the action.

The implied threat of civil war in these actions was made explicit by the Soviet Union in a number of ways. Radio Moscow, in its commentary to the West on these declarations, said:

The Communist parties in capitalist countries have warned the ruling circles of these countries that if the warmongers attempt to realize their plans, aimed against the Soviet Union, the working class will carry out its duty of international proletarian solidarity.[17]

A Soviet Army officer, writing in the newspaper of the Soviet High Commission in Germany, *Taegliche Rundschau,* spelled out the threat of invasion and civil war:

The declarations of the leaders of the Communist parties of France, Italy, Belgium, and the Netherlands, etc., have shown what attitude the democratic masses of the people in these countries will adopt if the Anglo-American imperialists should dare to kindle another war against the Soviet Union and the People's Democracies. If democratic forces in spite of all efforts for peace should not succeed in preventing another world war, the Soviet Army in the course of pursuing the imperialist aggressor naturally will be compelled to march into the territory of some West European states.[18]

*Izvestiya,* in the course of a review of the twenty-third volume of Lenin's works, took the occasion to draw a parallel between the current situation and Lenin's admonition to the workers during World War I to turn the conflict into a revolutionary struggle for power. Referring to the declarations of the French and other Communist parties in support of the Red Army, *Izvestiya* said: "if the imperialists try to drag them to the slaughter by force, they will unite and do everything to turn their weapons against the instigators of a new imperialist war." [19]

The foreign Communist movement was taking an extreme antinational position apparently for the dual purpose of demonstrating to Moscow its freedom from any Titoist taint and of communicating to the West Moscow's threat of civil disruption in the event of war. In such circumstances, all thought of peaceful coexistence was lost. Instead, the threatening tone of Soviet utterances and actions reached a climax in late March and early April 1949, as the negotiations on the North Atlantic Treaty entered their final round.

Throughout this period, the Soviet press professed its apprehensions not only about the treaty itself, but also about possible Mediterranean and Pacific pacts to follow, the development of Western military bases in Spain, and the incorporation of West Germany into the Western military alliance.

In diplomatic notes the Soviet government threatened to annul its wartime treaties of alliance with France and Great Britain. It denounced the proposed North Atlantic Treaty as incompatible with the United Nations Charter and announced the withdrawal of the Soviet Union, the Ukraine, and Belorussia from the World Health Organization. Soviet exports of chrome and manganese to the United States were drastically reduced. On Red Army Day, February 22, *Pravda* compared the United States' "policy of aggression" with that of Hitler and Japan and called for the strengthening of the army to counter American "saber rattling." The Soviet press revived memories of the Allied intervention during the civil war thirty years before, and anti-Americanism reached a new and more virulent extreme in the Soviet press. "The Mad Haberdasher" was one of fifteen plays in the current Soviet repertory carrying a crudely anti-American theme. Gorky's uncomplimentary vignettes of life in Chicago and New York were being reprinted in the Soviet press. An intensified censorship prevented foreign newspapermen from reporting the full extent of the anti-American propaganda in the Soviet press.[20] Charges of espionage were raised against some American newspapermen. The jamming of the Voice of America was increased. The Soviet Union ordered its consulates in Italy closed. Further reports of troop movements on the borders of Yugoslavia were circulated in Western Europe, and the Soviet Union revived the Macedonian question as a threat to both Greece and Yugoslavia. Border incidents with Iran increased, and the Iranian consulate in Baku was closed. In Eastern Europe, the continuing purges of national deviationists implied a general tightening of party ranks against any eventuality.

Despite — or possibly because of — this thunderous orchestration of threats of civil war, sabotage, invasion, strikes, treaty cancellations, parliamentary obstruction, and international working-class solidarity, the negotiation of the North Atlantic Treaty moved steadily forward. Once the treaty was signed in Washington on April 4, 1949, the great crescendo began to subside. Only a few rumbles remained to mark the transition to a new phase of Soviet efforts to check the further growth of Western power.

### The German Problem

The next immediate task for the Soviet Union in Europe was to forestall the formation of a West German government. To do this would require the reversal of a trend that had been building up momentum for more than a year, stimulated by the Soviet blockade of Berlin. During late 1948 and early 1949, the negotiations to translate into reality the agreement in principle among the three Western powers to set up a West German government out of their zones of occupation had been developing along a triangular pattern. The United States and Great Britain were confronted with French fears of the danger of a reconstituted central authority in Germany. At this point in history, the French seemed more preoccupied with the menace of revived German militarism than with the threat of Soviet aggression.[21] On the other hand, the British and Americans were dealing with an intricate domestic political pattern in Germany, where some thought was expressed of a compromise role for Germany, midway between East and West, and where many Germans feared that the formation of a West Germany would make German reunification less likely in the future.

By the time of the signing of the North Atlantic Treaty, there were signs that these difficulties were about to be surmounted. On April 8, 1849, a joint communiqué issued by the foreign ministers of the United States, Great Britain, and France announced their full agreement on all questions relating to the establishment and control of a Western German Federal Republic.[22] They had agreed that the military government would be terminated as soon as the republic was established and that occupation troops would remain for security reasons under a new and simpler Occupation Statute.

Everything depended now on getting German assent to these principles. After a period of intensive negotiations with the major parties and political figures of West Germany, the three Western military governors announced, on April 25, 1949, that agreement had been reached. Under a specific timetable, the approval of the new constitution by the Parliamentary Council at Bonn was expected by the middle of May and the new government was to be established by mid-July.

The American view of the strategic significance of these measures was described by General Clay, military governor of the American zone, in these terms:

The formation of an association of the free nations of Western Europe with Germany integrated therein will create lasting stability in Europe and will not only end the threat of Communist expansion but will make it difficult for the Communist front to keep intact. It is the only sure way to peace.[23]

Secretary of State Dean Acheson expressed the view that these measures, together with the recovery of Europe under the Marshall Plan and the strengthening of Europe under the North Atlantic Treaty, had changed the international atmosphere by putting strength into what previously had been a vacuum in Western Europe.[24]

Soviet calculations regarding the German problem at this juncture had to take account not only of the rapid progress of these negotiations for the establishment of the Federal Republic, but also of the consequences of the counterblockade and airlift and the general effects of the blockade upon the international situation.

The Western counterblockade had been stringently tightened in the early part of 1949, with economic effects upon East Germany and Eastern Europe that appeared to be seriously disadvantageous to the Russians.[25] This came at a time when the Soviet Union was pressing for an acceleration in the collectivization of agriculture in Eastern Europe, and it provided an additional source of political tension in an already difficult situation. In East Germany itself, living standards had continued to fall; they were low in comparison with West Germany and even of blockaded West Berlin. By March 1949, production in the three Western zones had reached 85 percent that of 1936 levels, compared with 50 percent in June 1948.[26] The political effects of this contrast, and of resentment against Soviet plant removals and reparation seizures, were reflected in the fact that in May 1949, despite heavy policing of the polls, one third of the voters in the Soviet zone cast ballots against the Communist delegates to the People's Congress and against the Russian plan for German unity. A Communist official on the scene was quoted as saying: "This is the greatest bankruptcy in the history of the Party." [27]

The success of the Berlin airlift also constituted an adverse factor, from the Soviet point of view, as a symbolic demonstration of Western power, determination, and technological capabilities. As if to cap its achievement, the airlift on April 16, the 294th day of the blockade, set a record of 1,398 flights in 24 hours, carrying a total of 12,941 short tons of supplies.[28] In terms of propaganda, the situation cast the West in the position of using its strength in a humanitarian cause, while the Soviet Union was seen as a power which used starvation as an instrument of policy. Moreover, although the airlift in itself provided a clear advertisement of the American intention to stand by commitments in Europe, the point was reinforced by several official declarations. In an extemporaneous talk on April 6, 1949, President Truman declared that he would not hesitate to use the atomic bomb again if it were necessary for the welfare of the United States and the democracies of the world.[29] This reassurance was reported as having had a heartening effect in France.[30] General Clay referred to this biggest assemblage of United States troops in Europe since the end of the war as a "symbol of our country's still firm will to fight for the rights of free men."

The significant point about the Berlin confrontation, however, was that it represented a wary test of will by measures short of force. The West did not try to break down the blockade by direct military action; it chose rather the flanking maneuver of the airlift and the nonviolent reprisal of the counterblockade. The Soviet Union, for its part, cautiously avoided provocative interference with the air corridors to Berlin. In the face of these mutual restraints, the West was able to frustrate the Soviet attempt to incorporate West Berlin on the chosen ground of political maneuvering.

Nevertheless, the tension of the confrontation and the uncertainty of whether the level of violence would be raised, either intentionally or by accident, provided a continuing stimulus to the further development of Western cohesion and military power. On April 8, 1949, the same day on which the three Western powers reported final accord on the establishment of a West German Federal Republic, the defense ministers of the five Brussels Treaty powers, with American and Canadian participation, announced agreement on a sweeping plan for the defense of Western Europe "to meet any attack from the East." [31] Four days later, the United States and Britain reported agreement on facilities in England to be placed at the disposition of the United States Air Force for atomic bombers. Plans for a radar warning net, approximately 900 miles in length, stretching from north to south across Western Europe, were also announced as evidence of the strides made by the military committee of the Western Union. On the following day, the three Western powers announced that they had all decided to reduce their scheduled dismantling of German industry and to liberalize restrictions on German industrial production.[32] The next day, the United States Congress passed an authorization of $5.4 billion to extend the European Recovery Program for another fifteen months. Within a few weeks, talk was reported from Europe of the necessity of the appointment of an American as commander-in-chief of the North Atlantic forces.[33] In May, the State Department announced that the administration proposed to request almost a billion and a half dollars for a military-assistance program to strengthen the defenses of Western Europe. In presenting the program, the State Department's "Peace Paper" described the current defenses of Western Europe as weak enough to invite aggression and declared: "the need to act now arises out of the insecurity and fears of Western Europe and of other freedom-loving nations of the world." [34]

All these measures, coming with increasing momentum in the spring of 1949, must have suggested to the Soviet leaders that they had to remove what Churchill had described as the harsh external pressures. The most obvious necessity was to terminate as gracefully as possible the Berlin blockade, which had not only failed of its purpose, but was becoming a greater disadvantage with each passing day.

An interesting example of the Soviet technique of feeling out the optimum terms available for achieving a desired purpose can be found in the sequence of steps by which the blockade was brought to an end during the first five months of 1949. In January, the Russians publicly indicated an exploratory attitude toward the possibility of bringing about an end to the blockade.[35] On January 30, Stalin chose to reply to a series of four questions submitted by an American newspaperman, J. Kingsbury Smith, which had some relevance to the blockade.[36] Two of the questions bore on the possibility of a declaration or pact between the Soviet Union and the United States expressing the peaceful intent of both countries; another question dealt with the possibility of a meeting between Stalin and Truman, and the fourth with the lifting of the blockade.

In response to the question concerning the meeting with President Truman, Stalin repeated that he would have no objection to it. When Smith cabled from Paris a further inquiry, asking Stalin's reaction to a report that a White House spokesman had quoted the President as willing to receive Stalin in Washington, Stalin replied that his doctors would not permit him to make so prolonged a journey, but offered to meet the President in the Soviet Union or Eastern Europe.[37] The President and the Secretary of State gave indications that this was out of the question while the blockade was in progress, and there the matter was to rest, despite indirect Communist efforts to prod the United States into taking the initiative on the project.

With regard to the problem of the blockade itself, the question as asked by the reporter was a sufficiently leading one to enable Stalin to state his terms without appearing to be a suppliant. (We cannot know whether the Russians selected this series of questions from among the many queries available at any one time for the purpose of putting out a feeler to the West, or even if they encouraged the asking of a question along these lines; or whether the Soviet government interpreted the interviewer's question as an unofficial feeler inspired by the United States government.) Smith asked: "If the Governments of the United States of America, the United Kingdom, and France agreed to postpone the establishment of a separate Western German State, pending a meeting of the Council of Foreign Ministers to consider the German problem as a whole, would the Government of the USSR be prepared to remove the restrictions which the Soviet authorities have imposed on communications between Berlin and the Western zones of Germany?" To which Stalin replied: "Provided the United States of America, Great Britain, and France observed the conditions set forth in the third question, the Soviet Government sees no obstacle to lifting transport restrictions, on the understanding, however, that transport and trade restrictions introduced by the Three Powers should be lifted simultaneously."

Two weeks later, there was a nibble on the line. In the delegates' lounge at the United Nations, Ambassador Phillip C. Jessup, acting under instructions, inquired informally of the Soviet representative, Ambassador Jacob Malik, whether Stalin's omission of the currency question as a condition of the settlement of the blockade had been intentional. Malik promised to look into the question. The Soviet Union allowed the matter to rest for thirty days. During that time, rigorous winter weather was still buffeting the airlift, which had been obliged to reduce food shipments in order to alleviate a crisis in coal, at one time reduced to a one-week supply. During that time also a committee of experts from neutral nations was still at work under the aegis of the United Nations secretariat on a possible compromise on the currency question. By the middle of March, however, it was apparent that the airlift was not only surviving but setting new records; that the United Nations committee of experts was reaching a dead end; that the Western powers were about to introduce a second currency reform, making the West mark sole legal tender in West Berlin; that the counterblockade was being intensified; and that the West was progressing rapidly toward the signing of the North Atlantic Treaty and the formation of a West German government.

On March 15, Malik informed Jessup that the omission of the currency question in the Kingsbury Smith interview had not been accidental and that the Soviet Union was willing to discuss currency along with the entire problem of Germany at a meeting of the Council of Foreign Ministers. In response to a further inquiry from Jessup about whether the Soviet government meant that the meeting of the Council of Foreign Ministers would have to precede the lifting of the blockade, Malik replied on March 21 that the Soviet government would agree to a lifting of the blockade providing the counterblockade were also lifted and a date set for the meeting of foreign ministers.

By this time, the attitude of the adversaries toward a lifting of the blockade appeared reversed. The Western powers, confident of the airlift, had their attention concentrated on breaking a deadlock among the West German parties on the revised Occupation Statute and a constitution and displayed no anxiety about rushing into negotiations. Special envoy Robert Murphy was hurried to Bonn to assist General Clay in urgent sessions with seventeen West German politicians. Only a few hours following the announcement that the German Social Democratic Party had accepted a compromise and that no further obstacle remained to an agreement between the occupying powers and the West German parties on a constitution, the official Soviet news agency, Tass, made public an account of the Jessup-Malik conversations, which had been conducted in secrecy, in an apparent effort to mobilize public pressure for a settlement.[38]

Soviet efforts to develop popular support in Western Europe for a more pliant policy on the part of the Western negotiators were having less and less effect. In March, Marshal Vasily Sokolovsky, who had been identified with the imposition of the blockade, had been withdrawn and rumors were circulated in Berlin that the blockade could be ended shortly.[39] Satellite diplomats were utilized to distribute broad hints that the lifting of the blockade would not be difficult to arrange.[40] Mass rallies of the Peace Movement were being held in New York during March and in Paris and Prague during April. Despite some nervousness in France about the concurrent Soviet threats against the signing of the North Atlantic Treaty, on the whole public opinion in Europe held firm against the Soviet gestures, and the hands of the Western negotiators were not forced by popular pressures for a settlement at any cost. An observer in Paris reported: "Although diplomats in Europe believe that part of the public may still be misled by Moscow's pacific gestures, they agree that never before has there been such widespread unwillingness in Europe to take Soviet utterances seriously in the absence of specific proposals." [41]

The Soviet Union endeavored to meet this demand for specific proposals by tentative suggestions that another current conflict could be resolved: the civil war in Greece. During April the Greek guerrilla government began to broadcast appeals for United Nations mediation of the conflict. On May 3, an important political leader of the Greek Communists was reported to have offered in Prague a series of proposals for a settlement.[42] On May 19, Tass quoted Andrei Gromyko, then the deputy foreign minister, as expressing Soviet willingness to talk over a settlement of the conflict on the basis of the proposals of the Greek guerrilla government. It was revealed that Gromyko had held a series of private conversations at the United Nations beginning in April with Dean Rusk, American Assistant Secretary of State for United Nations Affairs, and Hector McNeil, British Minister of State, on conditions for ending the Greek conflict. By this time, however, the Western position had been strengthened by the defection of Yugoslavia from the Soviet orbit and the consequent weakening of the Greek Communists. The State Department announced on May 20, in response to the Tass dispatch, that the United States and Britain rejected the Soviet suggestion and urged instead that the Soviet Union cease giving aid to the guerrilla forces. In fact, as it appeared later from Yugoslav sources, the Soviet Union had been opposed to the Greek civil war from the outset and had been urging the Yugoslavs to bring the operation to a close in January 1948, on the eve of the break with Tito.[43] After the split, the Soviets purged the "nationalists" among the Greek Communists, and this, with the closing of the border between Greece and Yugoslavia, brought an end to the civil war — without, however, giving the Soviet Union the advantage of being able to claim the action as a proof of its pacific intentions.

Meanwhile, finding that it was not possible to get the West to yield on the formation of a West German government or to withdraw the currency reform in exchange for a lifting of the Berlin blockade, the Soviet government determined, apparently in late March or early April, to accept a settlement in exchange for the minimum demand of a meeting of the Council of Foreign Ministers. In so doing, the Soviet Union may have hoped that the circumstances of a foreign ministers' meeting combined with a lifting of the blockade would achieve what the blockade itself had been intended to accomplish.

On May 4 the Soviet delegate to the United Nations reached final agreement with the British, French, and American representatives in New York, and on May 5 a four-power communiqué was issued, announcing that the blockade and counterblockade would be lifted on May 12 and that the Council of Foreign Ministers would meet in Paris on May 23, on "questions relating to Germany and the problems arising out of the situation in Berlin, including also questions of the currency in Berlin." [44]

For the Russians, the race had been lost. The Basic Law for the Federal Republic of Germany was signed at Bonn on May 23, the very day on which the meetings of the foreign ministers were to begin.

### The Sixth Session of the Council of Foreign Ministers

In retrospect, it appears that the Russians desired a meeting of the Council of Foreign Ministers not because they were prepared to modify positions for the purpose of negotiation, but in the expectation that the public pressure for a meeting in a conciliatory atmosphere would produce concessions on the crucial question of Germany. Failing this, the meeting would at least provide a face-saving way for the termination of the blockade.

That the Russians were out to create a conciliatory atmosphere, no one on the scene could doubt. "It is worth coming to Paris to feel the change in the political weather since the dark days of 1947," wrote one veteran diplomatic correspondent.[45] The Soviet foreign minister, Andrei Vyshinsky, was described as affable and diplomatic, in contrast to the stony coolness of Molotov at the previous session of the council. A Soviet magazine of comment on international affairs editorialized on the eve of the session: "There is not a single burning problem of the internal life of the peoples or of their foreign relations that could not find a positive solution under conditions of stable peace as part of peaceful international collaboration." [46]

There were other respects in which the Paris session differed from earlier meetings of the foreign ministers. At the first sessions, in 1945 and 1946, the three Western powers had been hesitant and

divided as they grappled with the problems of peace treaties for
Italy, Finland, and the states of Eastern Europe and sought a
formula for Trieste. Not until the meeting in Moscow in the spring
of 1947 did the French see themselves as aligned with the British
and Americans, rather than as a bridge between East and West. At
the fifth meeting of the council in London, from November 25 to
December 15, 1947, the West was united but in a weak diplomatic
position and still hopeful of finding a basis for settling the German
problem. The European economy was at its lowest point; the governments of Western Europe were unstable; violent strikes led by
the Communists had shaken France and Italy; the Marshall Plan
was still in the discussion stage; the Cominform had been organized
and was casting an ominous shadow over the continent. Molotov,
playing from a strong hand, saw no need for concessions. Following
the failure of the session, Secretary of State George C. Marshall
reported to the American people his conclusion that no settlement
would be achieved with the Russians so long as a power vacuum
remained in Europe.[47]

Less than a year and a half later, the sixth session of the foreign
ministers convened in a totally changed setting. The confidence of
the Western representatives reflected the change that had taken
place in the power relationship.[48] Western Europe had already
achieved a remarkable degree of economic recovery and political
stability. The internal Communist thrusts had been parried. The
North Atlantic Treaty was signed and on the way toward implementation with staff and military equipment. Western military
budgets had risen steeply. It was true that the American economy
had faltered, but it had recovered without experiencing the general
crisis anticipated by the Russians. The blockade had been a failure,
and the three-power reorganization of West Germany seemed
securely on its way.

Vyshinsky's assignment at the Council of Foreign Ministers
meeting was to undo the past. The Soviet position at the conference
amounted to a return to a four-power control of Germany, reserving

the right of veto; an international administration of the Ruhr, under four-power control; and the creation of a central economic council for all of Germany under four-power supervision. The slogan under which this position was advanced was "a return to the principles of Yalta and Potsdam." The Soviet foreign minister made no apparent effort to appeal at these sessions to the German sentiment for unification; his sole intent was to restore four-power control over a divided Germany. In effect, the Soviet Union was seeking, in its speeches at the conference and its appeals to the peoples of the Western countries, to revive the view of the German problem as a containment of German militarism, rather than as a decisive competitive factor in the European power balance. For their part, the Western ministers could see no advantage in returning to a situation in which the Soviet veto could once again be operative over the whole of Germany. In effect, said Secretary of State Dean Acheson, Vyshinsky was suggesting that a paralytic who had regained the use of three limbs should return to complete paralysis.

The conference adjourned on June 20 without agreement on Germany. The West had tried unsuccessfully to get Soviet acceptance for a Western-controlled corridor from Helmstedt to Berlin, but the only concrete results were a few minor arrangements regarding traffic into the city. At one point it appeared that an Austrian treaty might be agreed upon. The Soviet Union made a number of concessions, partly at the expense of Yugoslav territorial claims in Carinthia and Yugoslav reparation demands. Even this near-agreement evaporated, however, immediately after the close of the conference. Vyshinsky received fresh instructions from Moscow containing additional Soviet demands. The conference was reopened at his request, and the Austrian treaty was put back on the shelf for another six years.[49]

The failure of the conference occasioned no great surprise. It dramatized and culminated the failure of the Soviet effort to prevent a further shift in the balance of power in Europe by the West's gain of the major portion of Germany. The inability of the Soviet Union to prevent this was a decisive demonstration of its impotence at this stage.

In Germany, following its failure in the Council of Foreign Ministers to check the formation of a West German government, the Soviet Union now sought to delay the fruition of these plans by a campaign addressed to the West Germans, emphasizing neutrality and German unity. Through the National Front, which had been organized in the Eastern zone in May 1949, the Communists sought to develop a broadly based movement encompassing people of all classes and political convictions on both sides of the line in support of a program for German reunification, the conclusion of a peace treaty, and the withdrawal of occupation forces. Appeals to leading members of the West German parties and particularly to neutralist leaders were intensified and coordinated with a worldwide activation of the Peace Movement. With a few exceptions, the political leaders of West Germany had been innoculated against these appeals by the blockade, fresh in memory, and the campaign was without appreciable effect. The Federal Republic of Germany was formally established in September. The Soviet Union thereupon reactivated the movement toward a separate government for East Germany, which had been held in abeyance pending the outcome of the conference of foreign ministers and the subsequent unity and neutrality campaign.

Early in October, the German Democratic Republic was proclaimed in the Soviet zone of Germany, and the process of integrating it into the Soviet bloc was accelerated. Following the pattern of the Allied conversion from military to civilian authority in dealing with Germany, General V. I. Chuikov, chief of the Soviet military administration in Germany, announced on October 11 that a Soviet control commission would be installed and that the administrative functions previously exercised by the military administration would be transferred to the Provisional Government of the German Democratic Republic, as part of "the country's regeneration on democratic and peace-loving principles."

### The Low Point of Soviet Influence

During the months following the Council of Foreign Ministers meeting, Soviet influence upon the course of events in Europe continued to decline. Alternately blustering and conciliatory, Soviet rearguard actions appeared to have no effect upon the onward march of Western defense preparations. *Pravda* characterized it as "a new stage in the cold war," marked by "the growth of crisis phenomena . . . a new explosion of war hysteria in the USA . . ."[50]

These editorial fulminations referred to the outward signs of activity within the Western alliance. A Washington conference of the foreign ministers of the United States and the United Kingdom to coordinate defense and economic policies was succeeded by another conference, which also included the foreign ministers of all twelve NATO countries. The latter meeting resulted in the establishment of the North Atlantic Council and Defense Committee to carry forward the organization of the common defense. In the background, the Senate of the United States was deliberating large-scale expenditures for the shipment of military equipment abroad, in the face of a published intelligence estimate that five million Russian soldiers were believed to be under arms and possessed of the capability of advancing to the Atlantic Ocean without serious opposition.[51]

Minor concessions in negotiations were made by the Soviet Union in regard to the return to the United States of thirty ships obtained under Lend Lease (the negotiations had lasted two and a half years)[52] and in a slight easement in Soviet shipments of manganese and chrome to the United States (ostensibly in exchange for oilfield machinery). Other than this, the period was not marked by any major Soviet diplomatic activity.

In September 1949, the diplomatic isolation of the Soviet Union was further dramatized at the opening of the General Assembly of the United Nations. On issue after issue — Korea, Greece, the Balkan treaties, use of the veto, disarmament, Chinese representation — the Russian position received relatively little support outside the Soviet bloc. Perhaps the most stinging defeat was the election of Yugoslavia, over strenuous Soviet objections, to the rotating Security Council seat vacated by the Ukraine.

The opening address of Soviet Foreign Minister Vyshinsky to the General Assembly on September 23 was clearly directed toward enlisting public opinion to check the Western alliance in its almost daily augmentation of strength and cohesion.[53] Although he took his text from Stalin's interview in *Pravda* in October 1948, in which the policy of the leaders of the United States was characterized as aggressive and warlike, Vyshinsky also gave significant stress to statements by Stalin in 1934 and March 1939 concerning the Soviet belief in peaceful coexistence and in businesslike relations with all countries. This was a deliberate evocation of the period in Soviet policy of the Popular Front and of collective security against fascism. The language of Vyshinsky's indictment of the United States and Great Britain for "aggressive plans aimed at world domination" was tough and vitriolic, suggesting that his references to peaceful coexistence had not so much the intention of tempting the governments of the Western powers to change their course as of compelling them to do so by the pressure of an aroused public.

"A mighty mass movement for peace is constantly growing and developing in all countries," Vyshinsky declared, and the resolutions he proposed to the Assembly were to serve in the coming months as the program for that movement. The resolutions were: (1) a condemnation of the United States and British policy as aggressive; (2) an unconditional prohibition of atomic weapons; and (3) a peace pact among the five great powers.[54]

At this point, it becomes necessary to take account of the increasing emphasis in Soviet policy upon the Peace Movement. This auxiliary instrument, on which Soviet policy was to place increasing reliance in its efforts to check the growth of Western power, was a new phenomenon on the international scene, one which rewards examination in closer detail.

IV

# THE PEACE MOVEMENT AS AN
# INSTRUMENT OF DIPLOMACY

ONE of the fascinating aspects of Russia's policy in this period
was its dawning perception of the Peace Movement as a
novel and, hopefully, decisive factor in world politics. Here was a
target of opportunity — at its outset a spontaneous expression of
liberal and pacifist sentiment, regarded with suspicious disdain by
the Communists. Yet, within a year of its birth, it was to be brought
under Communist control, emptied of its social content, and so
broadened in its base of mass support that it became, for a time, a
more significant instrument of Soviet policy than the foreign Communist parties themselves.

In a limited sense, the Peace Movement was regarded by the
Soviet leadership as a defensive strategic instrument in a period
when the opportunity for further territorial gains in Europe was
more and more constricted by the hardening of geographical frontiers and the firming up of the new Western alliance. The Peace
Movement and other "front" organizations offered political rather
than territorial frontiers — opportunities for manipulating political
pressures within the West to circumscribe the freedom of action of
the Western governments. It was designed, as one official of the
Peace Movement expressed it, "to cut the hamstrings" of the
Western military program.[1] Specifically, the strategic functions of
the Peace Movement, in conjunction with the Soviet disarmament
proposals in this period, were to reduce the danger of war during
a period of maximum Soviet vulnerability; to neutralize the superior

atomic capability of the West by building up popular feeling against the use of the atomic bomb; to reduce the political advantages to the West of its atomic monopoly; and to weaken the West's aircraft delivery system by rendering the overseas airbases politically insecure. Ideologically, the Peace Movement enabled the Communists to enlist the support of parts of the bourgeoisie without having to make the concessions required by a popular front and to solicit the support of nationalist elements within the Western countries without sacrificing the "proletarian internationalism" of the Communist parties. On the plane of international politics, the Peace Movement provided a link with the emerging neutralist governments and the peoples of the underdeveloped areas; the Soviet Union called this coalition the "anti-imperialist front."

It is striking that an Italian Communist, trying to find a balance between Stalin's achievements and the condemnations at the Twentieth Party Congress, listed as a mark of Stalin's clarity of vision and understanding the fact that he "identified socialism with peace and thus facilitated the world-wide coalition of anti-imperialist forces." [2]

### Earlier Communist Attitudes toward the Peace Issue

A full awareness of these possibilities did not come all at once to the Communist leaders. Rather, it grew out of a series of improvisations, combining two long-familiar elements: the issue of "peace" and the technique of the "front" organization.

Traditionally, the Communist attitude toward pacifism had been at odds with the liberal opposition to war as an absolute evil. For Communists, war has its origin in the imperialist phase of capitalism. Until recently, the official Soviet position has been that war could only be wholly eradicated when capitalism had been eliminated. Tentatively at the Twentieth Congress in 1956, and somewhat more decisively at the Twenty-Second Congress in 1961, the Soviet leadership has modified this doctrine on the basis of a growing sobriety about the effect of modern weapons, and it now takes the position that war can be eliminated even before the final liquidation of capitalism. Historically, however, and up to the time of these congresses, war had been regarded by the Communists as good or evil depending on whether or not in the particular instance it served a "progressive" function in advancing the Communist cause.[3] (This yardstick is still applied by the Soviet leadership to those forms of local conflict which it categorizes as "wars of national liberation.")

Lenin was always scornful of pacifism, and this was heightened by the support which most member parties of the Second International gave to the war effort of their own countries at the outbreak of the First World War, despite a decision not to do so by the Stuttgart Congress of the Second International in 1907. His opposition to the war was based not on pacifism but on the necessity for "transforming the present imperialist war into a civil war," a slogan advocated by the "Zimmerwald Left" faction in 1915.

In November 1918, the first official foreign-policy act of the new Soviet regime was to issue a "Decree on Peace."[4] The document bore the ideological stamp of its origins. The "class-conscious workers" of England, France, and Germany were called upon to "bring to a successful conclusion the cause of peace, and, together with this, the cause of the liberation of all who labor and are exploited, from every kind of slavery and exploitation." Basically, it was designed to appeal to the universal war-weariness in behalf of a "just and democratic peace" and, like so many later Soviet appeals, to mobilize public pressures abroad in support of Soviet policies. As Karl Radek described it in retrospect on the occasion of the fifth anniversary of the revolution, Soviet policy was seeking "to arouse the popular masses in the Allied countries in order that the governments, under pressure from the masses, might sit around the table with us for peace negotiations and thus lead to a general peace which would be more favorable to us."[5]

The use of front organizations to mobilize popular support in the West had become a familiar device as early as 1921. Confronted with many troubles at home and adverse developments abroad, Lenin urged the tactic of temporary cooperation with other Left parties and a campaign to enlist mass support through subsidiary organizations of sympathizers, such as the Red International of Trade Unions, the Communist Youth International, and the International Workers' Aid Society. Both the front technique and the participation by Communist parties in broad coalitions were again utilized extensively during the defensive phase of Soviet policy between 1935 and 1939.

Soon after the conclusion of World War II, as tensions with the West began to mount, the Soviet government once more revived its efforts to enlist popular support in behalf of the peace issue and in opposition to the "warmongers" whom it accused of breaking the wartime alliance. In March 1946, during the crisis over the Soviet refusal to evacuate its forces from Iran, Stalin plainly sought to organize public pressures against the Western leaders. Asked in an interview about the causes of the prevailing fear of war, Stalin replied by attributing the responsibility to "the actions of certain political groups engaged in the propaganda of a new war and by these means sowing seeds of discord and uncertainty." "It is necessary," he said,

for public opinion and the ruling circles of all states to organize a wide counterpropaganda against these advocates of a new war and to secure the peace so that not a single action on the part of the advocates of new wars pass without due rebuff on the part of the public and press: thus to expose the warmongers without loss of time and give them no opportunity of abusing the freedom of speech against the interests of peace.[6]

A few months later, Stalin again identified "military-political adventurers" as responsible for the "clamor of a 'new war,'" for reasons of internal political advantage; they had to prevent the cutting of military budgets, he said, and to check demobilization lest it aggravate the capitalist problem of unemployment.[7] In this and a number of subsequent interviews, Stalin reaffirmed Soviet support for peaceful cooperation with other countries and denied the reality of Communist aspirations to world revolution in favor of the doctrine of "socialism in one country."

Over the following months, as relations worsened between the Soviet Union and the West, Soviet statements became increasingly explicit on the role of the "peace-loving" populations of the West in helping to check the policies of their governments. In his anniversary speech of November 6, 1946, Andrei Zhdanov dwelt upon the animosities shown by the Western governments toward the Soviet Union at the Paris Peace Conference. He argued that the hope for peace rested with those in the West who could restrain the warlike tendencies of their leaders.[8]

At the founding meeting of the Cominform in September 1947, Zhdanov restated this general argument in what was to become a famous directive.

It must be borne in mind that a great gulf lies between the desire of the imperialists to unleash a new war and the possibility of engineering such a war. The peoples of the world do not want war. The forces that stand for peace are so big and influential that if they are staunch and determined in defense of peace, if they display fortitude and firmness, the plans of the aggressors will come to grief. It should not be forgotten that all the hullabaloo of the imperialist agents about the danger of war is designed to frighten the weak-nerved and unstable and to extort concessions to the aggressor by means of intimidation.[9]

Although the peace motif was reflected in the hortatory title bestowed by Stalin upon the Cominform journal, *For a Lasting Peace, For a People's Democracy!,* the main thrust of the Cominform was indicated by the second phrase in the newspaper's title. The counterassault against the Marshall Plan outlined by Zhdanov in militant terms took the form of violent strikes in the West and a drive to establish Popular Democracies in Eastern Europe, including the Communist coup in Prague. Such tactics hardly encouraged "all sincere friends of peace" to associate themselves with the Russian cause, as Molotov hopefully invited them to do.[10] Reaffirmations of the Soviet belief in peaceful coexistence, as in Stalin's exchanges with Stassen in 1947 or Wallace in 1948, could scarcely win over a significant bloc of non-Communists in Western countries so long as the actions of the Soviet Union continued to reflect a bellicose and sectarian orientation.

### The Origins of the Peace Movement

The organization which was to be used by the Communists as the nucleus of the Peace Movement had its beginnings in France during February and March of 1948. Called "Combattants de la Liberté," the movement was organized by Yves Farge, an editor of a provincial newspaper who had distinguished himself in the Resistance by helping many of his countrymen avoid deportation to Germany for forced labor. He had attracted further attention in 1946 as minister of food by his vigorous prosecution of black marketeers in high places.[11] In organizing the Combattants de la Liberté, Farge was seeking to compete with De Gaulle for the aura and organization of the former Resistance movement, and its slogan of antifascism was clearly directed against De Gaulle.

Whether the Farge organization was wholly spontaneous in origin is difficult to judge, but in about a month's time the Cominform took note of the new group as "a national movement for defense of the principles and rights of the French Resistance," and described the purposes of the organization in terms indistinguishable from the current Communist line. According to the Cominform, the new movement "calls upon all Frenchmen, irrespective of religion and political beliefs . . . to influence public opinion, the Government and local authorities in order to defend national independence, to thwart the machinations of the neo-fascists and strengthen the Republic, to prevent the re-entry into public life of traitors and collaborators, to create a genuine people's army, and to end the war in the French colonies."[12] Local committees, reported the Cominform, were being formed throughout France.

The next step was to develop an international base for the new movement. This was to come in August 1948, with the World Congress of Intellectuals for Peace, at Wroclaw (Breslau) in Poland. Organized by Polish Communists, the congress was successful in

attracting a number of prominent non-Communists, including Julian
Huxley from England, O. John Rogge from the United States, and
Abbé Jean Boulier, a French priest who was to have repeated difficulties with the Church because of his activities as a leader of the
Peace Movement. One of the difficulties in recruiting a large number of non-Communists from France to attend the congress was
its unfortunate timing: it coincided with the August holidays in
France. However, the efforts of some non-Communist participants
from France and elsewhere to defend the cause of world brother-
hood can be read between the lines of such Communist accounts
of the congress as the following:

> Some delegates tried to divert the Congress along channels of a color-
> less cosmopolitanism, with the aid of which certain groups servilely
> camouflage American imperialism's fantastic plans for world domination.
> In the course of discussion this cosmopolitanism, which is a negation
> of the sovereignty and national independence of peoples, was denounced
> as one of the main weapons used by the ruling imperialist clique to lull
> the vigilance of the peoples, and win over to their side a large section
> of the intelligentsia who in this way become accomplices of the im-
> perialists in their schemes for world domination.[13]

If any final illusions remained in the minds of those who had
hoped to give the session a liberal character, they were thoroughly
dispelled by the chairman of the Russian delegation, Alexander
Fadeyev, head of the Soviet Writers' Union, who climaxed the
congress with a violently anti-American speech.

At the end, an International Liaison Committee of Intellectuals
for Peace was elected, with headquarters in Paris and national committees in each of the forty-six countries represented, to continue
the work of the congress. The choice of intellectuals as a major
target group was by no means a random one, as may be seen from
a lead editorial in the *Cominform Bulletin,* entitled, "Work Among
Intelligentsia — One of the Prime Tasks of Communist Parties."[14]
The intellectuals in whom the Communists had a special interest
were scientists troubled by the consequences of their work on

nuclear weapons, writers and artists disturbed by the excesses of the congressional investigations of Communists in American life, and, particularly in France, those who saw the increase of American influence in Europe as a threat to European culture. American soft drinks and movies became symbols of a "cultural invasion," an accompaniment to the extinction of national independence by American imperialism. The flavor of this appeal is indicated by the following paragraphs from the Cominform editorial:

Following in Hitler's footsteps, and acting in exactly the same way — organizing pogroms and violence, purging the teaching staffs of schools and colleges, throwing people into jail, having them shadowed, outlawed and so on — the ruling circles of the United States, steadily introducing fascism into the cultural life of the country, have, in the course of the past three years, outstripped the German fascists.

Entire branches of scientific-technological and cultural thought are doomed to stagnation and destruction. International reaction, headed by the American imperialists, is pouring money into the development and manufacture of weapons of mass annihilation and into the recruitment of its troubadors among the bourgeois philosophers, writers and poets.

The synthetic nature of the Soviet use of the genuine sentiment for peace among intellectuals was unconcealed in this militant appeal: once the United States is equated with Hitler, what is there to do but fight? The same issue of the *Cominform Bulletin,* commemorating the recent death of Zhdanov, paid tribute to his zealous exposure of "the putrid moral bases of bourgeois culture," his castigation of "the theory of 'pure art.' " Whether this praise would have been convincing to many Western intellectuals seems doubtful in view of the negative reaction expressed by non-Communist and even Communist intellectuals in the West toward Zhdanov's harsh strictures against Soviet artists and writers. Nor, indeed, was the atmosphere rendered more favorable by other aspects of Zhdanov's influence which still characterized Soviet international policies at this time: the harshness of the Soviet attack upon Yugoslavia's venture into national Communism, the blockade of Berlin, and the violent wave of Communist strikes in Western Europe. Against this unpropitious background, Laurent Casanova, the French politburo's "apostle to the intellectuals," undertook to woo the non-Communist intelligentsia while keeping the Communist intellectuals from breaking discipline.

Casanova has been described as a "former lawyer of Corsican origin . . . a ponderous and obstinate theorist . . . whose cold intransigence is well known, standing as a gray eminence and perhaps as the future chief of the party." [15] Under the guidance of the ideological section of the Central Committee of the French party, headed by Casanova, an intensive campaign was opened to deal with the "dangerous political tendencies" among intellectuals within or close to the party. Casanova described bluntly "the disagreement of certain Communist intellectuals with the Party's position in the ideological struggle," referring specifically to the decision on Tito and Zhdanov's speech on philosophy and the arts.[16] He set out to overcome these difficulties by strengthening the network of party schools and training programs, by issuing a new French edition of Lenin's *Materialism and Empiro-Criticism,* and by establishing in December 1948 a new journal, *La Nouvelle critique,* "a review of militant Marxism," whose columns opened a wave of self-criticism among Communist intellectuals.[17]

One of Casanova's main jobs, which he shared for a time with Charles Tillon, a leading Communist and a former Resistance leader, was to transform the Peace Movement in France, with the reluctant collaboration of its original leaders; he did this so well that it came to have little resemblance to its original form and purpose. Successive changes of title told the story. By November 1948, Farge's Combattants de la Liberté had become the Assises des Combattants de Liberté et de la Paix. Shortly, "Paix" preceded "Liberté," and finally "Liberté" disappeared altogether — a symbolic acknowledgment that the social content of the original movement had been swallowed up in the catchall slogan of peace. Anti-Communist forces in France made the dropping of "Liberté" a keynote of their campaign to discredit the Communist-led organization.

At one point during the behind-the-scenes conflict between Casanova and Farge over the character of the movement, in September 1949, Casanova laid the basis for a rival French branch of the world Peace Movement. The head of the French Communist Party, Maurice Thorez, came up from the south of France to arbitrate the dispute. Thorez formally decided it in favor of Farge who, as a symbol of non-Communist participation, was essential to the party's purposes. Farge's organization, by then known as the Combattants de la Paix, remained the sole French arm of the Peace Movement, but the victory proved to be a hollow one, for the content of the organization was shaped in time to Casanova's specifications. Casanova's partner on this assignment, Tillon, although more flexible by temperament and more agreeable to the non-Communist officials in the movement, sought to make use of it as an instrument for bringing the Communists to power in France, rather than as a device for changing the orientation of the "bourgeois" government; this deviation was to be one of the causes of his fall from Communist grace four years later.

On October 29, 1948, a great impetus to the Communist exploitation of the peace issue on a massive and organized world-wide basis was provided by Stalin's interview in *Pravda* which called upon "the social forces in favor of peace" to unseat by political action the leaders of Great Britain and the United States who were following "a policy of unleashing a new war." Stalin's interview, reinforced and made explicit by Molotov in his speech on the anniversary of the revolution a week later, became a basic directive to the Communist movement, calling for political action based on a broad coalition of antiwar social forces.

The first tactical application of this directive followed within a month, producing a popular response which surprised even its sponsors. Summoned by the Farge organization, a National Congress of Peace and Freedom drew an estimated twelve thousand delegates from all over France, plus thousands of Parisian onlookers and several trainloads of Italian sympathizers; the mass meeting was held at the Porte de Versailles on November 27, 1948. After hearing speeches by Farge, Abbé Boulier, and Tillon, the delegates passed resolutions calling for the creation of local Councils for the Defense of Peace and Freedom and appealing for popular support in the "struggle against the government which is betraying the national sovereignty, conducting social and colonial repressions, preparing odious legislation and which is striving, contrary to the will of the nation, to plunge the country into war." [18] The first task of the local councils, Farge declared, should be to develop a protest movement against the Western European defense staff which was being set up in France by Field Marshal Montgomery.

The Communist leaders were impressed with the power of the peace symbol to evoke a public reaction, and they made no secret of the fact. "If the fruits carry out the promise of the flowers," wrote Jacques Duclos, secretary of the French Communist Party, "we can expect to see develop across the country a formidable movement for freedom and peace, a movement which will shatter the criminal plans of the people in the government and the seditious Gaullists, who are all in the service of the American imperialists." [19] "One of the most important events since the liberation of France from the German fascist occupation," was the *Cominform Bulletin*'s evaluation of the public response to the National Congress. [20]

One reason for the extravagant enthusiasm for the Peace Movement at this juncture was that the French Communist Party was just then reeling from the dismal failure of the miners' strike of October-November 1948 (it had been called to force a change in French national policy). At a time when a reliance upon the mass action of the proletariat was proving to be a disappointment and, even worse, a positive disadvantage, a new approach suddenly and unexpectedly began to pay dividends. The implications of this experience were most clearly drawn in an article by Georges Cogniot, member of the Central Committee of the French Party and editor-in-chief of *L'Humanité*.[21]

> It can be said that the National Congress for Defense of Peace and Freedom opens up a perspective for the unification of the democratic forces on a far wider scale than that achieved in the past by the People's Front . . .
>
> The broad movement now unfolding in France against the policy of aggression fully confirms the basic idea of Comrade Stalin [that is, in the *Pravda* interview of October 29, 1948], the greatest strategist of the struggle for peace, that the peoples will compel the instigators of a new war to retreat . . . This is a battle . . . for the alliance of the worker elements belonging to the non-proletarian strata of the population, and of the middle classes with the working class . . . the situation now unfolding in France calls for an ever greater consolidation of the people . . .

This article by Cogniot sounded a new note, heralding the approaching thaw but not immediately dispelling the frost. Cogniot served notice, with the apparent concurrence of the Cominform, that the "hard" line had not produced results in France and that a broader tactic was required. The mass action of the proletariat, which Zhdanov had warned should not be underestimated, had in fact been overestimated. The working class was not powerful enough nor "politicized" enough to halt the French government's alignment with the Western defense alliance. If there was to be any hope of bringing about a change of policy in France, a broader class alliance was necessary and the peace issue provided the means of creating it. This was the import of Cogniot's post-mortem on the miners' strike and the National Peace Congress.

This new point of view was to become the ascendant one in the French Party only after it had become apparent that the brief and superficial "peace offensive," launched by Cachin in January 1949 and swamped by Thorez' intransigent declaration of support for the Red Army in February 1949, had failed to overcome the political isolation of the Communists or to check the continuing mobilization of the Western nations.

*From Wroclaw to the Waldorf*

While Thorez was delivering his defiant declaration and the French party was publicly celebrating the Red Army, the foundation was being laid for the next series of international measures to be applied by the Peace Movement. On February 24, 1949, the International Liaison Committee of Intellectuals for Peace, appointed at the Wroclaw Congress, met in Paris and announced a series of meetings to be held in several major cities. The most important of these were to be a Cultural and Scientific Conference for World Peace in New York in March and a World Peace Congress to be held in Paris in April. The call was issued jointly by the peace organization and the Women's International Democratic Federation, one of the oldest and most active of the Communist-controlled front organizations. At its Second World Congress, held at Budapest in December 1948, the women's organization had announced that it was turning its full energies toward support of the peace campaign.[22] The two organizations cast their nets wide, addressing their appeal "to all democratic organizations which have a natural concern for the defense of peace, to all persons devoted to progress in their country: trade unions, women's organizations, the youth and their international federations, peasant organizations, cooperative groups, religious groups, cultural organizations, scholars, writers, journalists, artists, democratic political figures." [23]

Particularly in the case of the New York conference, which was held at the Waldorf Astoria Hotel on March 25–27, an effort was made to reach the largest possible following and to avoid offending the sensibilities of fringe supporters by keeping the resolutions as general as possible. At its conclusion, the organizers fought off demands for specific resolutions condemning United States policy and the North Atlantic Treaty, for the sake of "defining an area of agreement on peace among many persons of widely diverse views on other subjects." [24] As adopted, the resolutions expressed support for the United Nations, a defense of cultural freedom in America from the consequences of the cold war, and a pledge of continuing contact with the world Peace Movement. This represented a low-pressure, broadly based, and carefully limited approach, aimed at rallying several varieties of opposition to the North Atlantic Treaty in the very homeland of the Soviet Union's principal adversary. Coincidentally with the conference, Henry Wallace announced a plan to invite a number of European peace leaders to join him in barnstorming the country. (The project was hampered by the inability of several of the invitees, including Pierre Cot and Konni Zilliacus, to obtain visas for travel to the United States.) At the same time, the Central Committee of the Italian Communist Party pledged itself to fight against the North Atlantic Treaty by organizing a nation-wide peace front, and peace conferences were also held in the course of the year in Bucharest, Tokyo, Budapest, Mexico City, and Moscow.

The center of the movement, however, was in France. There its political objectives could be declared more openly and its prospects were more promising. The French still felt a lingering fascination for the concept of the Third Force, not only in domestic politics but also as a French mission to mediate among the Great Powers. The profound fear of a revived Germany and of an aroused Soviet Union struck a powerful chord in French hearts. Moreover, the tradition of French intellectuals' identifying their progressive aspirations with the Soviet cause went back to the "Clarté" group in the early twenties, which included among others Anatole France, Romain Rolland, and Henri Barbusse. These factors rapidly made the Peace Movement a political force of considerable portent in France. There at least the Soviet Union could hope that the commitment of the government to the Western alliance could be reversed by popular resistance. As one Soviet commentator wrote, "This enormous movement for international peace is evidence that the politicians who are organizing the Atlantic bloc are building on sand. The popular movement of the struggle for peace is confidently led by the French Communist Party. Every day brings new evidence that all progressive forces of the country are rallying around the Communist Party."[25]

To demonstrate that the Atlantic pact was built on sand was the objective of the first of the Peace Movement's "signature campaigns," the collective letter to President Truman denying that the French government represented the will of the people of France in adhering to the North Atlantic Treaty. During February, March, and April of 1949, an intensive campaign on behalf of this oversimplified proposition reached hundreds of thousands of people throughout France, according to *L'Humanité*. It proved so useful a device for involving large numbers in a simple token action of support that it was to become the model technique of the Peace Movement.

Shortly before the April meeting of the World Peace Congress in Paris, the North Atlantic Treaty was signed. The Soviet Union began to mute the shrill propaganda with which it had tried to prevent this action and turned to the peace congress for its next great effort. In the next issue of the *Cominform Bulletin*, the leading editorial made it clear that, with the signing of the North Atlantic pact, the Communist movement was turning its full attention to the Peace Movement as a major instrumentality and was counting heavily upon the forthcoming congress. "The Peace Congress will become an historic landmark," it predicted.[26]

But the editorial also pointed toward a change of emphasis to be followed by the Communist parties. "The struggle for peace has entered a new, sharper phase since the North Atlantic Pact was signed," began the editorial, with significant emphasis. "The American millionaires, anti-Soviet provocateurs, stock exchange gangsters and fascist-minded obscurantists are trying to kindle the flames of a new war which will doom millions of people to death and destroy the heritage of centuries of world culture and progress." Despite the violence of language, however, the editorial contained a significant intimation of the broadening of the class base of the Peace Movement. Its readers must have raised their eyebrows at the following paragraph:

The vast mass of the workers, peasants, intellectuals, women and young people, *including elements of the democratically-minded national bourgeoisie in the colonial and capitalist countries,* is taking part in the struggle for peace headed by the great Soviet Union and the Communist Parties. This movement is made up of all kinds of people, regardless of their religious belief, the color of their skins, or party affiliation. [Italics added.]

The shift of emphasis indicated by this formulation is apparent when it is compared with an editorial on the same subject and in the same publication only two weeks earlier, before the treaty was signed. The operative paragraph in the first editorial read:

The North Atlantic Pact is designed to exploit the national treachery of the European bourgeoisie who fear the growing power of the people's forces. This bourgeoisie is going to the Anglo-American imperialists for help against their own peoples and is in a hurry to use the North Atlantic bloc as a new "holy alliance" in a world reaction to defend capitalism and support colonial slavery.[27]

It should be noted that by referring to the "national treachery of the European bourgeoisie," the Cominform sought at one and the same time to identify itself with the forces of nationalism and to present the fight against the North Atlantic Treaty as a class struggle. The allusion to a new holy alliance not only recalls the system of diplomatic alliances of the early nineteenth century, but specifically refers to the Catholic sources of support for the Western alliance and was transparently intended to evoke an anticlerical response in France and Italy.

In contrast, the formulation advanced after the signing of the treaty opened the effort to rally a wider basis of popular support against the policies of the West European governments. In the April 15 editorial, the phrase "regardless of their religious belief" was a directive to seek Catholic rank-and-file support, despite the orientation of the leadership of the Christian Democratic parties; the phrase "regardless of party affiliation" was an "antisectarian" directive to seek collaboration with rank-and-file members of the

Socialist and Christian Socialist parties wherever possible. All energy
was to be concentrated, the editorial indicated, on making the
coming World Peace Congress in Paris a broadly based enterprise.
The Peace Movement was to be used to break out of the political
isolation into which militant and antinationalist tactics had cast the
Communist parties.

Despite the efforts of its organizers to emphasize the participation
of non-Communists in the congress, the Soviet press wrapped the
event in a maternal embrace, printing column after column of
supporting resolutions from all over the world. The congress was
clearly intended to mark the most strenuous bid of the Peace Movement for universal influence, and the Russians may have had hope
of persuading some of the shakier NATO signatories to withdraw.
In the words of Moscow Radio, the congress would represent "a
powerful wave of world-wide protest against the plans of the
promoters of the Atlantic Pact." [28] It went on that the recent news
about the signing of the treaty "confirmed fully the foresight of
the man of genius, the leader of the Soviet people, Stalin, who
stated that too vivid are the memories of the last war and too great
are the social forces for peace for the pupils of Churchill to succeed
in the field of aggression."

The French Communist Party, which had a key organizing role
to play in the new campaign, was hampered by an internal conflict
over the degree to which working-class demands should be subordinated to the needs of the Peace Movement. The reluctance of
the party to put aside the theme of the class struggle in favor of
a broad peace appeal embracing elements of the bourgeoisie reflected a resistance among the militants, who found it difficult to
give up what they regarded as the traditional function and attitudes
of the party. This "sectarian narrowness" among the rank and file,
*L'Humanité* said editorially, "holds back the activity of the Party
and its policy of union." [29] At a decisive national conference of the
party in Montreüil five days after the signing of the North Atlantic
Treaty, Thorez and Duclos hammered away at the theme: "Peace

is the decisive question of the hour." They insisted upon a "union of all those who do not want war" and called for a policy of the "outstretched hand" to the socialist and Catholic workers and to the non-Communists of the left.[30]

Although the militants in the party continued to fume against what they regarded as opportunism and the leadership to fulminate against what it called the sectarianism of the militants, the party nevertheless proceeded to lay the foundations for the next stage of the peace campaign. A new organization was formed in France to handle the arrangements for the forthcoming World Peace Congress — Les Intellectuels pour la Paix — apparently an outgrowth of the International Liaison Committee. Its secretary was Jean Lafitte, former secretary to Maurice Thorez and until 1950 director of the Documentation Section of the French Communist Party.[31]

A massive Soviet delegation originally expected to number fifty-two was reduced to eight by action of the French government, which limited the number of visas for delegates from each of the Communist countries. The excluded delegates, numbering one hundred sixty-eight, joined with several hundred other participants from Eastern Europe and Asia to hold a supplementary peace congress in the parliament building at Prague, simultaneously with the Paris meeting.

The delegates from fifty countries who did manage to get to Paris found it gaily decorated with Picasso doves. The Salle Pleyel, which was to be the headquarters of the congress, was lavishly garlanded. On April 20, the First World Congress of Partisans of Peace was opened by its chairman, Frédéric Joliot-Curie, French High Commissioner for Atomic Energy. "We are not here to ask for peace," he said, "but to impose it. This Congress is the reply of peoples to the signers of the Atlantic Pact. To the new war they are preparing we will reply with a revolt of the peoples." [32] Among others who spoke in the same vein were Pietro Nenni, leader of the Italian left-wing socialists, Yves Farge, and Alexander Fadeyev.

Nenni stressed that the World Peace Congress was not a gathering of pacifists. "Unity of the peoples," he said, "is the best weapon in the struggle for peace. Unity is necessary in order to render null and void the obligations the governments have assumed in signing the Atlantic Pact, and to reduce this pact to a scrap of paper." [33]

Five days and many speeches later, the congress closed with a manifesto and a resolution "in the name of 600 million supporters of peace," which condemned war, the atom bomb, colonialism, violations of the United Nations Charter, and the rearming of Western Germany and Japan, in language which carefully avoided identifying the offending nations.[34] Identical resolutions were simultaneously voted at the Prague session. As at the New York conference, differences had arisen between those who had wanted more pointed resolutions and those who felt it important to be able to begin the manifesto with the preamble: "We, men and women of different nations, beliefs, and convictions . . ." The guiding spirits of the meeting walked a verbal tightrope to avoid alienating the peripheral supporters, as was acknowledged by Louis Aragon, the French Communist writer who guided the drafting.[35]

To continue the work of the World Peace Congress, as it came to be called, a Permanent World Peace Committee was designated, with headquarters and an executive bureau in Paris. The congress also established a magazine of the world Peace Movement entitled *In Defense of Peace,* to be published in several languages. National Councils of Partisans for Peace were to be established in each of the participating countries, wherever they had not been organized previously.

The congress did not pass without being challenged in its claim to be the sole spokesman for the popular aversion to war. On April 30 an International Day of Resistance to Dictatorship and War was held in Paris by a group of anti-Communists. The action was sponsored by a Rassemblement Démocratique Révolutionnaire, led by David Rousset and Jean-Paul Sartre; among its American members were Sidney Hook and the writers, James T. Farrell and

Richard Wright. Competing with the Communists for leadership of the widespread opposition to war, the counterrally met under the slogan, "Peace through freedom and freedom through peace." The group attacked antidemocratic practices in the United States, but it also explicitly identified totalitarianism as one of the chief causes of war. Another counterattack continued to enliven Paris throughout the following years — a series of satiric posters signed "Paix et Liberté," which jousted against the Communists and the Peace Movement with typical Gallic humor.

### Communist Expectations of the Peace Movement

The Soviet Union was frank to speak about the relation of Communists to the Peace Movement and about the purposes of this peace effort. The role of the world Communist movement as the guiding nucleus of a broad mass movement in the name of peace was explicitly stated, again and again, in unmistakable public directives to the parties. The following is a characteristic example from this period:

The Communist and Workers' Parties are in the vanguard of the struggle for peace. They welcome close cooperation with members of other political parties who share the desire of the peoples for peace.

The Communist Parties clearly realize that the struggle for peace today is the principal task of the democratic camp of the world progressive forces. That is why the Communists of all countries constitute the advanced and organized detachment in the great army of fighters for peace.[36]

Nor was there any reticence in stating bluntly that the function of the Peace Movement was to bring pressure upon the Western governments in support of Soviet diplomatic objectives. An illustration of this is to be found in an *Izvestiya* editorial of the period, commenting upon the World Peace Congress and its relationship to the May Day slogans of 1949, which had just been circulated by the Communist Party of the Soviet Union. The principal theme of the slogans that year was the "brotherly union of the peoples of

Britain, the United States, and the Soviet Union" against the "aggressive plans" of the Western governments.[37] Said *Izvestiya*:

The Soviet emphasis on the cleavage between the plain peoples of the United States and Britain and the warmongers does not necessarily mean that the government has abandoned hope of reaching a peaceful settlement with the West. Rather, it has been a reflection of the hope that popular resentment against war *will cause the Western governments to modify their programs,* thus establishing the prerequisites for the possibility of new high-level efforts to resolve world tensions.[38] [Italics added.]

Particularly in the case of France, this did not seem an unreasonable expectation, and, if France could be pulled out of the Western defense structure by popular pressure, the entire structure would collapse. In France, the issue of German rearmament and the restoration of any German state, partial or unitary, aroused visceral feelings of great intensity among the entire populace. And this sentiment, fanned by a growing neutralism, anti-Americanism, resentment against the rising cost of military expenditures, and, above all, by a profound fear of another war, made Soviet expectations of public pressures upon the French government not at all farfetched.

Warning signs of the spread of neutralist sentiment to moderate conservatives could be seen in a startling front-page article in *Le Monde* by Étienne Gilson. Returning from a trip to the United States, Gilson wrote that Europe would be safer if it remained neutral than if it were to accept the "illusory protection" of the North Atlantic Treaty.[39] The Communists, who had always castigated neutralism on the grounds that "who is not for us is against us," now began to show some appreciation of the potentialities of this trend. Without identifying itself too closely with Gilson, *L'Humanité* accepted his statement as a confirmation of the Communist charge that the government parties were "the new collaborators," aiding the Americans "to buy French blood with dollars for a war against the Soviet Union." [40]

During the late spring and summer of 1949, the increasing apprehension of war, compounded of nervousness among the French at the Soviet reaction to the signing of the North Atlantic Treaty, helpless frustration over the restoration of Germany's position and influence in Europe, and widespread anti-Americanism, gave substance to the Communists' claim that they had won the support of other groups in France. A French contributor to the *Cominform Bulletin* was not overstating the situation by much when he wrote in May:

A long path has been traveled since the time when the call of the intellectuals who met at the Wroclaw Congress was received either with a sceptical smile in certain circles of the French intelligentsia or was greeted with a conspiracy of silence. Today the overwhelming majority of French intellectuals realize that peace is really in danger, that civilization is threatened and that the time for complacency is over.

There is hardly an intellectual in France who would dare to vouch for the peaceful intentions of the United States; there is hardly an intellectual who does not realize — even if he lacks the courage to proclaim the fact — that the U.S. imperialists are driving toward war, are planning to unleash war.[41]

In the eighteen months that had passed since Zhdanov's speech at the founding of the Cominform, his exhortations to utilize popular pressures in the West to inhibit the growth of Western power had acquired organized form in the Peace Movement and had become a dominant activity of the foreign Communist parties, providing a means for political collaboration with intellectual and bourgeois elements. It provided also a fresh instrument capable of being directed toward specific and current Soviet objectives.

Starting in mid-1949, when Soviet policy was chiefly concentrated against the formation of a West German state, the issue of German remilitarization became one of the principal slogans of the Peace Movement. The Soviet Union had been pressing to get the Berlin blockade lifted before the West could resolve the French and German obstacles to a new Occupation Statute and Basic Law for the Federal Republic. While the German Communists were seeking to enlist West Germans in a national front, the Peace Movement, and particularly the French branch of the movement, sought to mobilize popular pressure upon the Council of Foreign Ministers, meeting in Paris in June on the German issue. Whether this represented a serious estimate or hyperbolic encouragement, Soviet sources claimed that the Peace Congress had compelled the Western powers to agree against their will to the meeting of the foreign ministers and had influenced the outcome of the conference.[42] It is possible that the Soviet government may have overrated the efficacy of these pressures upon the conference itself. While Foreign Minister Vyshinsky did his utmost to create an atmosphere of lowered tension at the conference, he offered no substantive change in the Soviet position, apparently anticipating that popular pressure on the conference would at least oblige the Western leaders to defer their plans for creating a separate West German state. At this point, the pressures were still insufficient to do this, but during the following years they were to contribute substantially toward the delay in West German rearmament with the additional military contribution to the Western defense alliance (Khrushchev noted this at the 1961 party congress).

During the summer of 1949, following the fruitless meeting of the Council of Foreign Ministers, the Peace Movement continued to seek broader support among non-Communists. Although its Communist sponsors during this period acclaimed the Peace Movement as an important factor in the victory of the "anti-imperialist camp" at the Paris meeting, it felt that "present objective conditions" provided the basis for a still wider unity of action by the party in the framework of the Peace Movement. To the *Cominform Bulletin,* Laurent Casanova reported that the Central Committee of the French Party felt "that results did not correspond to the existing possibilities . . . We have not yet put an end to manifestations of sectarian narrow-mindedness which injure the Party's relations with the masses." [43]

In a new appeal, the French Central Committee spelled out the breadth of unity of action which the Communist leaders had in mind: "Communists, Socialists, Catholics, Republicans of all shades,

Patriots and Resistance fighters, by our union and our action, let us affirm forcefully our will to peace, our opposition to the Atlantic Pact, our firm resolution to defend republican liberties." [44]

During the same meeting of the Central Committee of the French party on July 1 and 2 at Saint-Ouen at which this appeal was issued, new attention was also being paid to events in the Far East. In their accounts of world developments, the French party leaders now began to place foremost the advances being made by the Chinese Communists, apparently to counterbalance the current decline of Communist fortunes in Europe. In the list of the party's current objectives, the slogan of ending the war in Vietnam by a peace treaty with Ho Chi Minh took second place only to the continuing fight against the Atlantic Treaty.

The actions of this period, although not notably effective, made a particular effort to harness French nationalism to the cause. On Bastille Day, July 14, the party attempted to organize large public demonstrations against the Atlantic Pact, dramatizing its effort to recover the "banner of national independence" which Thorez had dropped in February. Again on August 5, upon the arrival in Paris of General Omar N. Bradley, then chief of staff of the United States Army, a similar effort was made. This demonstration, formally sponsored by the Partisans of Peace in defiance of a government prohibition, led to numerous injuries and arrests, which the Communist leaders felt "strengthened and tempered the broad unity of all peace supporters, irrespective of their political convictions and religious beliefs." [45] To the refrain of the *Marseillaise,* symbolizing the appeal to nationalist sentiments, crowds under Communist leadership marched past the American Embassy in Paris carrying banners denouncing the Atlantic Pact.

However, it was not until the spring of 1950, after the Stockholm meeting of the World Peace Committee that the movement was to reach its full scope of operation. By that time, the general setting of international relations had changed considerably, and Soviet policy had begun to move in a new direction.

# V

# EFFECTS OF THE CHANGING
# POWER BALANCE

A FEW hours before Soviet Foreign Minister Andrei Vyshinsky began his opening speech to the General Assembly of the United Nations on September 23, 1949, an event occurred which was to make the speech an anticlimax. An announcement by President Truman, issued simultaneously by the British and Canadian governments, reported the recent detection of an atomic explosion in the Soviet Union.

This achievement, in conjunction with the final Communist victory on the mainland of China, was to have a profound effect upon the Soviet outlook. In the nine months which intervened between these events and the outbreak of the Korean War, the uncertain course of Soviet foreign policy reflects the existence of two conflicting trends, both based on an assessment of the changing power balance in the world, but drawing quite different implications for policy from this circumstance.

One of the elements of uncertainty in the Soviet calculations was the effect which the bomb and the Chinese victory might have on the likelihood of war. The news that the Soviet Union had developed an atomic weapon three years earlier than had been anticipated by American scientists was a further spur to the mobilization of the West. Within four days of the President's announcement, the United States Congress by a heavy majority approved a $1.3 billion Mutual Defense Assistance Program, restoring almost half a billion dollars that had been cut by the House during August. On the following day, Congress gave its approval to a foreign-aid program of $5.8 billion, including more than $3.6 billion for the continuation of aid to Marshall Plan countries. The decisive stimulus for this legislation, quite outspokenly, was the Soviet atomic explosion. In Washington, officials expressed uncertainty over whether the Soviet Union would use the weapon to launch a new peace offensive or to play upon the fears of an atomic war in Europe, making "the mastery of the atomic secret the supreme weapon of terror." [1]

The first response of the Soviet Union, however, was to keep the entire matter in as low a key as possible. On the day following Truman's announcement, Radio Moscow broadcast in English a Tass dispatch which deplored the concern that had been raised by the event. "There are not the slightest grounds," said Radio Moscow, "for the alarm that is being spread on this account by certain foreign circles." [2] Perhaps, it added, some large-scale blasting on hydro-electric or other construction projects may have been involved, "using the latest technical methods." [3] As for Soviet possession of an atomic bomb, this could scarcely be regarded as news, said the Soviet broadcast, since Molotov had indicated on November 6, 1947, that the secret of the atomic bomb was already nonexistent. No effort was made by the Soviet Union at this time to use the event for purposes of intimidation. Pending the passage from first atomic weapon to the acquisition of a stockpile of atomic bombs, Soviet spokesmen cautiously avoided generating great fears of Soviet nuclear power lest it have the effect of increasing the immediate danger of war.

Similarly, in regard to China the first Soviet reactions were cautious. The breathtaking speed of the Nationalist collapse and the Communist advance may have caused as much surprise in Moscow as it did in Washington. At the beginning of 1949, the main forces of the Kuomintang north of the Yangtse River had been destroyed and Peking was under seige. In January, the Nationalists had sent a delegation to ask the Communist terms of peace. The reply was an ultimatum to surrender. On April 20, 1949, the Communists breached the Yangtse River line and swarmed southward. By May, Shanghai had fallen; by September, the Chinese Communists, after twenty-eight years of revolutionary struggle, controlled the mainland; on the first of October, the Chinese People's Republic was proclaimed. There are reports suggesting that the Soviet leaders may have anticipated a stabilization of the Nationalist regime in the south of China for a long period. Almost to the end, the Soviet Union maintained correct relations with the Nationalists. In January and February 1949, the Soviet Union was reported negotiating through its consul in Urumchi, capital of Sinkiang Province, with representatives of the Nationalist government for economic rights which would give the Soviet Union a dominant position in the province.[4] Irritation on the part of the Chinese Communist leaders "by the blatant Soviet expansionism into China at the expense of Chinese Communism" was reported by an American journalist,[5] although further information and more direct evidence on this point is still lacking. With regard to southern China, he reported, "there is some suspicion that Moscow, fearing the too rapid growth of Mr. Mao's power and the possibility of his heretical tendencies, is seeking to stabilize this southern belt — the remnant of Nationalist China — in order to be in a better position to deal with Mr. Mao." Yugoslav sources quote Stalin as saying in February 1948 that the Chinese Communists were acting against Soviet advice in continuing their advance against the Nationalists but he acknowledged that the Chinese had been right to do so. "True, we, too, can make a mistake!" Stalin is reported to have said. "Here, when the war with Japan ended, we invited the Chinese comrades to reach an agreement as to how a modus vivendi with Chiang Kai-shek might be found. They agreed with us in word, but in deed they did it their own way when they got home: they mustered their forces and struck. It has been shown that they were right, and not we." [6]

A responsible British writer refers to a conference in southern Hopei in July 1948 to determine military strategy for the autumn campaign, at which a leading Chinese Communist who had just returned from Moscow was reported to have served as Stalin's emissary.[7] Stalin's preference, according to the report, was that there should be no all-out offensive to crush the Kuomintang and seize power; the civil war should continue on a guerrilla basis. The reasons advanced for the Soviet preference were that the continuation of the civil war would weaken the United States by inducing it to pour arms into China, that a third world war was not imminent, and that the Chinese Communists could therefore afford to wait. The report goes on to say that Chou En-lai rebutted the Soviet position, arguing that China was exhausted by nearly twelve years of invasion and civil war, that one hard push would dispose of the Kuomintang regime, and furthermore that the possibility of World War III was not to be excluded.

The tone of cautious reserve with which the Soviet and world Communist press followed the progress of the Chinese Communist advance during the spring and summer of 1949 tends to strengthen these fragmentary reports. In the *Cominform Bulletin,* for example, a restrained May Day editorial saluted the victories of the "national-liberation armies of China," and a small inside story in the same issue reported the occupation of Nanking.[8] The first substantial reporting of the advance was carried without prominence in mid-June, indicating uncertainty about the possibility of further American intervention in China and concluding that the Chinese Communists "have still a great deal to do in order to completely crush the resistance of Kuomintang reaction and transform China into an independent democratic state."[9] It was not until October, following the proclamation of the Chinese People's Republic and the Soviet recognition of the new regime, that major attention was given to the victory. In contrast with the tentative and general reference to Asia in the November 1948 speech on the anniversary of the revolution ("the peoples of Asia are in motion"), on the same occasion a year later there is a full-throated confidence expressed in the march of history in Asia.

We do not know how much Soviet enthusiasm over the Communist advance in Asia was tempered by Stalin's anticipation of the difficulties of extending his control over the new revolutionary epicenter, as Djilas suggests,[10] and how much by his uncertainty regarding the effect upon the United States of the Communist victory in China. It is clear in any case that the advance raised new opportunities as well as new problems for the Soviet leadership at a time when a provisional stabilization appeared to exist on the European frontier of the Communist orbit. The victory in China not only carried with it sufficient prestige to compensate for the failure of the Berlin blockade; it also called attention to the dynamic front in Asia. Nationalist rebellions in Indonesia and Indochina, civil conflicts in the Philippines, Burma, Malaya, and Korea, plus signs of disturbance in the French and British territories of North Africa and the Middle East, may have deepened Soviet opinion that, true to the Leninist prophecy, the weakening of the capitalist base would be achieved not by a direct assault in Europe, but by severing the colonial appendages in Asia and the Middle East. This shift in perspective was to have, as we shall see, a profound effect upon Soviet strategic thinking.

## The New Configuration of Power

The changes in the world power balance which were taking place in this period did not represent merely shifts in relative advantage between one side and the other. They also brought about certain significant changes in the nature of the relationship itself. The development of the Soviet atomic weapon and the Communist victory in China did more than add a quantitative advantage to the Soviet power position: they contributed to an altered configuration in the distribution of power. The tendency toward a bipolar distribution of power in the postwar world now began to show signs of becoming a more complex and differentiated pattern.

A number of other factors also contributed to this tendency toward multipolarity, a tendency which presented the Soviet leaders with opportunities for maneuver outside their orbit as well as dangers within it. It is one of the ironies of this period, for example, that the impact of the mobilization of American military power began to affect Europe with a feeling that the Soviet pressure upon Europe had begun to recede. Previously the European concern had been whether the United States would commit itself to the defense of Europe against a Soviet threat. Now the popular mood reflected a fear that the United States would overreact, thus unnecessarily involving Europe in warlike challenges. The drop in the revival of European living standards by the military deflection of American policies was beginning to incur resentments in Europe, and, further fed by worries about American bellicosity, this stimulated a neutralism which had heretofore received only limited and tentative expression. The governments of Western Europe, still firmly committed to the Western alliance, found their mass support diminishing in the face of a growing popular preference for an independent role for Europe, detached from and in some degree hostile to American policy. This trend was encouraged by the growing realization that the development of the Soviet atomic weapon gave the Russians the capability of pulverizing the cities of Europe.

The centrifugal tendency was also fed by the development of a number of divisive issues within the Western alliance. The Communist victory in China introduced, especially between the United States and Great Britain, the thorny issue of the diplomatic recognition of Communist China and the representation of China in the United Nations. Not only did the economic revival of Germany and Japan serve to diminish the bipolarity of the previous period by introducing potential nuclei for new power groupings, but, even more, the question of their military revival became the most painfully divisive problem within the Western alliance. In particular, the issue of West Germany's relationship to the North Atlantic Treaty Organization became central, often overshadowing the question of how to defend Western Europe against Russia's massive power.

Finally, it was becoming apparent in this period that nationalism, far from having suffered a violent death in the war, proved to have been only temporarily stunned. It was destined once again to become the most potent political force of the age. As nationalism reemerged in the advanced industrial countries of Western Europe, the nascent movement toward a larger European political entity was detoured into a series of specific functional agreements on coal and steel, the balance of payments, and military planning. Moreover, the awakening of nationalism in Asia and Africa not only sapped the strength of the European colonial powers, but inflamed their relations with the United States over differences in their respective colonial policies. That the Soviet sphere was not itself immune to the fragmenting force of resurgent nationalism had already become evident in Tito's resistance to Soviet threats and in the recurrent and even intensified purges of nationalist tendencies within the Communist parties of Eastern Europe (this was the period of the Rajk and Kostov trials), as well as in the frenetic campaign against "bourgeois nationalism" among the Ukrainians, the Georgians, and other national minorities within the Soviet Union.[11]

Given these diverse and somewhat contradictory forces, it is not surprising to find similarly conflicting responses within the Soviet Union itself. Further, it is necessary to remind ourselves that any calculation of relative power advantages rests upon elements which are by nature somewhat imprecise, often intangible, and not altogether comparable. Moreover, what is politically consequential is at base a subjective estimate of these elements. All these considerations are reflected in the seesaw interplay between two Soviet modes of behavior, rooted in two different outlooks: one restrained, indirect, optimistic about the way history seems to be going; the other, defensively militant, anticipating imminent attack. Each mode had its spokesmen; often they used the same slogans, though with very different inflections. The curious character of Soviet policy in 1950 stems from the oblique collisions between these two tendencies.

## Confidence and Coexistence

The spirit of exuberant confidence in history was most strikingly illustrated in the anniversary speech delivered in November 1949 by Georgi Malenkov, once again in the ascendancy since the death of Zhdanov. In contrast to the defensive tone of Molotov's speech on the same occasion the year before, Malenkov spoke with assurance: "We are entitled to say with confidence that the forces of democracy and socialism are growing, while the forces of capitalism and warmongers are suffering a loss." The greater part of his speech was a balance sheet of Soviet credits and Western debits.[12]

First of all, there was the growth of the Soviet economy. "Our national economy has not only attained its prewar level but has surpassed it. We have every reason to believe that the first postwar Five-Year Plan will be completed ahead of time." Malenkov's figures were carefully selected and for the most part couched in percentages, but the essential reported fact was a 20 percent increase over the previous year in gross industrial output.

Then, the borders had been secured. Malenkov's *tour d'horizon* is worth reproducing in full, to give a sense of its tone:

Never in all its history has our country had such just, well-ordered state frontiers as it now has. Glance at the map. In the west, the Ukraine has brought together all her Ukrainian people into one family. The historical injustice in relation to the borders of Belorussia and Moldavia has been righted.

In the west there is no longer East Prussia, which for centuries constituted a base for attack on our country. Further north new frontiers have been defined quite securely in the interests of strengthening the defense of Leningrad. In the Far East, the chain of Kurile Islands has assumed a new significance, promoting the security of our country, while Sakhalin Island, now restored as a single unit, plays a greater role than when it was cut in two, in the defense of the Soviet Union.

Never before in all its history has our country been surrounded with neighboring countries so friendly to our State.

Calling the roll of the satellite states of Europe, Malenkov spoke with satisfaction of the contrast between the present "loyal and friendly" regimes and their hostile predecessors. And to the east there was the Mongolian People's Republic, the Korean People's Democratic Republic, and, above all, the "great and friendly neighbor, the Free People's Republic of China."

Recalling Lenin's prophecy of 1923 that the decisive factor in the conflict between capitalism and Communism would be the massive populations of Russia, India, and China, Malenkov hailed the "historic significance" of the Communist victory in China. With it, he foresaw a "new, considerably higher stage" of the "national struggle of liberation of the peoples of Asia, the Pacific Ocean basin, and of the whole colonial world," and "an important strengthening of the positions of the world democratic and anti-imperialist camp." It was in this particular context that he saw the balance as having shifted in favor of the Soviet sphere. From this point on, the effect of the anticolonial revolution upon the world balance of power was to have an increasing importance in the Soviet perspective.

With regard to the other new major factor in the world situation — the Soviet possession of an atomic weapon — Malenkov carefully modulated his expressions of boastful defiance of the West in the interest of a broader impression of peaceful intent. However, there was no mistaking the evident relief at no longer being under the shadow of what he called "American atomic diplomacy," in spite of the previous Soviet outward attitude of indifference to the atomic factor in warfare.

Three years before, in responding to a question from the British newspaperman, Alexander Werth, Stalin had made a reply which now took on added significance:

I do not believe the atomic bomb to be so serious a force as certain politicians are inclined to consider it. The atomic bombs are intended to frighten the weak-nerved, but they cannot decide the outcome of war, since atomic bombs are by no means sufficient for this purpose. Certainly monopolist possession of the secret of the atomic bomb does create a threat, but at least two remedies exist against it:

    a. Monopolist possession of the atomic bomb cannot last long.

    b. Use of the atomic bomb will be prohibited.[13]

Now that the first of Stalin's prophecies had been validated, Malenkov permitted himself and his Moscow audience a few defiant jibes at the West, carefully avoiding any belligerent implication. He indicated that in the event of war the American continent would not now be immune from attack. He predicted that another war would bring about the end of world capitalism, but he added: "We do not want war and we shall do everything possible to avert it. But let no one imagine that we are intimidated by the fact that the warmongers are rattling their weapons. It is not we, but the imperialists and aggressors, who would fear war."

In support of his theme of the contrast between the peaceful intentions of the Soviet Union and the warmongering West, Malenkov made a point which reinforced his emphasis upon the historical inevitability of the triumph of Communism:

If in the hands of the imperialists atomic energy is a means for the production of lethal weapons, a means of intimidation, an instrument of blackmail and coercion, in the hands of the Soviet people it can be and must be a mighty instrument of technical progress on a scale never witnessed before, an instrument for the further rapid development of the productive forces of our country.

Complementing this emphasis upon the peaceful uses of atomic energy, Malenkov restated the Soviet proposals for the condemnation of war preparations abroad and the unconditional outlawing of atomic weapons; these were to become the stripped-down program of the Peace Movement during the following period. Malenkov also hailed the world Peace Movement as an historically unprecedented development and as another favorable factor in the world situation from the Soviet point of view. In his assessment, the importance of the Peace Movement and of other organizations concentrating on the peace issue, such as the World Federation of Trade Unions, the International Federation of Democratic Women, the World Federation of Democratic Youth, and the International Student Union, could hardly be overestimated as a "force capable of curbing the aggressors."

On one further point Malenkov claimed a net gain for the Soviet sphere: the formation of the German Democratic Republic. Quoting Stalin's assessment of the event as "a turning point in European history," [14] Malenkov added that "European and consequently international peace cannot be insured without the correct solution of the German question."

Against this catalogue of advances on the Soviet side, Malenkov painted a dark picture of stagnation, decline, and desperate warmongering on the part of the West. He reaffirmed the Soviet conviction that the capitalist economies of the United States and Western Europe were approaching a severe economic crisis. As evidence he cited labor unrest and high unemployment (the period from September 1949 through March 1950 was marked by intermittent strikes in the steel and coal industries in the United States), the recent devaluation of currencies in Western Europe resulting from the United States recession of 1948–49, the disorganization of international trade among the countries of the West, and an alleged decline in the standards of living in Western Europe. The Marshall Plan and the foreign military-assistance programs he described as desperate measures to save the American economy and establish American hegemony over both the economies and the colonial possessions of the Western European countries. "Let those doomed by history rage in fury!" exclaimed Malenkov in conclusion. "We are firmly convinced that the triumph of socialism and democracy throughout the world is inevitable."

The critical point is that the force of Malenkov's argument pointed to the need for a right-wing policy, not as a defensive retreat, but as a new form of advance. His vigorous restatement of the adherence of the Soviet Union to a policy of peaceful coexistence was not accompanied by any hint of substantive concessions in policy. On the foreign-policy side, his speech contained only procedural and atmospheric measures intended to reduce international tension, eliminate any external stimulus to Western mobilization, and inhibit the freedom of action of Western governments — a Big Five peace pact, outlawing the atomic bomb, returning to the Potsdam terms for Germany, support for the Peace Movement. Meanwhile, the affirmative emphasis of the speech was upon consolidation within the Soviet Union, in full confidence that the forces of history favored the strengthening of the Soviet sphere.

An indication that this point of view continued to have authoritative support at the very top came a month later in the special edition of *Pravda* on the occasion of Stalin's seventieth birthday, December 21, 1949. Among the articles written by prominent members of the party, leading attention was given to Malenkov's significant emphasis upon Stalin's belief in the necessity of peaceful coexistence. For a brief time, this line was linked with the possibility of bilateral talks with the Americans. When an American correspondent, Harrison Salisbury, filed a dispatch in February 1950, reporting that the Soviet leadership was prepared to meet with United States leaders in a two-power effort to resolve atomic and other differences, the story was held by the censor for about thirty hours (presumably being checked with the Kremlin) and then passed without any deletions.[15] During the following weeks, a whole series of dispatches by Salisbury reporting statements from *Pravda* and *Sovetskoe gosudarstvo i pravo* (Soviet State and Law) indicating a Soviet interest in a peaceful settlement of disagreements with the United States was passed without deletions, although no relaxation of the censorship was extended to other American correspondents. Salisbury understood the relaxation in his case to mean a Soviet interest in floating a trial balloon over Washington.

Early in February, in the course of a general election campaign in Great Britain, Churchill had proposed personal conversations between Stalin, Truman, and the next British prime minister. The project was supported by some United States senators, and Truman was urged at his press conferences to say whether he favored the proposal or would revive his earlier intention to send Chief Justice Vinson or some other emissary to Moscow. Truman parried the questions until after the British elections, when he made it clear that there were no divergencies between himself and the views expressed by his Secretary of State, Dean Acheson, that direct talks with the Russians would be unavailing until the West had sufficiently strengthened itself to give the Soviet Union a motivation for actual settlement rather than diplomatic maneuver. In any case, bilateral talks between the United States and the Soviet Union were regarded in Washington as a divisive threat to the Western alliance. By early March, the President made it clear that he had no intention of going to Moscow, and the trial balloon passed from the scene without further effect (other than the alienation of French and, to a lesser extent, British public opinion which had been favorably disposed toward the possibility of top-level talks with the Russians).[16]

Even after this negotiation project was dropped, however, the official emphasis upon peaceful coexistence continued. In March, for example, an authoritative commentary in *Pravda* responded to "questions from readers" with an emphatic reaffirmation that "the Soviet Union in all its policies proceeds from the fact of the inevitability of the coexistence for a protracted period of the two systems — socialism and capitalism." [17] All of Stalin's reassurances to Western interviewers on this point over the preceding three years were reviewed by *Pravda,* as they were on a number of other occasions during this period.

It often happens, during phases of Right emphasis in policy, that an opportunity is found for a fresh review of Lenin's classic ideological statement, "Left-Wing Communism: An Infantile Disorder." And so it was in this period. In April, a lengthy article in *Pravda* by a leading Soviet theorist called attention to the thirtieth anniversary of Lenin's essay.[18] Ponomarev's article was clearly intended to be an explicit directive to Communists the world over. (A former official of the French Communist Party in an interview observed that a careful reading of the Soviet press provided the principal source of guidance for the party.)

After the usual criticisms of both Right and Left deviations — this is another convention invariably followed to ward off later criticisms from either direction — Ponomarev issued a clear warning against the main danger of left-wing doctrinairism: denial of "the necessity for compromise, for agreements and detours in the practical activity of the proletarian parties." The following explanation is unusually explicit:

The Leninist-Stalinist principles of strategy and tactics demand that in the propagation of their line the Communists should combine the most stringent loyalty to the ideas of communism with the employment of detours in attaining their aim . . . The Communist Parties, while maintaining an irreconcilably revolutionary line, must combine it with maximum flexibility . . . The Communists must, by taking part in parliaments, municipal governments and trade unions, skillfully combine the struggle for the ultimate aim of the proletariat, for socialism, with the defense of the every-day demands of the workers and of all the working people, with the defense of peace and democracy. Without the continued, daily work in those organizations to which in the course of decades the workers of the capitalist world have become accustomed, the isolation of the Right-wing Social-Democrats cannot be counted on nor can a mass political army for the victory over the bourgeoisie be organized. It is necessary to enter all organizations where the masses are . . .

Hailing the role of the Peace Movement in drawing "masses of the people into an active political life," Ponomarev left no room for misunderstanding in the following directive regarding the broadening of the class target of the Communist movement: "In their struggle for victory over imperialism, the Communist Parties are rousing to political life the broad masses, not only of proletarians, but of semi-proletarians, the masses of the peasants and of other strata of the petty bourgeoisie."

## Militancy and Fear of War

Another approach to policy was also being voiced in the Soviet Union, one dominated by an overhanging belief in the inevitability if not the imminence of war and by a consequent belief in the necessity for militant action against the bourgeoisie. This, of course, cut across the peaceful-coexistence line in practice, leading to contradictions and cross currents at every level, from the top of the Soviet leadership to the local cells of the foreign Communist parties. It was not until the final offensive in the Korean War had been defeated in the spring of 1951 that the more indirect and less bellicose line became more or less clearly dominant.

The highest-level spokesman for the militant policy emphasis was Molotov. The following paragraph neatly illustrates how Molotov stayed within the framework of the dominant slogans of the day and still managed to infuse them with a militant content. In a series of election addresses by members of the Politburo in March 1950, in which Malenkov reaffirmed the readiness of the Soviet Union to be "an active participant in all honest plans . . . for averting a new war and for preserving peace throughout the world," Molotov said:

We stand squarely for the Leninist-Stalinist principles of peaceful coexistence of the two systems and for their peaceful economic competition. But we are well aware of the truth that so long as imperialism exists there also exists the danger of fresh aggression; that, given the existence of imperialism and its rapacious plans, wars are inevitable. Therefore the supporters of a lasting peace among peoples must not be passive, must not turn into empty pacifists engrossed in phrases, but must wage a daily, obstinate, and ever more effective fight for peace, enlisting the masses of the people in it and not stopping short of necessary measures when faced by imperialist attempts to unleash new aggression.[19]

Another articulate spokesman for this point of view was Mikhail A. Suslov, a secretary of the Central Committee of the party, member of its Organization Bureau, and chief of the Central Committee's Department of Agitation and Propaganda.[20] Suslov's two major responsibilities during this period were in the realm of ideology and in the guidance of the foreign Communist parties. In connection with this second responsibility, Suslov conducted an important meeting of the Cominform in the second half of November 1949,[21] at which the militant line was laid down in explicit terms, calling for combative action by the member parties under the banner of a "struggle for peace." In his assessment of the world situation, which was the principal report at the conference, Suslov argued that the recent gains in Soviet power had greatly increased the immediate danger of war.[22] He called attention to the intensified Western military preparations which followed upon the Soviet atomic explosion. Not only had the United States increased its overseas military-assistance programs, but it was now reported to be proceeding with the development of an even more powerful explosive — the hydrogen bomb. (The revelation was first made in a television broadcast on November 1, 1949, by Senator Edwin C. Johnson, a member of the Joint Congressional Committee on Atomic Energy. Official confirmation came in an announcement by President Truman on January 31, 1950. The decision, which at this stage was limited to a determination of the technical feasibility of the thermo-nuclear weapon, was a direct result of the Soviet atomic explosion.[23]) Furthermore, Suslov could point to persistent speculation from Washington, despite official denials, regarding plans for rearming West Germany.

"The change in the correlation of forces in the international arena in favor of the camp of peace and democracy," a resolution based on Suslov's speech warned, "evokes fierce anger and rage among the imperialist warmongers." The resolution went on to spell out the familiar Soviet "death throes" analysis of the cause of war:

The Anglo-American imperialists hope, by means of war, to change the course of historical development; to solve their external and internal contradictions and difficulties; to consolidate the position of monopoly capital and to gain world domination.

Aware of the fact that time works against them, the imperialists feverishly and hastily hatch various blocs and alliances of reactionary forces to realize their aggressive plans . . .

Historical experience teaches that, the more hopeless things are for imperialist reaction, the more it rages and the greater the danger of military adventures.

In its indictment of the warlike intent of the West, the Cominform statement cited the North Atlantic military alliance, the enlargement of military budgets in the West, the establishment of American military bases overseas, the development of West Germany and Japan "into centers of fascism, revenge and springboards for aggressive plans," and charged the West with refusing to prohibit the atomic weapon, frustrating a peaceful settlement of relations with Germany and Japan, whipping up war hysteria, undermining the United Nations, and — as had been claimed at the Rajk trial — conspiring against the Popular Democracies.

Under the flag of anti-Communism, Suslov depicted a new "holy alliance" of warmongers, the forces of imperialism, fascism, the Vatican, and right-wing socialists. Their immediate purpose, he affirmed, was an attack on Eastern Europe, to be followed by a frontal assault on the national-liberation movement, including the Communist governments in China and North Korea.

Following this analysis, Suslov directed the Communist and workers' parties to subordinate their entire activity to the central task — the "struggle for peace." Among the "vital tasks" assigned to the Communist parties of Western Europe, three were essential: (1) to intensify the use of the Peace Movement and broaden its platform to include "all genuine peace supporters, regardless of religious beliefs, political views and party affiliation"; (2) to identify the "struggle for peace" with the "struggle for national independence," so that the Peace Movement could be used as a politically effective force against the "bourgeois governments which have become direct lieutenants of aggressive United States imperialism"; (3) to strengthen working-class unity on the basis of a "United Front from below."

To explain the current meaning of the "United Front from below" formula — a characteristic left-wing tactic — was the assignment given to Palmiro Togliatti, secretary general of the Italian Communist Party. Togliatti and his party had been known to prefer the broader coalition tactics, and his selection to make this report was a familiar Communist device for demonstrating that even the most articulate spokesman for the opposing tactic was now toeing the new line.

An analysis of Togliatti's report makes it clear that what was intended for the countries outside the Soviet orbit was a mixed strategy based on a concentric design.[24] The outer circle, identified in Communist language as "the national unity of all democratic forces," was to be made up of the broadest possible coalition on the simplified platform of "peace and national independence." This would include all peace supporters of whatever affiliation: Catholics, nationalists, nonparty intellectuals, and other elements of the middle class. Here was to be the instrumentality for bringing about a change of government and a shift in the orientation of the country involved away from the Western bloc. Guiding this circle from within was to be another coalition, based on "working-class unity" — the Communists plus rank-and-file socialists and Catholic workers. (In the special case of Italy, this also included the left-wing socialist movement, leaders and all.) At the center of this concentric series of levers of power, finally, was to be the Communist Party itself, guiding the working-class movement and through it the politically more effective coalition of democratic forces. The party continued to assert its commitment to the ultimate goal of a socialist transformation of each country, but its immediate purpose was to multiply its day-to-day effect upon the foreign policies of the nations involved.

Although the distinction may be a confusing one to the un-inititiated, it is essential to recognize that, in the Communist mind, this new line was one step removed from the popular-front strategy of the thirties — a "higher stage." It did not require each party to enter into agreements with the leadership of the socialist and center parties and, therefore, did not require any dilution of the ideology or program of the Communist Party. But it aimed to achieve the same effect by attracting rank-and-file support from the other parties on the basis of local, *ad hoc* efforts at collaboration on specific action programs. The non-Communist Left in France, as it turned out, persistently misunderstood this strategy. It hopefully read into each new swerve of the party an effort to re-create the popular front of the mid-1930s, despite explicit denials by the Communist leaders.

The dialectic was stretched to the breaking point by the effort of this complex strategy to satisfy everyone: it included the "class struggle," but it also had a place for nationalists and the middle classes; it could play the parliamentary game to form new governments and change policies, but it could also lead the Communists to power. This is the claim expressed in characteristic Communist language by the following paragraphs of the Cominform's November resolution:

The unity of the working class movement and consolidation of all democratic forces is essential not only to solve the daily tasks of the working class and of the working people; it is essential also to solve the cardinal issues confronting the proletariat as a class leading the struggle to abolish the power of monopoly capital, and to reorganize society along socialist lines.

On the basis of successes achieved in creating unity in the ranks of the working class movement, and in the consolidation of all democratic forces, it will become possible to develop the struggle in the capitalist countries for the formation of governments which would rally all patriotic forces opposing the enslavement of their countries by United States imperialism; governments which would adopt a policy of a stable peace between the peoples, put an end to the armament race and raise the living standards of the working people.

In an editorial commenting on the resolution, *Pravda* observed that they were "aimed at mobilizing the broadest masses of the people for the struggle against the threat of a new war."[25] It was apparent that, while the Soviet leadership as a whole felt increased confidence as a result of the Soviet atomic explosion and the Communist victory in China, two varying lines of policy thinking were built upon the common base. One, expressed in the Suslov directives to the Cominform, proceeded from a sense of heightened vulnerability in the immediate period and called for a sharpening of the "struggle for peace." The other, formulated by Malenkov, seemed confident that a policy of peaceful coexistence would damp down the Western mobilization and create the conditions for the ultimate victory of Communism without war. To the confusion of the outside world, both used the slogan of "peace." In the hands of Molotov and Suslov, however, the "struggle for peace" was indistinguishable from a call to war.

### Problems in Applying the Dual Policy

Despite these differences in outlook, Soviet foreign policy in action displayed considerably more verve and ingenuity in this period than it had shown during the succession of defeats suffered in the spring and summer of 1949. In addition to the sporadic appeals for peaceful coexistence and hints of possible top-level settlements with the United States, the Soviet Union was actively occupied with the consolidation of the new situation in Asia. The prospect of new gains in the Far East found enthusiastic expression at a conference, in Peking, of the Asian-Australian branch of the World Federation of Trade Unions during November 1949. The bureau which it set up seemed destined to serve as a Far Eastern counterpart of the Cominform. Between December 1949 and February 1950, Mao Tse-tung and a large group of Chinese Communist officials were in Moscow, negotiating a series of agreements with the Soviet Union, including a thirty-year Treaty of Friendship, Alliance, and Mutual Aid, directed against Japan and any country allied with it. Other agreements provided for the delivery of machinery and equipment, for increased trade, and for Soviet credits amounting to $300 million to be repaid by Chinese foodstuffs and raw materials. Joint companies were set up by the two countries to handle civil aviation development, the exploitation of oil and nonferrous mineral resources in Sinkiang Province, and the operation of the Changchun Railway in Manchuria. Accompanying the latter agreement was a pledge by the Soviet Union to evacuate its forces from Port Arthur and Dairen (Dalny).[26] In addition to the negotiation of these and other intergovernmental agreements, the top leaders of the two parties doubtless took the opportunity to coordinate their strategies in the broader field of world politics, although further information on this aspect of the meeting is not yet available.

Meanwhile, at the United Nations, Vyshinsky was pressing the Soviet proposal for a five-power peace pact. This would, of course, have brought Communist China into the circle of great powers. Moscow also intended to prevent "the organization of any military, aggressive groupings and pacts," as Vyshinsky explicitly stated in opening the debate.[27] The ambiguous character of this ostensible appeal for peaceful collaboration was further underlined by the Soviet boycott of the Security Council which began in January over the issue of Chinese representation.

The Peace Movement was also drawn into the broad effort to circumscribe the freedom of action of the Western governments in developing an alliance and to deny the West any political or military advantage from the one weapon in which they had superiority. The effectiveness of this effort was, however, partially undercut by other Soviet actions. This was a time of heavy-handed violence in Eastern Europe. The trial and execution of Laszlo Rajk in Hungary sent a wave of revulsion through the entire Western world, and this feeling was deepened by the public degradation of Traicho Kostov and other Bulgarian leaders. In November, the Soviet Union designated Marshal Konstantin Rokossovsky as minister of defense in Poland; at the same time, Warsaw announced the expulsion of Wladyslaw Gomulka, Marian Spychalski, and Zenon Kliszko from the Central Committee of the Polish United Workers' Communist Party and then from the party itself, on charges of bourgeois nationalism. This was also the period of the most virulent anticosmopolitan campaign within the Soviet Union against intellectuals and artists, and this too contributed to the unreceptivity of Western liberals and intellectuals to the Soviet-sponsored peace appeals.

From November 1949 until April 1950, the deputies to the Council of Foreign Ministers continued to wrangle fruitlessly over the terms of an Austrian treaty. When Moscow insisted in May that the treaty would depend upon a resolution of the Trieste issue, this widely strengthened a feeling that the Soviet Union had no serious interest in coming to a settlement at that time.

Two further incidents brought international tension to a high although not explosive level: a "little blockade" of Berlin in January and February of 1950 and the shooting down by the Soviet Union of an American navy plane over the Baltic area in April. In an exchange of notes, the Soviet Union claimed that the plane had crossed the coast near the Russian base at Libau, Latvia, and had opened fire on investigating Russian fighters, whereas the American note insisted that the plane had been unarmed. With this, the incident was closed, except for the decoration of the Russian airmen involved with the Order of the Red Banner.

The operational difficulties faced by the Soviet Union in carrying out its hot and cold policies in the international Communist movement are well illustrated by the turbulent developments within the French Communist Party in late 1949 and early 1950. It soon became apparent that the party was faced with disaffection in both directions. This was evident at the plenum of the Central Committee of the French party, which was held on December 9 and 10 to propagate the Cominform resolutions. The militants in the party, it appeared, were reluctant to emphasize the peace issue over the wage issue and objected strenuously to the instruction to cultivate the rank-and-file socialist and Catholic workers, against whom so many local battles had been fought. Although Maurice Thorez, in his closing speech, denied allegations that opposition tendencies existed within the party and even among the leaders of the party, the monitory tone of his speech left no doubt about the party's difficult situation. "Two lines cannot exist in the Party," he warned. "The Party has one line — a revolutionary, proletarian, Lenin-Stalin line of the Communist Party. This general line cannot be questioned in any Party organization. Not a single Party branch or Party unit will allow it." [28]

This admonition came as part of a caustic attack upon "soft" deviators and served to establish the orthodoxy of his position. Many Communists of bourgeois origin, said Thorez, had shown "vacillations or doubts with regard to the USSR and the People's Democracies." This was presumably an allusion to the widespread negative effects of the Rajk trial and execution, the violent Soviet attack upon Tito, and the Thorez declaration of support to the Red Army on French soil. The Party could well do without those who are so easily shaken, said Thorez.

Turning to the militants, Thorez reproved them for not giving sufficient support to the collection of peace signatures and other activities of the Partisans of Peace and Freedom. The message was skillfully couched in a tone and language of extreme militancy, evoking the spirit of struggle and revolutionary sacrifice. He suggested, as an outlet for their militant spirit, that they support the struggle for peace by "practical actions": refusal to produce, transport, or unload war matériel. He recognized that the Communists, and particularly those who worked in the trade unions, had to take account of the economic struggle, but he chided them for not realizing that the peace issue had to come first. Only through the struggle for peace could real gains be made on the economic front. Only by organizing a mass movement for peace could a change of government be brought about in France, "a government of domestic unity which will satisfy the demands of the working people, restore and extend the freedom of the people, and bring France back to the camp of democracy and peace. In this way we shall lead our country along the road towards Socialism."

But Thorez went even further in his effort to awaken the militants to the tactical possibilities of the peace issue as a means of doing what, in existing circumstances, a frontal assault could not do — that is, lead the Communists to power in France. In a passage remarkable for its explicitness, Thorez declared:

As far as the government is concerned, the Information Bureau Resolution holds that the mass peace movement can lead to power, [that it is] a formula still broader, if possible, than our slogan of a Government of Democratic Union. Read that again! . . . It is not a question of beginning all over again with 1934 or 1936. It is a matter of promoting a government of peace and national independence by means of the action of the masses, which has been decisive in this period, and will again be decisive this time.

The other major presentation to the Central Committee was made by Jacques Duclos, who argued, and with greater plausibility, not that the broad line would lead the Communists to power in France but that it was required by the international situation. "We must not lose sight of the fact that, by the admission even of the American imperialists, France is considered the cornerstone of what they call the 'Western defense.' This underlines the importance of the role which falls to us French Communists in the gigantic struggle of the camp of peace against the imperialist camp." [29]

One reason why neither of these arguments carried much weight in persuading the party militants to subordinate the economic struggle to the broader peace issue was that this was a time of renewed economic unrest in France. The wage issue was a live one, and workers were restless. Food prices, which had shown some decline in the first half of 1949, had begun to rise again in September. Industrial production had not maintained the promise of the early part of the year. Wheat acreage had not increased, as had been expected. The franc had been devalued as a result of the still alarming dollar gap. On October 6, the Queille government had fallen because of its inability to produce agreement on the budget. The restiveness of the French workers was made evident by a twenty-four-hour nationwide demonstration strike staged by the Force Ouvrière on November 25, calling for a full return to freedom of collective bargaining. Although the CGT and the CFTC joined in the strike, the Communist leaders did not succeed in their efforts to take over the strike or to prolong it beyond the original twenty-four hours.

The party resolved its dilemma by merging the two issues. "Bread" and "peace" became twin slogans in the wave of "hiccup strikes" which swept across France during the early months of 1950. By this device the party achieved several important advantages. It was able to utilize, rather than having to repress, the pressure from the rank-and-file trade unionists for action in the face of declining real wages. It could also use the strikes to develop collaboration in local situations between the CGT, the FO, and the CFTC, thus furthering the "United Front from below." Finally, the wage issue provided some protection against prosecution for strikes in defense industries.

On the latter point, it was the government that now found itself in a dilemma. Following the Central Committee meeting of December 1949, the party had intensified its program of "practical actions" for peace. This euphemism was used to describe those strikes which were intended to impair Western defense preparations. It was also implied that these actions could be of insurrectionary significance in case of war.[30] A direct target was now provided by the signing, in January, of a bilateral agreement between France and the United States under the Mutual Defense Assistance Program, under which military supplies were to begin flowing to France in April. The Communist Party at once called upon its members among dockers and railway workers to refuse to handle the shipments. As long as these strikes were nominally related to wage demands, they could claim constitutional protection.

Under the direction of André Marty, the party also intensified its campaign against what it called the "dirty" war in Indochina, and for this purpose many port strikes were called. During this period the Communist press claimed hundreds of local practical actions for peace: a strike at an armory at Toulon; a strike in the chemical factories of Marseilles; a strike of nine hundred building workers at Bec d'Ambes against the construction of an American fuel base; a mass meeting of dockers at Marseilles to stop work on the *Athos,* bound for Vietnam; protest strikes by dockers at Dunkirk, Boulogne, and Calais against the use of troops for loading military equipment for Vietnam.

With difficulty, the leadership of the French Communist Party kept this militant line of action going side by side with a broad appeal for support from non-Communist groups. In February, Marcel Servin, the member of the Central Committee in charge of the training of cadres, pleaded for support for these "two main aspects" of the party's work: "the development and sharpening of the class struggle in France, on the one hand, and the policy of a broad unity essential to save peace, freedom and our national independence, on the other." He decried the "sectarianism still existing among rank-and-file Communists and local functionaries — a sectarianism which arises from a lack of confidence in the strength of the working class, and which leads to isolation." [31]

This two-pronged and somewhat contradictory tactic was given the blessing of the international Communist movement. An editorial in the *Cominform Bulletin* on the occasion of the twenty-sixth anniversary of the death of Lenin found full sanction for this course of action:

The Communist and Workers' Parties in the capitalist countries, especially in France and Italy, are skillfully leading the battles of the working masses — guided by Markist-Leninist strategy and tactics which have been tested by the Bolshevik Party. They combine the struggle for the interests of the working class and peasantry with the struggle for peace and the national independence of their countries . . . rallying all democratic, patriotic forces against the shameful subordination to American imperialism. [32]

Two weeks later, in calling attention to a number of incidents in which workers had refused to produce or unload munitions and had held up the dispatch of troops to the colonies, the *Bulletin* expressed the hope that such practical actions would contribute to the political education of nonparty elements: "The supporters of peace are beginning to understand, more and more, that only their own growing concrete struggle can bridle the frantic warmongers . . . For the supporters of peace, practical action is the main method of struggle against the policy of unleashing war." [33]

Aroused by the economic cost of these waves of strikes,[34] and by the obvious threat to its defense program, the French government rallied to parry the new tactic. In January the president of the republic declared that strikes intended to hamper the national defense would be considered unconstitutional. In March the government introduced an Anti-Sabotage Bill in the National Assembly. Despite, or perhaps because of, the extremely violent obstruction offered by the Communist deputies, this bill was passed on March 8, 1950. It provided for the imprisonment of persons found guilty of sabotage, of the destruction of arms, or of efforts to demoralize military personnel.

Despite the Communist slogan, "Not a single docker will unload ships with American ammunition!" the first shipment of American arms under the Mutual Defense Assistance Program was unloaded at Cherbourg the following month without incident. In the presence of French troops and police, backed by a firm government stand, the threatened interference did not materialize, and the strike movement petered out. While denouncing the government's countermeasures as fascist, a member of the Politburo acknowledged that the strike movement had passed its peak by mid-March.[35]

Once again, the Communists had run through a minor reprise of the 1947–48 experience: the militant tactics had been relatively ineffective and had instead produced undesirable countereffects. The violently obstructionist tactics in the National Assembly, the strikes, the talk of mutiny and civil war, strengthened the shaky Bidault government by presenting it with an external threat. Despite the

resignation of the socialist ministers in February, the government
— now reconstituted with a center of gravity farther to the right
than any government since the liberation — remained in office
until June. The party's riposte to the strong measures against the
strikes was to evoke the familiar call for unity against fascism.
This was the burden of the report of *Pravda*'s correspondent in
France at the time, Yuri Zhukov, who wrote: "Continuing to
sound the alarm, the progressive public of France calls on all republicans, regardless of political convictions or religious beliefs, to
unite and resist the fascist threat just as they did in 1934–36." [36]

Yet the militant prong of the peace campaign — the form of
action euphemistically called "direct," "concrete," or "practical" —
had served a number of purposes less immediately apparent. It
had provided satisfying work for Party militants, had served to
organize and train cadres for insurrectionary duties in case of
war, and had provoked a degree of repression which might in
turn open the way to a revival of the "antifascist" alliance with
non-Communist groups. These factors may help to explain why
the Communists persisted in this militant accompaniment to the
signature-collecting Peace Movement appeal, which was in the
process of becoming the central focus of Soviet operations in
Western Europe.

### The Stockholm Peace Appeal

Impressed by the popular responses to the peace congresses held
in April 1949 at Paris and Prague, the Soviet Union perceived in
the world Peace Movement a significant addition to the strength
of the Communist camp. As we have seen, Malenkov in his November 1949 anniversary speech hailed the movement as a historically
unprecedented factor in world affairs, capable of inhibiting the war
potential of the Western powers. This confident estimate was constantly reaffirmed in Soviet analyses of the international situation.
An editorial in a historical journal of the period, for example, says:
"The new and remarkable event of modern times is the emergence

for the first time in the history of mankind of the organized peace front headed by the USSR." [37] All Communist parties were directed, in the Suslov resolution at the November 1949 meeting of the Cominform, to make the Peace Movement the "pivot of [their] entire activity." [38]

The Peace Movement itself was passing through several stages of development in its search for the most effective way to put to use the popular response aroused by the peace slogan. A "peace ballot," aimed at drawing into the movement "people who voted for other parties" and circulated to mark World Peace Day on October 2, 1949, claimed seven million signatures in France by the end of the year. The first meeting of the Permanent Committee of the movement, elected at the April congress, was held in October at Rome for the purpose of expelling the Yugoslav delegates. With this out of the way, an inner bureau met two months later in Paris to proclaim the following catchall program:

End the armaments race by curtailing war budgets and reducing armed forces; outlaw the atom bomb; end military intervention against the peoples — in Indonesia, Malaya, Burma and Viet Nam; stop repressions against the Partisans of Peace; end the war of nerves by concluding, within the framework of the United Nations, a Peace Pact between the Great Powers. [39]

At the third session of the Permanent Committee, held in Stockholm on March 15–19, 1950, its general secretary, Jean Lafitte, a member of the French Communist Party, exhorted the Peace Movement to emulate the "concrete actions" against war already taken by the dockers, railwaymen, and factory workers of France, Italy, Belgium, and Holland in refusing to transport or manufacture arms. [40] The Stockholm session called for a second world peace congress, to be held in Italy during the fourth quarter of 1950. It also established a program of international peace prizes.

However, what was to prove to be the master stroke of the movement was the proclamation of a new campaign of mass signatures patterned on the successful experiment of the peace ballot in

France. For this campaign, the program of the Peace Movement was simplified to a single and universally appealing proposition: "Ban the atomic bomb!" As presented by the chairman of the Permanent Committee, Frédéric Joliot-Curie, the Stockholm Peace Appeal was a work of propaganda genius:

We demand the unconditional prohibition of the atomic weapon as an instrument of aggression and mass extermination of people, and the establishment of strict international control over the fulfillment of this decision.

We will regard as a war criminal that government which first uses the atomic weapon against any country.

We call upon all people of good will all over the world to sign this call.[41]

The full energies of the Peace Movement were now concentrated upon a massive signature-collecting campaign in behalf of the Stockholm Appeal. By the end of the year, its organizers claimed 500 million signatures. Although the majority of these came from behind the Iron Curtain, impressive totals were claimed for other countries: 15 million from France, almost 17 million from Italy, 2.5 million from the United States.[42]

The campaign fitted perfectly into Soviet strategic requirements. Sidestepping the complexities of the problem of inspection and control that had arisen in the United Nations discussions of disarmament, the appeal sought to mobilize public opinion against the use of atomic weapons. By attaching a moral stigma exclusively to the atomic weapon as against other instruments of war, the appeal would neutralize the very form of military power in which the West still had an advantage. To the extent that Western superiority in atomic weapons could be neutralized, the Soviet advantage in conventionally armed forces could be enhanced while the Soviet Union was accumulating a sufficient atomic stockpile. In his interview with Alexander Werth in 1946, Stalin had cited two "remedies" against Western superiority in the field of atomic weapons. The first, the development of an atomic weapon by the Soviet

Union, had been achieved in September 1949. Stalin's second remedy was an international prohibition against the use of the atomic bomb, and this was the purpose of the Stockholm Appeal.

Although there is no clear evidence that the Stockholm Appeal was launched with foreknowledge of the impending invasion of South Korea, this contingency may have been in the minds of some of its Communist sponsors. This possibility is strengthened by the preparations for clandestine operations which had been made and by the insurrectionary overtones of the so-called concrete actions for peace, such as strikes against the transportation of war matériel.[43] The issue of the *Cominform Bulletin* which reported the session at Stockholm also devoted six full columns to an account of the border tensions in Korea, pledging its support to the Korean people, led by the People's Democratic Government of North Korea, for the attainment of a "united, independent democratic Korea."[44] Communist sources later claimed that the success of the Stockholm Appeal had been a decisive factor in inhibiting the American forces from using the atomic weapon in the course of the Korean War.[45]

### Division of Functions in the Communist Movement

As the Stockholm campaign gathered momentum in the spring of 1950, it became clear that a division of functions was needed between the Peace Movement and the Communist parties. The militant side of the "struggle for peace" — the organization of "practical actions" against the manufacture or transportation of war matériel — became the direct responsibility of the Communist parties, leaving the Peace Movement less encumbered in its effort to organize the "broadest possible alliance of the popular and national forces."[46]

The reasoning behind this separation of functions was explained in a front-page article in the *Cominform Bulletin* on March 31, 1950, by Jorge Amado of Brazil, a member of the Permanent Committee of the World Peace Congress: "With the intensification of

the active struggle of the working class against war (strikes, refusal to load or transport war materials, mass demonstrations)
under the leadership of political parties, trade unions and public organizations, the Peace Movement will rally around the call for the
prohibition of the atomic weapon all people of good will throughout the world . . ." The field of action of the Peace Movement
must be wider than that of the Communist Party and the trade
unions: "It unites people in various walks of life, and of all kinds
of philosophic, political and religious convictions. Any narrowness
in exposition and application of slogans may diminish substantially
the scope of the movement and create the danger of a breakaway
by certain groups of peace supporters."

In order to enlarge the scope of its appeal, the Peace Movement
increasingly sought to dissociate itself from any direct identification
with the Communist parties. For their part, the Communists
found irksome the role of guide to a movement whose program
they did not wholly control. From the beginning, the Communists,
even while appreciating the mass leverage offered by the Peace
Movement, had squinted with suspicion at the mixture of pacifists,
liberals, and dilettantes with whom they felt themselves obliged
to deal. "A strange mixture of illusion and reality," one member
of the French Central Committee wrote of the Peace Movement.[47]
Another paid it this left-handed compliment: "French Communists
should participate in every manifestation of the peaceful will of
our people, even if this will is expressed in terms still tainted with
confusion or incomprehensibility." [48]

In order to give the Peace Movement the appearance of independence, it was necessary not only to have at least some prominent
non-Communists among its leaders, but occasionally to allow them
to take positions which strained Communist tolerance. In at least
two instances, however, the non-Communist leaders of the French
branch of the Peace Movement displayed such a degree of independence that they were subjected to punitive action by the party.
These incidents involved a more or less independent attitude to-

ward the Yugoslav issue and an outspoken resistance to the Soviet switch to an endorsement of German national forces in March 1952. In the former case, a leading member of the Peace Movement was expelled from the movement; in the latter, the Peace Movement was obliged to suspend publication of its magazine.

Some hint of the problem faced by the French Communist Party in getting its members to work side by side with non-Communists was conveyed in the following section of the address by Maurice Thorez to the Twelfth Congress of the party, held at Gennevilliers from April 2 to 6, 1950:

We believe it useful to declare once again that we Communists, while reserving our right to express our viewpoint under all circumstances, fully recognize the right of all other genuine peace supporters to have their views on different matters, including such an important question as the profound reasons for the new danger of war and about the ways and means necessary to safeguard peace.[49]

The main brunt of Thorez' five-hour speech to the party delegates was a stern lecture to the "sectarians." The most serious shortcoming of the party, he said, was its underestimation of the danger of war and the refusal of the sectarians to accept a peace campaign which had to reach out for middle-class support. "Peace hangs by a thread," he declared, and the principal task of the party must therefore be to support the Stockholm signature campaign.

Thorez added a significant nuance to the Party's slogan, "For a government of democratic unity." Now the slogan was to be, "For a true government of national union." The delegates understood that a national union went clear across the political spectrum, whereas a government of democratic unity had covered only the left side of the spectrum. To make his meaning clear, Thorez, in his closing speech, called upon "all Frenchmen, irrespective of political or philosophical views and religious convictions, to intensify the struggle against the instigators of war, for the restoration of the national independence of France, and to save peace." [50] What this subtle shift meant to the members of the party might be expressed in non-Communist language as follows: the key issue at this moment is the international situation, not domestic social change. Because of the requirements of Soviet foreign policy, we are to emphasize action whose chief purpose will be to restrain the Western-oriented government of France. Therefore, we will pick up allies anywhere across the board in French politics, right or left, provided they also oppose the present French government.

In the meantime, the other function of direct party action was also dealt with at the Twelfth Congress. In a lengthy discourse on "how to stop the Vietnam war, in Europe," the leading Party militant, André Marty, discussed the subject of his special responsibility: the implicit encouragement to mutiny on the part of troops assigned to Indochina. The full text of Marty's speech was published in the party's weekly newspaper for its leaders, *France nouvelle,* but not in *L'Humanité.* In the full version, it was clear that Marty was expanding the program of "concrete actions" against the transport and manufacture of war matériel into an explicit plan for subversion in France, with the Communal Peace Councils transformed into "levers" of action against the government.[51]

At the congress, a banner stretched across the stage proclaiming the party's familiar declaration: "The people of France will not, will never, make war against the Soviet Union." Speaking as a delegate from the Seine Department, Frédéric Joliot-Curie declared that no Communist or "progressive" scientist would ever contribute a fragment of his scientific knowledge toward a war against the Soviet Union. As a consequence, within the month he was dismissed as High Commissioner of Atomic Energy. This dismissal was only one act in an extensive purge of Communists from the Atomic Energy Commission, the armed forces, and other sections of the French government.

Nevertheless, the momentum of the Western mobilization continued, in France and elsewhere in Western Europe. Despite the best efforts of the French Communist Party, the large number of signatures on the Stockholm Peace Appeal, a growing neutralist sentiment among the people as a whole, and a losing battle against a recalcitrant budget (on June 24, the Bidault government fell on a technical wage issue), the government continued to strengthen France's ties with the Western alliance. During April and May of 1950, the Western powers, impelled by a mounting sense of urgency, reached agreement on an "integrated defense of the entire North Atlantic area" by "balanced collective forces." The Western foreign ministers, meeting at London on May 11–13, began to approach gingerly the delicate problem of how to include West Germany in the Western alliance. The Schuman Plan for a coal and steel community, announced in May, further advanced the prospects for a functional integration of the economies of Western Europe. Toward the end of May, a resolute response by the Western powers faced down a threatened "march on Berlin" publicly planned by the Communist-led Free German Youth.

By the spring of 1950 it was apparent that the contradictory blend of intimidation and blandishment which characterized Soviet policy in this period, as well as that of its foreign instruments, was not effectively decelerating the increase of power and cohesion in the West. Then in June came the event which illuminated the entire international horizon like a battlefield flare by night — the attack on South Korea.

# VI

# SOVIET POLICY DURING THE KOREAN WAR: FIRST PHASE

THE Korean War is one of those events which confirms the description of international relations as an art rather than a science. From deceptively small beginnings, this curious episode was to explode into a traumatic experience for the entire world. Even after its end, the conflict was to leave behind many unsolved questions. As the prototype of the modern concept of limited war, the Korean War sharply posed the question of the meaning of victory in such circumstances. For the United States, its self-imposed restraints comprised a major trial of the spirit. There were many other military implications, among them questions concerning the capability of modern airpower to interdict primitive lines of supply, the potential usefulness of tactical nuclear weapons, the function of overseas bases, and the uses of conventional forces in the nuclear age. As an experience in international politics, the Korean War provoked debate over whether advanced planning could have anticipated that the political circumstances of an attack, rather than the strategic importance of the area involved, might be a determinant of the response; whether lack of precision in the definition of United States' interests and intentions may have been a factor in the Communist decision to attack; whether the intervention of the Chinese Communists might have been anticipated or forestalled; and whether Communist negotiating techniques do not fundamentally alter the character of modern diplomatic negotiation.

Among the most interesting and still uncertain aspects of the war is the question of its relation to the general foreign policy of the Soviet Union. At the time, the prevailing interpretation on this point came to be that the Communist attack on Korea signaled the opening of a new and more militant world-wide policy. Apprehension was aroused about the possibility of other attacks: if, as some thought, Korea was to be regarded as a diversionary feint, then aggression might be expected against Iran, Yugoslavia, or Western Europe.[1] In any case, it was thought ominous that the Russians appeared willing to accept whatever risk of general war that the Korean action might involve. American officials were reported as feeling obliged to reconsider their previous judgment that the Soviet Union would hesitate to use force to achieve its purposes, at least until 1952 to 1954, when it was expected to reach a higher level of military strength.[2]

In retrospect, however, it appears that this interpretation of the Korean attack as a sign of a heightened general offensive tendency may have been an error. It is true that the action appeared to be a departure from the conservative policy toward the direct use of force which Russia had been following since the end of the war. It seemed to go beyond the essentially reactive character of Soviet militancy that had been keyed to a sense of temporary vulnerability. It also appeared to conflict with the uneven movement of Soviet policy toward calming international tensions in order to check Western mobilization until Russia could become strong enough to secure a favorable power position. What appears to have been decisive in influencing the Soviet leaders to depart from these policy trends were three major considerations: the impelling floodtide of the Chinese revolutionary impulse, the need to check American moves toward establishing a military outpost in Japan, and the apparent prospects for a quick, self-contained success in Korea.[3]

The very length of the discussions between the Chinese Communist leaders and the Russians in Moscow from December 1949 until the middle of February 1950 suggests that the magnitude of the issues went beyond the publicly announced agreements on trade

and mutual assistance. Whether the impending attack on South
Korea was dealt with during these prolonged conversations can
only be surmised, but it seems probable that an action involving
so considerable a movement of forces and supplies during the
next few months and so extensive a coordination of policies would
have required advance planning at the time of the conference.[4] The
state of mind of the Chinese Communists is difficult to reconstruct,
but indications suggest that theirs was the heady feeling of a revolutionary movement that had just triumphed against great odds and
now felt capable of "licking the world." Particularly if one takes
into account the provinciality of the Chinese Communist leadership, its limited knowledge of and visceral hatred of the Western
"imperialists," it seems probable that the Soviet Union was faced
with a situation in which the Chinese were prepared to drive
ahead, with or without the Russians, to round out the victory by
attacking the Western salient in Korea, the Nationalist stronghold
on Formosa, and the Western colonial positions in Indochina. This
put before the Russians a painful dilemma: even if they preferred
to be cautious, which is by no means clear, they would lose whatever influence they hoped to exercise over the Chinese revolution
and, specifically, would lose their dominant position in North Korea.

It seems a plausible conjecture that the Moscow talks included
Soviet support for China's declared territorial aspirations, in view
of the reported substantial deliveries of Russian tanks, trucks, and
heavy artillery to North Korea in April and May of 1950[5] and
the concurrent redeployment of North Korean Communist divisions
which had been active in the Chinese civil war. It also seems probable that a coordinated Chinese Communist assault on Formosa was
planned for the summer of 1950.

On the international front, the Russians' efforts to gain acceptance
for the new Communist government appeared to be carefully
calculated to pace the lifting of the Chinese isolation with the
consolidation of their own influence over the new regime. Moscow's diplomatic support for the new government had been ex-

pressed in two ways: first, by its proposal for a Big Five peace pact, which was intended to win Western recognition of Communist China as a great power; and, second, by its insistence upon Chinese Communist representation in the United Nations. Although this insistence was reinforced by the Soviet delegation's walk-out from the Security Council on January 10 (it stayed away for six and a half months), in practice it appeared that Soviet tactics impeded the acceptance of the new Chinese government into the family of nations. Such an effect may not have been unintentional.

At this point it is worth recalling that a major revision in United States policies toward Japan was then in progress, stimulated by increasing international tensions, the Communist victory on the mainland of China, and Soviet intransigence in regard to a peace settlement with Japan. In 1948 and 1949, the United States had begun to modify its occupation policies in Japan, replacing the earlier emphasis upon social reform with measures intended to strengthen Japan politically and economically as a point of defense against further Communist expansion in the Far East. At the same time, the United States began to take steps toward a Japanese peace treaty, with or without the Russians. The Soviet Union, virtually excluded from a voice in the occupation of Japan, took the position that only the Council of Foreign Ministers, in which it had a veto power, possessed jurisdiction over a treaty with Japan. Having experienced the Soviet uses of the Council of Foreign Ministers in regard to Germany, the United States called a conference of member governments of the Far Eastern Commission (not to be considered as a meeting of the FEC), which the Soviet Union could not obstruct. By the turn of the year 1949–50, diplomatic preparations for a separate peace treaty with Japan were actively under way.[6] It was understood that the treaty would be accompanied by an arrangement to assure the United States the continued use of air, land, and naval bases in Japan and would also provide for the development of Japanese defense forces.

From the Communist point of view, the prospect was not appealing. Communist potentialities in the Far East would be clearly limited by the continuation or expansion of American military power in Japan, the one advanced industrial nation in the Far East. It is significant that the new Treaty of Friendship, Alliance, and Mutual Assistance between the Soviet Union and the Chinese Communists was proclaimed as a preventive measure against aggression by Japan or any state united with Japan.[7]

In a related move, the Soviet Union called upon the Japanese Communist Party to reverse its present line and shift to violent tactics against the proposed American defense arrangements with Japan. The directive was conveyed openly, in a *Cominform Bulletin* article on January 6, 1950, which criticized the previous policies of the Japanese Communist Party in seeking to form a "democratic people's front." The time had come, said the Cominform directive, for "revolutionary struggle." Reminiscent of the Zhdanov rebuke against the French and Italian parties in 1947, the directive appeared to represent a further extension of the militant inflection which Suslov was then encouraging among the European Communists, but it included none of the efforts to gain broader support from other classes which tempered the hard line in Europe.

Despite the opposition of a moderate faction, militant elements within the Japanese Communist Party mounted violent demonstrations and riots throughout the country, culminating in an attack on American military personnel on May 30, 1950.[8] It cannot be established that the new tactics were intended to prepare the Japanese party for a clandestine role against American forces in anticipation of the outbreak of war in Korea; but it would have been a reasonable precaution to take as part of an effort to neutralize American power in the Far East. It may have appeared reasonable to the Russians that a brief and successful action against the Republic of Korea would not only eliminate a Western salient against the Communist sweep of Asia, but would also help to render the American position in Japan politically untenable by stirring up Japanese public opinion with this demonstration of Communist power. Militarily, the installation of strong Communist forces on the lower Korean peninsula may have been expected to checkmate the consolidation of American bases in Japan.

That the Communists did not anticipate serious resistance in Korea seems indicated by the limited number of forces brought to bear. In the absence of outside support to the Republic of Korea, these would undoubtedly have sufficed to accomplish the assigned task within a period of several months. This assumption may have been based upon the results of previous military probes and an erroneous reading of the American reaction to these probes. The North Korean attack on June 25, 1950, had been preceded by a long and unsuccessful effort to undermine South Korea by means of Communist penetration units and by border harassments of increasing intensity. The withdrawal of the main body of United States troops from South Korea by mid-1949 despite these provocations reflected a judgment on the part of the American authorities that Korea would not be of prime strategic importance in the event of general war; the troops were required to fulfill the American commitment to Europe. This withdrawal, and statements by American officials that Korea did not lie within the American defense perimeter,[9] may have been understood by the Communists as a renunciation of American national interests in the area. The Soviet Union may have been tempted to dismiss the importance of the United Nations as a defender of the Republic of Korea in view of the fact that the organization as a military power was yet untried; nor were any effective military preparations then in sight.

Whether these were the intentions and expectations that prompted the act of aggression, the event, as it turned out, radically altered the situation in Asia, the United States, and Western Europe, and did so in a way that proved adverse to Communist interests.

Whatever flexibility appeared to have been developing in the American position toward Communist China since the publication of its White Paper in August 1949 was now wholly at an end. The United States Seventh Fleet was despatched to the Formosa Straits to guard against a possible Communist assault against the Nationalist government. The Chinese Communist regime now faced not only a hardened diplomatic situation in the United Nations, but a transformed military situation on Formosa: instead of the weak and vulnerable Chinese Nationalist government, the Communists were confronted with a military power firmly committed to the defense of the island. If an invasion of the island of Formosa had indeed been part of the original plan, it was now clearly out of the question.

It may have been the case that the Soviet leaders now attributed to the United States a deliberate intention to mislead them in order to produce the situation that resulted and to justify further American military action in the Far East.[10]

The first effects of the Korean War in the United States itself was to make politically feasible a great expansion of military expenditures. Plans for substantially higher defense levels, which had been drawn up by the National Security Council after the Soviet atomic explosion in September 1949, had so far remained largely unrealized because of the budgetary inhibitions of a congressional election year. Now these plans were hurriedly put into force. Within the next few months, the curve of defense expenditures in the United States rose almost vertically. Three supplementary appropriations by Congress brought Department of Defense appropriations for the fiscal year 1951 to a total of $48.2 billion, as compared with $13.2 billion in fiscal 1950. In fiscal 1952, the total rose to more than $60 billion.[11]

A trend toward curtailing the number and use of overseas bases was immediately arrested by the outbreak of the war. Within a short time, the United States Air Force in Great Britain was trebled in size, with the addition of jet fighters and B-50 strategic bombers. The United States also doubled its draft goals for the armed services, gave extensive economic powers to the government under the National Defense Production Act, increased its stockpiling of strategic materials, and greatly increased foreign military assistance, particularly to the nations of Southeast Asia. Diplomatic exploration of a separate peace treaty with Japan was now accelerated, and a Japanese national police reserve, organized to replace American troops transferred to Korea from Japan, started the process of remilitarization in Japan.

Despite outspoken divergencies on the future of Formosa and the recognition of Communist China among the United Nations allies (particularly between Great Britain and the United States), the fact was that the United States was now in the position of conducting a military campaign against Communist aggression under the aegis of the United Nations. These were the immediate consequences of the Korean War as far as the United States was concerned.

### Korea and the Defense of Western Europe

From the Soviet point of view, an even more serious consequence was the impetus which the Korean War gave to the Western defense of Europe. At a later stage, the war was to place serious strains upon the Western alliance, but its first impact was to heighten the sense of common danger and to provide fresh stimulus for a greater Western military effort. The attack also served to stimulate the rearmament of Western Germany and to implant in the minds of Western policy makers a military preoccupation in their estimate of Soviet intentions.

In the summer of 1950, both Britain and France announced substantial increases in military expenditures and in the numbers of men under arms, on the condition of added American assistance. A French note conveying this information also appealed for an immediate increase in the number of British and American ground forces to be stationed on the continent, as a guarantee of Western preparedness.[12] This assurance was given by Truman in September, together with an increase in Mutual Defense Assistance funds for the European allies. American troops and an American commander-in-chief for NATO were now to be deeply involved in the defense of Europe.

American spokesmen bluntly raised the question of including West German troops in the Western defense system with added urgency as a result of the attack on Korea.[13] These developments were spurred on by intimations from both Moscow and the German Communist leaders that West Germany might expect to share the fate of South Korea.[14] Such tactics comprised the major Soviet effort to take advantage of the crisis atmosphere in Europe resulting from the Korean attack, but its effect was directly opposite to what the Russians might have wished. Although for a time the Soviet Union tried to capitalize on the fruits of intimidation which their action had harvested, the hesitation and inconsistency with which this was done tend to discount the possibility that intimidation in Europe was an intentional element in the Soviet plan of attack. In the main, the threats only accelerated trends adverse to Soviet interests.

Plans for the rearmament of West Germany, already in the air before the Korean attack, began to move rapidly forward in the atmosphere of crisis which now prevailed. Meeting in May 1950, the three Western foreign ministers had already urged the speeding up of Germany's re-entry into the "community of free peoples of Europe." In August, West Germany was represented for the first time in the Consultative Assembly of the Council of Europe at Strasbourg. At that session Winston Churchill called for "the immediate creation of a unified European Army subject to proper European democratic control and acting in full cooperation with the United States and Canada."[15] Churchill later added that Germany ought to be included in any European army.[16]

The first large step in this direction was taken by the three Western foreign ministers at their September 1950 meeting in New York. Agreement was reached to terminate the state of war with Germany and to revise the Occupation Statute, granting new powers to the West German government, while also relaxing controls on the levels of German industrial production and shipbuilding. The three nations promised to strengthen their forces in Germany and at the same time guaranteed the West German republic that any attack upon it or West Berlin would be treated as an attack upon themselves. As a concession to French sensibilities, the communiqué issued after the meeting declared that the ministers did not have in mind the re-creation of a German national army.

One month later, the French government combined the earlier proposal for a European army with one for the strengthening of NATO. The Pleven Plan, as it was called, was designed to offer safeguards against the resurgence of German national military power. Approved in principle by the French National Assembly on October 25, the Pleven Plan proposed that the European army be composed of contingents at the smallest possible unit level — of battalion or brigade strength — and that the army be under the direction of a European minister of defense, who would in turn be subject to a European council of ministers and assembly.

After modifications to take account of an American desire for a somewhat larger and quicker recruitment of German combat groups of not more than six thousand men each, the North Atlantic Treaty Organization Deputies and Military Committee announced in December their complete agreement on the political and military recommendations for German participation in a "West European integrated defense force." By the middle of December, the three Western foreign ministers at their meeting in Brussels were able to reach agreement in principle upon a West German military contribution to the defense of Europe. They also approved the replacement of the Occupation Statute by a Contractual Agreement and a security pact, as well as the appointment of General Dwight D. Eisenhower as supreme commander of NATO forces in Europe.[17]

The Soviet leadership reacted vehemently to this alarming prospect of German rearmament. Its first effort was an attempt to head off the danger by calling for a four-power conference of foreign ministers on the demilitarization of Germany. One month after the New York meeting of the Western foreign ministers, the Soviet Union made formal protests to the three powers and summoned a meeting of the foreign ministers of the states of Eastern Europe, including East Germany, at Prague. A communiqué following this meeting on October 21 called upon the four powers to issue a proclamation against the remilitarization of Germany and to return to the terms of the Potsdam agreement.[18] The communiqué also urged the creation of an all-German constituent council on the basis of equal representation of East and West Germany, to prepare for the unification of the country.

Following a rejection of the Prague declaration as "a return to old and unworkable proposals," by Secretary Acheson on October 25,[19] the Soviet government addressed diplomatic notes to the three Western powers on November 3, formally proposing a conference of foreign ministers on the basis of the Prague resolution. A flurry of other diplomatic notes followed in quick succession: a personal letter from Grotewohl to Adenauer on November 30, restating the proposal for a constituent council; further notes from the Soviet Union to the British and French governments on December 15, characterizing the rearmament of West Germany as a breach of their respective treaties of alliance with the Soviet Union. These notes were patently designed to encourage the numerous hesitations which had been expressed in both countries over the danger of proceeding with the rearmament of Germany in the face of an uncertain Soviet reaction.

On December 22, the three Western governments delivered identical replies. They were willing, they said, to attend a conference provided it dealt with the German problem within the framework of the basic causes of tension between the powers. This Soviet effort to block or delay the rearmament of Germany by calling for an immediate conference of foreign ministers was thus turned aside for the time being. In deference to British and, particularly, French public opinion, an outright rejection of the Soviet proposal was avoided by the three Western governments. A conference of deputy foreign ministers did result from the diplomatic exchange, but not until the spring of 1951; by then the European army project had been advanced one stage further.

By the winter of 1950–51, Soviet diplomacy appeared relatively ineffective in checking these developments. Its principal thrust — to open up fissures in the anti-Communist alliance — identified no significant strains in the wave of unity engendered by the Soviet-sponsored aggression in Korea.

To the American charge that the Korean War demonstrated an increasing aggressiveness on the part of the Soviet Union, Moscow replied with an identical charge against the United States. In his order to the United States armed forces of June 27, 1950, President Truman had declared: "The attack upon Korea makes it plain beyond all doubt that communism has passed beyond the use of subversion to conquer independent nations and will now use armed invasion and war." [20] In an answering statement, Gromyko replied on July 4 that by its action "the United States Government went over from a policy of preparing aggression to outright acts of aggression in Korea's domestic affairs, on a course of armed intervention in Korea . . ." [21] Drawing a significant analogy between the Korean conflict and the American civil war, Gromyko insisted that intervention by outside powers was unwarranted. Further, he argued, the United Nations intervention was illegal in view of the fact that the Soviet Union and Communist China had not been represented in the Security Council at the time of the decision to intervene.

### Russia Seeks to Limit the Consequences

On August 1, Jacob Malik, Soviet representative to the United Nations, returned to his seat on the Security Council. Rotation had delivered the presidency of the council into his hands, and he used the opportunity to the full for a month-long indictment of the

United States and for parliamentary obstruction. His charges of aggression and of "inhuman, barbarous bombing" were to provide daily fare for the Peace Movement around the world. Malik concentrated his fire on divisive issues: the seating of Communist China in the United Nations, the protection of Formosa, the strategic views of General MacArthur. On these matters even as staunch an ally as Great Britain was having trouble in reconciling all its differences with American policy.

Malik may have had another objective in returning to the council. By this time, although the United Nations forces had been driven into the small Pusan perimeter, it was clear that a quick Communist military victory was no longer possible, that the future could bring only a continued stalemate or a United Nations counteroffensive. The Communist cause had suffered the disadvantages of the refortification of Formosa and the world-wide defense mobilization of the West. There are some indications that the Soviet Union at this time may have been exploring the possibility of a diplomatic compromise to restore Korea to its prewar status quo.[22]

One of the developments which may have encouraged the Soviet Union to sound out this possibility was an Indian effort to find a compromise solution. Although India had voted for the Security Council's initial resolutions against aggression in Korea, it quickly returned to its preferred role as a neutral mediator. On the first of July, the Indian ambassador in Peking secretly proposed a compromise which would involve the seating of Communist China in the United Nations and the return of the Soviet Union to the Security Council.[23] Encouraged by restrained Chinese Communist editorial responses, on July 13 Prime Minister Nehru sent personal messages to Stalin and Acheson, expressing the desire to localize and if possible end the Korean conflict by breaking the deadlock on the Chinese representation issue. The Soviet premier found the proposal agreeable; the American secretary of state did not. In the long run, the Indian proposal may have contributed to the beginning of the Communist appreciation of the advantages to be gained by treating the neutralist nations as potential allies, rather than as automatic members of the imperialist camp.

In the Security Council, Malik now sought unsuccessfully the *ad hoc* representation of the Communist Chinese regime as an interested party in the Korean affair, modifying his previous demand that the regime be granted a member's seat in the United Nations. He also developed the "civil war" analogy advanced by Gromyko in July and demanded that both Pyongyang and Seoul be represented during the Security Council sessions. This also marked a concession on his part, in view of his previous refusal to recognize the legitimacy of the government of the Republic of Korea. By treating the matter as a civil war, the Russians were not only setting up a legal argument against intervention but were refusing to accept responsibility for the North Korean attack.[24]

Despite these modest indications of an interest in a compromise settlement, however, the Soviet representative was unsuccessful in causing the United Nations to break its stride. The decision of the United Nations allies to persevere was strengthened by the turning of the tide of battle which occurred at this time. By mid-August, the United Nations forces won their first major battle, and it seemed evident that the North Korean attack had spent itself. By mid-September, following the United Nations amphibious landings at Inchon, the counteroffensive seemed well on the way. The Western delegates began to talk of the extension of freedom to the entire peninsula, rather than returning to the boundary at the thirty-eighth parallel.

Failing to restore the prewar situation and to obtain even the temporary seating of the Chinese Communists and the North Koreans at the Security Council session, Malik issued an ominous warning on August 22 that the United States would bear the responsibility for the widening of the conflict which would result from a continuation of the fighting. Undaunted, the General Assembly on October 7 passed a resolution which, by deliberately ambiguous implication, authorized the United Nations forces to continue their advance across the thirty-eighth parallel into North Korea. By the end of October, United Nations forces had reached a point on the Yalu River, North Korean prisoners were being taken at the rate of three thousand a day, and the war appeared to be almost over.[25]

The Soviet Union's world position had deteriorated rapidly in the few months since the war began. A sense of the contemporary feeling about this deterioration is conveyed in an American news account of the gains in Korea, which summarizes the "startling change" in the world situation since the war began four months before:

Then, on the eve of the Communist aggression, these were the world highlights: the U.S. Congress was quarreling over extending a standby draft law. There were plans and more plans for the defense of Europe, but few soldiers in the line and few weapons for them. The U.N. was in the backwash of world events. Russia's attitude was tough and self-confident. She had not turned up at a U.N. Security Council meeting for half a year.

Now the highlights are these: The U.S. is becoming a military giant. A vast rearmament of the West is on in grim earnest. The U.N. is a revitalized organization. Russia obviously is greatly disturbed by the whip-lash reaction to the North Korean adventure. The Soviets, back at the United Nations, want to talk things over with the West.[26]

The annual speech on the anniversary of the Russian revolution, delivered on November 6, 1950, by Bulganin, illustrated the Soviet response to these trends. "The ruling circles of the United States are pursuing a policy of unleashing a new war . . . intensifying the armament drive, inflating military expenditures, increasing the strength of the armed forces," but the Soviet Union was doing its utmost to consolidate peace and cooperation among peoples.[27] Emphasizing Stalin's statements concerning the possibility of peaceful coexistence among states having different economic systems and ideologies, Bulganin asked: "What could be more direct and clearcut than the repeated proposals of the Soviet government aimed at preventing the unleashing of a new war and at extending inter-national cooperation?"

In a speech notable for its defensive tone and concentration on domestic economic achievements, Bulganin permitted himself one paragraph of bristling defiance:

It is high time for these gentlemen to learn that the Soviet people do not belong to the weak-nerved (applause), and that threats cannot frighten them (prolonged applause). History shows that our peace policy is not a sign of weakness. It is time for these gentlemen to learn that our people can stand up for themselves (prolonged applause), stand up for the interests of their country, if necessary, with arms in hand (stormy, prolonged applause).

However, Bulganin softened the implied threat by reaffirming the theme that "the Soviet people stand for peace," and as evidence he cited the fact that the entire adult population of the Soviet Union had signed the Stockholm Appeal. The Peace Movement, he said, was continuing to grow in importance as a result of the increased danger of war and would, in the end, "frustrate the plans of the warmongers."

Indeed, during this period Soviet policy appeared to place in-creasing reliance upon the Peace Movement — a result of the apparent ineffectiveness of Soviet diplomacy and the Communist parties in the face of the world-wide reaction to the Korean War. The decision to throw the full resources of the Peace Movement against the United Nations intervention in Korea was made at a meeting of its Permanent Committee, held at Prague in August. Reporting the decisions of this meeting, *Pravda* carried the following directive as a paragraph in bold-face type: "The immediate stopping of the bloody intervention of the United States imperialists in Korea — this is the demand of hundreds of millions of people striving towards peace." [28]

How this was to be applied in practice was set forth in an editorial directive which appeared in the *Cominform Bulletin* on Septem-ber 22, 1950. Calling for a "new phase" in the Peace Movement, the editorial declared that the time was ripe for an "extension of the program of the movement." This was to mean both an increase in militant political action and an effort to reach out for a broader following. "Life is raising before the Peace Movement new, militant tasks," said the Cominform editorial, praising the "direct action" of the working classes of France, Italy, Belgium, Holland, and Australia; the evasion of military service by youth in the United States, Britain, France, Belgium, and Yugoslavia; and particularly the refusal of some French conscripts to serve in Indochina. The extension of the movement, it was explained, meant enlarging the political content of its program while seeking at the same time to strengthen its non-Communist coloration.

To carry out these tasks, the Peace Movement was summoned to its second world congress. Originally scheduled for Genoa, the congress was shifted to Sheffield, England, in an effort to reach a wider audience. However, because of the British government's refusal of visas to about two hundred of its delegates, the congress was postponed. It was finally opened in Warsaw on November 16.

The main business of the congress was to launch a second worldwide signature campaign, on the model of the successful Stockholm Peace Appeal. The Warsaw Appeal, however, was more detailed and included many principal objectives of current Soviet policy. Non-Communist speakers who sought a Peace Movement program less closely identified with Soviet objectives were attacked as "Titoist." [29] In a formal "Address to the United Nations," the appeal demanded an immediate five-power peace conference, to include Communist China; an immediate end to the war in Korea and the withdrawal of all foreign troops from that country; opposition to the remilitarization of Germany and Japan; termination of the United States neutralization of Formosa; an end of the war in Vietnam; a ban on all weapons of mass destruction and a one-third to one-half reduction of all armed forces by the great powers; a restoration of trade and cultural relations between East and West; an investigation of American war crimes in Korea; a reduction of all military budgets;

opposition to aggression, colonial oppression, and racial discrimination.

The Warsaw congress also made some significant organizational changes. The World Peace Committee, enlarged from 138 to 220 members, was reorganized as the World Peace Council. Its work was to be directed by an executive committee of thirty, with responsibility for maintaining a liaison with other front organizations. The movement, which claimed more than seventy-five national peace committees and a hundred and fifty thousand local committees,[30] seemed to be emerging as an organization paralleling the Cominform and potentially rivaling the United Nations.

In the course of the following year, the intensive campaign for support of the Warsaw Appeal produced a claimed total of 562 million signatures — one quarter of the world's population. More than 90 percent of these were from Iron Curtain countries.[31] How much effect these campaigns had upon the world political situation is difficult to judge, but a preliminary result may have been its unifying symbolic action. It was only after a new turn in the international situation produced a marked rise in neutralist and pacifist sentiment in Western Europe that the Peace Movement was to find a more fertile soil for its activities. Ironically, that change was largely brought about by the intervention of the Chinese Communists in Korea.

# VII

# SOVIET POLICY DURING THE KOREAN WAR: SECOND AND THIRD PHASES

ONCE it had become clear that the initial assault would not sweep the Korean peninsula and that the attack had generated an adverse world-wide response, the Soviet Union set about to contain the conflict and to reduce its effects. By probing divisive issues to maximize strains within the Western alliance, by heightening exploitation of the peace issue to increase popular pressures upon the Western governments, and by somewhat uncertain diplomatic efforts within the United Nations, the Soviet Union sought to compel the United Nations forces to withdraw from Korea and to restore the status quo in circumstances as favorable as possible.

These measures were not effective, however, while the United Nations was experiencing success in its first test of arms. Each bulletin from the advancing United Nations forces further stimulated the euphoric feeling that Might was at last making Right, that the age-old dream of a world rule of law was being realized on the Korean battlefield. Against this exhilarated drive for total victory in Korea, Jacob Malik's tentative and ambiguous offers of compromise in the Security Council during August and once again in early September were unavailing. Seeking to head off the crossing of the thirty-eighth parallel by United Nations forces, Vyshinsky made one further diplomatic effort in the General Assembly in early October. Vyshinsky's resolution held out the promise of an all-Korean election, in return for a cease-fire and a withdrawal of all foreign troops from Korea, with the Chinese Communists participating in a United Nations Commission to observe the elections. The Soviet proposal gained no support outside the Soviet bloc. Instead, the General Assembly passed a resolution which implicitly authorized the unification of Korea by force. This resolution was voted on October 7, just ahead of the news that the forces of the United Nations had swept across the thirty-eighth parallel.

The two phases of Soviet policy which followed this development were closely keyed to the rise and fall of Communist fortunes in the Korean War. At first, the massive Chinese intervention in November 1950 produced a serious deterioration in the United Nations military position and within the Western alliance, and a consequent hardening of Soviet policy. Then, after the defeat of the final Chinese Communist offensive in May 1951, the Soviet Union began to turn once again toward conciliation.

What role the Soviet Union played in the Chinese intervention in Korea is not clear. In his study of the Chinese entry into the war, Whiting tentatively concludes that Soviet influence was a contributing rather than a determining factor in the Chinese decision.[1] From the Soviet point of view, the danger that the United States, intoxicated by its success against the Communist forces in North Korea, might feel encouraged to take the offensive in Asia and elsewhere may have appeared greater because of a number of impassioned statements made at this time by highly placed American military and civilian officials. They urged not only an extension of the Korean War but a more aggressive strategy against the Communist bloc as a whole. Although these statements were disavowed by the President, and some of the officials involved were dismissed from their posts, the Soviet and Chinese leaders may have not known whether to give the statements or the denials greater credence. Another factor in this calculation may have been the air intrusions over Chinese territory attributed to the United States Air Force by the Chinese Communist authorities.[2] It is possible, therefore, that the Soviet Union, to the extent that it had a voice in the matter, deemed the Chinese entry into the war a relatively low-risk means of discouraging the United Nations and the United States from persevering in their intention to conquer the whole of Korea.

Indeed, there is some indication that the first entry of Chinese "volunteers" into the fighting was tentative, for it was followed by a pause in the advance; this may have been intended to allow for time to determine whether the United Nations would now withdraw or whether the United States would react by more extreme measures.[3] When, as it turned out, neither of these anticipated consequences resulted and the intervention met with unexpected military success, the attack was further developed. On November 26, in response to a "general assault" launched two days earlier by General MacArthur's forces, the Chinese unloosed a massive counter-offensive. The strength of the Chinese attack rapidly drove the United Nations forces back below the thirty-eighth parallel with heavy losses. Almost overnight, the United Nations victory had turned into a disastrous rout. For a time it appeared as if the entire United Nations army, which included a high proportion of United States troops then under arms, might be lost. Whatever the initial Soviet judgment in regard to the Chinese intervention, it now appeared that a drastic shift in the world power situation might be in the making, and this possibility dominated both Western and Soviet policy during the following months.

### Effects of the Crisis in the West

On December 16, 1950, Truman declared the United States to be in a state of national emergency. In a broadcast to the nation on the previous day, the President announced an increase in American armed forces from 2.5 million to 3.5 million, a substantial acceleration of defense production, and the introduction of stringent controls over the economy. In a short time, Congress passed a supplementary defense appropriation in excess of $20 billion.[4]

One effect of the atmosphere of heightened tension in the United

States was the triggering of what came to be called the Great Debate on foreign policy, a debate which was to have repercussions within the Western alliance, and in turn upon Soviet policy.

Strong conflicts of opinion over United States foreign policy had been evidenced in the period preceding the congressional elections, held on November 7. Widespread impatience with the human and material costs of the Korean War, the indecisive character of that conflict, and the restraints imposed by diplomatic alliances had all been focused into a single issue: a lack of confidence in the Department of State. Among the factors which raised the attack to frenetic levels was the traumatic reaction in the United States to the unexpected and — from the public point of view — inexplicable Communist victory in China during the previous summer and fall. Charges of widespread disloyalty on the part of public officials and of treason in the conduct of foreign affairs became commonplace in the United States.

The responsible part of the debate concerned a question of policy. In December 1950, when the situation in Korea appeared most desperate, among the additional defense measures announced by the President was the designation of General Dwight D. Eisenhower as Supreme Commander of the North Atlantic forces in Europe and a reaffirmation of the American intention to station additional troops in Europe. This intention was challenged by former President Herbert Hoover in a speech on December 20 which touched off the Great Debate. Hoover challenged the value to America of its continental allies and raised doubts about the commitment of further men and matériel to Western Europe. He urged the United States instead to concentrate on building up its sea and air power in order to be ready to defend the Western hemisphere.[5]

Two other prominent Republican leaders, Senator Robert A. Taft and Governor Thomas E. Dewey, picked up the issue, and as the attack gathered fury in Congress it expanded to include a variety of dissatisfactions. Aroused by the sudden, humiliating, and frustrating turn of events in Korea, there were many who, following the line advocated by General MacArthur, urged that the war be carried to mainland China. Others expressed concern about the President's authority to commit American troops to Europe without congressional approval. Differences were aired concerning the possibilities of an alternative defense system based more extensively upon air and sea power. Some urged a re-examination of the fundamental assumptions of American foreign policy; others frankly gave voice to a resurgent isolationism. Concurrent allegations by Senator Joseph R. McCarthy that the State Department was deeply penetrated by Communists heightened the emotional fervor of the controversy.

Finally, after lengthy hearings before the Senate Committees on Foreign Relations and Armed Services, the debate was brought to an end in early March with the adoption of a Senate resolution supporting the main lines of administration policy.[6] Although the direction of United States foreign policy remained unaltered, the debate weakened popular and legislative support of the administration's program. Abroad, the internal conflict over fundamental commitments further strained the confidence of the Western alliance, already badly shaken by a number of serious divisive issues.

One indication of the anxiety of the British government and public over American reactions to the events in Korea was the hurried trip to the United States by Prime Minister Clement Attlee in early December 1950, undertaken within an hour after receiving a press-conference report that Truman was considering the use of the atomic bomb in Korea. The report, as it turned out, had been based upon a misinterpretation of a routine response to a leading question and therefore incorrectly implied a change in the administration's thinking. The episode illustrates the jittery atmosphere of the period; there was particular anxiety abroad over the differences between the administration and General MacArthur regarding the extension of the Korean War to the mainland of China.[7] These differences finally led, on April 11, 1951, to the recall of MacArthur,[8] which in turn caused another round of debates and congressional committee hearings.[9]

Relations among the Western allies were also being worn thin by other issues. One was the question of the export of goods from Western Europe to Communist countries. Although many restrictions on trade with Eastern Europe had been voluntarily accepted by the Western European allies, the pressure of economic necessity and a belief in the moderating effect on the cold war of trading with the East resulted in the continued shipment to the Communist countries of goods which many in the United States Congress deemed of strategic importance. The result was the passage of two legislative measures in 1951 (the Kem Amendment to a routine appropriation bill and the Battle Act) which prohibited, in certain circumstances, the shipment of American aid to countries engaged in East-West trade in "strategic commodities." The issue raised bitter feelings on both sides of the Atlantic.

Another troublesome issue was the heavy purchasing by the United States of scarce raw materials after the outbreak of the Korean War, causing sharp increases in their prices to the detriment of the Western European economies. The growing American strategic interest in Spain was another political irritant in much of Western Europe, partly because of residual feelings regarding the Spanish Civil War, but also because this interest cast some doubt on the United States' commitment to the defense of the continent. American resentment against its allies for not giving additional support to the war effort in Korea was matched by British and French resentment against the United States for insufficient appreciation of their burdens in Malaya and Indochina. British troubles in Iran during this period were compounded by suspicions of American competition for a larger share of the world petroleum market. French difficulties in Africa were similarly exacerbated by rumors of American commercial ambitions in the area.

Of all the causes of interallied tension in this period, however, the most serious was the persistent problem of the military strengthening ot West Germany. Within France particularly, American pressure for rapid action on a West German military contribution to the Western defense system seriously aggravated internal political conflicts. The United States, on the other hand, found it difficult to understand British and particularly French eagerness to accept renewed Soviet invitations to another round of four-power conferences on Germany, and thus to delay consummation of the interallied agreements on West Germany.

## A Period of Communist Toughness

All these conflicts within the Western alliance were followed with close attention by the Soviet Union and were interpreted as confirmation of the anticipated "internal contradictions" of the capitalist world.[10] The theme of internal contradictions as a factor in the inevitable weakening of the Western alliance was to play an increasingly important role in Soviet analyses in the following period. As we may see from Stalin's final essay in 1952, this was later to become a key element in the emergence of a divisive peaceful-coexistence policy, which rested upon the expectation of imminent conflict among the capitalist states and the early collapse of the "imperialist world system." For the moment, however, at the turn of the year 1950–51, while the Chinese Communists were still driving back the United Nations forces in full retreat, the Soviet Union apparently saw no reason to move in a conciliatory direction.

This was, on the contrary, a period of uncompromising hardness in Sino-Soviet behavior. Despite the urgent appeals of the United Nations Cease-Fire Committee, strongly supported by the emerging Arab-Asian bloc, the Communists showed no signs of wanting to resolve the Korean conflict. A representative of Communist China, General Wu Hsiu-ch'uan, who appeared in New York on November 24 in response to an invitation of the United Nations Security Council issued almost two months before, stood firm on a demand that the only basis for a cease-fire would be a withdrawal of United States forces from Korea and Formosa. When a resolution was presented to the Security Council appealing to Communist China not to intervene in Korea on the basis of an assurance concerning its "legitimate interests," it was vetoed by the Soviet Union on November 30, by which time China's full-scale attack was well under way. Despite renewed promises from the cease-fire group to arrange a conference on Far Eastern problems coincident with a cease-fire in Korea, General Wu left for Peking on December 19, wholly unresponsive to the United Nations overtures. His parting words warned that a world war might result from the American intervention in Korea and Formosa.

On New Year's Day of 1951, the second large-scale Chinese offensive in Korea began, with Russian-designed jet fighter planes in use for the first time in considerable numbers.[11] In apparent coordination, the Communist-led Vietminh forces in Indochina abandoned guerrilla tactics and on December 26 launched the first of a series of frontal assaults upon the French army in the Red River delta.[12] A further indication of the Sino-Soviet judgment that this was a time for military action rather than diplomacy can be found in the Chinese Communist invasion of Tibet, which was launched in October notwithstanding the friendly relations that had prevailed between Peking and New Delhi and the services performed by the Indian government as a diplomatic go-between with the Chinese Communist regime.[13]

In Europe, too, the Communist line showed signs of hardening in this period, which was characterized by the *Cominform Bulletin* as one of "sharpening class struggle." A new level of anti-American virulence was reached by Piotr N. Pospelov, former editor of *Pravda,* currently head of the party's Department of Agitation and Propaganda, in his speech on the twenty-seventh anniversary of Lenin's death, January 21, 1951; it made a sharp contrast to the same speaker's emphasis on peaceful coexistence on the same occasion the year before.[14] In the presence of Stalin and other Soviet leaders, Pospelov signaled the reopening of a campaign in the Soviet press bitterly attacking the United States for its part in the intervention in the Russian Civil War, a theme often invoked during militant phases of Soviet policy.

Further evidence of militant intent was the effort of the French Communist Party to mount strikes and demonstrations on the occasion of General Eisenhower's visit to NATO headquarters in Paris on January 9 and 24. The effort, however, was unsuccessful. In Eastern Europe, the harsh treatment of American citizens also indicated no Communist interest in creating a conciliatory atmosphere. An American businessman, Robert A. Vogeler, was released in April 1951 after more than seventeen months in a Hungarian prison on charges of espionage, in return for the reopening of Hungarian consulates in New York and other concessions. In the same month, however, an American newspaperman, William N. Oatis, was arrested in Czechoslovakia on similar charges.[15] International tension was also heightened by further purge trials within Czechoslovakia, Poland, and Bulgaria.

At this point, Stalin chose to make one of his occasional interventions in the international situation, his first public statement on foreign affairs since his interview with Kingsbury Smith regarding the Berlin blockade two years before. On February 16, 1951, Stalin granted an interview to *Pravda,* in the form of answers to five questions, which serve to define the tone and direction of Soviet policy in this period. Although the interview provided a cue for the Peace Movement, which was holding an international meeting the following week, the immediate occasion for the interview appeared to be Stalin's desire to make a political rebuttal to Prime Minister Attlee's statement in the House of Commons that the Soviet Union, far from demobilizing after the war, had been increasing its armed forces.

Stalin characterized the Attlee statement as "slander." He asserted that the Soviet Union had in fact carried out a demobilization in three stages, from 1945 to 1948.[16] No state, he argued, could have carried out the massive reconstruction of its economy, expanding its hydroelectric and other resources as the Soviet Union had done, and at the same time have multiplied its armed forces without falling into bankruptcy. In turn, Stalin accused Attlee of prevarication in order to justify the armament drive in Britain and to deceive the British people into supporting "the new world war being organized by the ruling circles of the United States." If Attlee were really a supporter of peace, asked Stalin, why had he rejected the Soviet proposals for a five-power peace pact, an immediate start on the reduction of armaments, and a ban on the atomic bomb? Why had he prohibited the meeting of the world peace congress in Britain in November?

The other questions and answers in the interview concerned the war in Korea. If Britain and the United States rejected the proposals of the Chinese Communists, said Stalin, "the war in Korea could only end in defeat for the interventionists." This was not because the American and British generals and officers were inferior to those of China and Korea, he added, but because they realized they were fighting an unjust war.

In response to another question, Stalin characterized as "a shameful decision" the resolution passed by the General Assembly of the United Nations two weeks earlier condemning Communist China as an aggressor. Here Stalin was playing upon British sensitivities. Anxious not to create further impediments to the ultimate conciliation of the Chinese Communists, the British had with great reluctance given their support to this resolution, which had been advanced by the American delegation under the pressure of domestic political considerations. Stalin drove the knife into a tender spot. The United States, he said, was turning the United Nations into an instrument of war. Ominously, he added: "The United Nations Organization is therefore taking the inglorious road of the League of Nations. In this way it is burying its moral prestige and dooming itself to disintegration." Stalin was echoing arguments that had been heard in the House of Commons itself and that had been advanced in the General Assembly by representatives of the Arab-Asian bloc, particularly India, during the debate on the American-sponsored resolution. Did Stalin, then, think that war was inevitable? No, he replied, at least not at the present time. The "aggressive forces" in the United States, Britain, and France were "thirsting for a new war," but they could be held in check by the "peace-loving forces" in these countries.

There then followed two paragraphs which were to be much quoted in the Communist press during the next months as a directive to the Communist Parties and the Peace Movement:

Peace will be preserved and consolidated if the peoples will take the cause of preserving peace into their own hands and defend it to the end. War may become inevitable if the warmongers succeed in entangling the masses of the people in lies, in deceiving them and drawing them into a new world war.

That is why the wide campaign for the maintenance of peace, as a means of exposing the criminal machinations of the warmongers, is now of first-rate importance.

Stalin concluded the interview by reaffirming in familiar terms the peaceful aims of Soviet policy.

To Western eyes, the paragraphs cited above may have appeared to be only the repetition of familiar propaganda themes, but to the newly reorganized World Peace Council, which was holding its first meeting from February 21 to 25 in East Berlin, the operational significance of Stalin's statement was clear.

Originally scheduled for Geneva, the meeting had been transferred to Berlin because of the objections of the Swiss authorities. A further difficulty arose when Frédéric Joliot-Curie, chairman of the council, had been unable to obtain a transit visa across West Germany. The main report was therefore presented by Pietro Nenni, the vice-chairman, who picked up and developed the line indicated in the Stalin interview. The council enlarged the proposal for a five-power peace pact that had been advanced at the Warsaw Peace Congress in November and strengthened it by adding a preamble designed to appeal to "all men and women of good will, all organizations that hope for peace . . . whatever may be their view of the causes that have brought about the danger of world war." It condemned in advance any refusal to accept the proposal "as evidence of an aggressive design on the part of the Government in question." [17] Accompanying this appeal, now launched as a new signature campaign, was a series of resolutions protesting the remilitarization of Germany and Japan, denouncing the United Nations resolution against Communist China for its intervention in Korea, and demanding an immediate conference for the peaceful settlement of the Korean problem, together with the withdrawal of all foreign troops from Korea.

## Focus on Germany

The main emphasis of the Peace Movement at this point, however, was not upon Korea, where the Chinese Communist armies were still advancing, but upon the problem of Germany. This was foremost among the concerns of the Soviet Union. It seems probable that both the timing of the World Peace Council session and its location had been set with an eye on the deputy foreign ministers' conference on Germany which was to convene within a week. The *Cominform Bulletin* emphasized the special significance of the fact that the Peace Council was meeting in the heart of Germany, "the western part of which the US-British imperialists are intensively turning into a jumping-off ground for unleashing a new war, into the powder-barrel of Europe." [18]

The entire effort of the French Communist Party and the French branch of the Peace Movement was now concentrated on the German issue. At a meeting of the Central Committee of the French party shortly before the Berlin meeting of the Peace Council, Jacques Duclos, now the acting leader of the party,[19] significantly alluded to the decisions of the Brussels NATO conference in December as a confirmation of the analysis projected by Zhdanov at the founding meeting of the Cominform three years before.[20] "France occupies a particularly responsible sector" in the peace campaign, he wrote a week later, and "for the French people the struggle against restoring the 'Wehrmacht' is unquestionably the essential problem in the general struggle for peace." [21] He called upon the party and the Peace Movement to carry out a house-to-house drive throughout France for signatures to a petition which said simply: "I am against rearming Germany!" In less than three months, the French branch of the Peace Movement claimed that six million signatures had been affixed to the "referendum." [22] One of the actions of the Berlin meeting of the World Peace Council was to plan an International Conference for the Peaceful Settlement of the German Problem, to meet in mid-May in Paris.

The timing of this emphasis upon the German problem was related to the central attention this issue was receiving in Soviet diplomacy. Following the September conference of the Western foreign ministers in New York, at which the first steps were taken toward arranging for a German military contribution, Soviet policy had been galvanized into a series of diplomatic countermaneuvers: the Prague conference of East European foreign ministers, protests to the three Western capitals, a proposal on November 3 for a four-power foreign ministers' conference, and notes to the British and French on December 15 attacking the proposed rearmament of West Germany as a violation of the Anglo-Soviet and Franco-Soviet treaties. When the Western powers agreed to hold a preliminary session preparatory to a foreign ministers' conference to discuss the broader causes of East-West tension, rather than the German problem alone, the Soviet Union on December 30 accepted the proposal, although it continued to insist that Germany be discussed before other subjects. After further diplomatic exchanges, a deputy foreign ministers' conference convened on March 5 at the Palais Rose in Paris, for the purpose of drafting the agenda for a conference of their principals. [23]

What was most significant about the conference of the deputies was not its failure to reach an agreement even on the agenda, but the striking shift which it revealed in the focus of Soviet concern. During the first month of the conference, the Soviet Union showed eagerness to have the German issue first on the agenda, in an effort to forestall Western progress toward rearming West Germany. Conversely, the Western powers, and particularly the United States, were determined to put the fundamental causes of tension first on the agenda, both for reasons of logic and to avoid the very delays which the Soviet Union desired. Toward the end of March each side brought up, perhaps for bargaining purposes, other contentious issues. Gromyko threw in the problem of Trieste; Philip Jessup, the American delegate, raised the question of human rights in Rumania, Bulgaria, and Hungary. Both sides had added the issue of reduction of armaments, in different forms.

Suddenly, at the very end of March, the attitude of the Soviet delegate changed. Whatever degree of accommodation had been achieved was now lost, as the Soviet representative tabled two thorny new items: the North Atlantic Treaty and American bases in Europe and the Near East. From this point until it dissolved on June 21, the conference made no progress toward an agreement. The length of the conference stemmed from the reluctance of any of the participants to accept the responsibility for its termination, particularly in view of the general election in France on June 17.[24]

An explanation of this shift in Soviet tactics may be found partly in the conference itself, but even more in the events that were taking place in Europe. Within the conference room, the first month of discussions had made it clear that the Soviet hope of opening up differences among the three Western powers would be disappointed. Despite Stalin's *Pravda* interview of February 16 and the best efforts of the Peace Movement and the French Communist Party to bring pressure upon at least the French delegate, the three Western governments remained firmly united at the conference table, whatever their disagreements were in private.

But another and probably more important factor was the fact that serious delays had been developing among the Western powers outside the conference over the implementation of their decisions regarding Germany. In two sets of simultaneous discussions — in

Paris among the Western European states on the Pleven Plan and in Bonn between the Western High Commissioners and the West German military advisers — the complex problems encountered gave assurance to the Soviet Union that the rearmament of West Germany was by no means imminent.[25] The Soviet Union may have concluded, therefore, that divisive political tactics and the manipulation of popular pressures were not likely to produce a foreign ministers' conference on favorable terms at this time but that, in any case, the difficulties of the Western allies in moving from agreement in principle to agreement in realization on the problem of German rearmament made the matter less immediately urgent than it had seemed a few months before.

## The Beginning of the Third Phase

Whatever assurance the Soviet leadership may have felt as a result of the dilatory Western progress on the German problem must have been more than balanced by unfavorable developments at this time elsewhere in the world. Not only was the tide of battle in Korea now beginning to turn against the Communists, but the galvanizing effect upon the West of its near-defeat at Chinese hands was now beginning to produce results which must have alarmed the Soviet leadership.

By the latter part of February 1951, the second great Chinese offensive had been spent. By March, the United Nations forces were once again crossing the thirty-eighth parallel.[26] The third and final Chinese offensive, begun in April and renewed in early May, was held and thrown back by the reinforced United Nations troops. When, on May 24, the UN forces resumed the offensive, they inflicted extremely heavy casualties and captured large numbers of Chinese and North Korean prisoners.[27] Although the fighting had now reached a point at which only moderate territorial gains were registered, the United Nations had secured a line roughly approximating the thirty-eighth parallel and was at a considerable advantage in regard to the ratio of casualties.

Elsewhere in Asia, the situation held little comfort for the Communist cause. The frontal assault of the Vietminh in Indochina had by this time proved a failure, and Ho Chi Minh's forces had been obliged to return to guerrilla warfare.[28] The United States had been pushing steadily ahead with arrangements for a peace treaty with Japan and a security treaty which would reserve to the United States the right to maintain military bases in that country. Defense agreements were under active negotiation between the United States and the Philippines, Australia, and New Zealand.

Alarmed by its near-disaster in Korea, the United States was displaying a driving determination to redress the power imbalance as quickly as possible. Perhaps the most telling aspect of this development from the Soviet point of view was the powerful growth of American strategic air power. In January 1951 the President's State of the Union message called for an expansion of the American Air Force to ninety-five air groups, approximately double the pre-Korean strength, with far more formidable equipment. Soviet industrial sites would be within range of the projected aircraft even from bases in North America. In the meantime, arrangements were made to strengthen the overseas-base structure, which would immediately extend the reach of American airpower. In February it was announced that five airfields in Morocco were to be built for the United States Air Force, in addition to the large bases being developed at Wheelus Field in Libya and at Dhahran in Saudi Arabia. American air units in Austria and Germany were being reinforced and reorganized as the Twelfth Air Force, a tactical unit with headquarters at Wiesbaden. In Britain, an American strategic bombing force was being further strengthened and reconstituted as the Third Air Force.[29]

Other signs of the United States' intention to increase its power position must have been apparent to the Soviet leaders in the high mobilization goals recommended by Truman in January 1951. Military-aircraft production capacity was to be increased to 50,000 units annually; tanks, to 35,000. The armed forces were being increased to 3.5 million from the 1.5 million at the outbreak of the Korean War. Defense expenditures were being projected at a rate of more than $60 billion for the next fiscal year, as contrasted with a rate of $12 billion two years before. Military and economic foreign aid was called for at a level of $10.6 billion for the following fiscal year, as compared with $4.5 billion for the previous year, and an increasing share of this was to be directed toward military purposes. The Russians can have been in no doubt that the war in Korea, and particularly the shock of the Chinese Communist advances, had made these increased appropriations politically possible in the United States.[30]

Among American government leaders, the possibility that the Korean War might develop into an all-out war with the Soviet Union had increasingly stimulated support for the intensive concentration of resources upon the hydrogen-bomb program, as well as for an expansion of the production of atomic weapons.[31] The Soviet Union required no intelligence system to become aware of this development, since the matter was widely discussed in the American press.

In Europe, although its land forces amounted at the moment to no more than fourteen to sixteen divisions, NATO's potential strength may have given the Soviet leaders some concern. With four additional American divisions scheduled to be added in 1951 to the two already stationed in Europe, the United States was unmistakably committed to the defense of Europe. In early 1951, General Eisenhower assumed command of the NATO forces and by April the Supreme Headquarters of the Allied Powers in Europe (SHAPE) had been activated. The same month saw the signing of the treaty for the establishment of the Coal and Steel Community among six European nations, including the Federal Republic of Germany. In May the United States proposed the formal addition of Greece and Turkey to NATO. In April it was announced that Yugoslavia, in addition to the economic assistance it had been receiving, was now seeking military assistance from the West.

To many Europeans, these developments reflected an alarming tendency in American policy. What was to the American administration an urgent necessity — the replacement of "situations of weakness" with "situations of strength," in the words of Acheson — seemed to many articulate critics abroad an undue preoccupation with the military aspects of the world situation and a rigidity of political policy. To the Soviet leaders, these steps toward mobilization of Western power may have seemed even more foreboding. The Chinese attack in Korea had nearly produced a dramatic defeat of American power; it did succeed in provoking a period of quarreling and suspicion within the United States and between the United States and its allies. Now that the Chinese assault had been thrown back, however, trends in American policy were seriously adverse to Soviet interests. The near-disaster had galvanized the American government — executive and legislative branches alike — and, whether as a result of the Great Debate or of the course of events in Korea, American Far Eastern policy was rapidly losing the flexibility and disinterestedness of previous years and was now showing a decreasing resistance to the possibility of widening the conflict in the Far East.[32] Whether or not they perceived a cause-and-effect connection between the high degree of international tension and the efforts to increase Western power and harden Western policy, the Soviet leaders now sought to remove the cause and lower the level of world tension.

On June 23, 1951, two days after the conference of deputy foreign ministers in Paris had come to its dreary end, one month after the beginning of the decisive defeat of the third Chinese offensive in Korea, the Soviet Union gave an open sign of its interest in a cease-fire in Korea. The chosen harbinger was once again Malik, the same representative to the United Nations who had given the first indication of a Soviet interest in terminating the Berlin blockade two years before. In a broadcast, one of a series sponsored by the United Nations, Malik expressed the belief that the Korean conflict could be settled and declared that the first step should be the opening of discussions between the belligerents for a cease-fire and an armistice providing for the mutual withdrawal of forces from the thirty-eighth parallel.[33]

The willingness of the American government to accept a cease-fire at the thirty-eighth parallel had been indicated in testimony given during May and June at joint congressional hearings on the recall of General MacArthur.[34] In an interview between the Soviet deputy foreign minister and the American ambassador to Moscow on June 27, the Soviet government officially reaffirmed its interest in a settlement in Korea, limited for the present to purely military questions.[35] Contact was then established by radio between the respective military commanders in Korea, and arrangements were made for the beginning of the truce talks in July. The United Nations offensive promptly came to a halt, thus relieving the Chinese Communist forces of the danger of a complete rout.

With this initiative, Soviet policy entered a period of relative quiescence. For a time, no strong sense of direction was in evidence. Yet, by this very holding back, the Soviet Union was beginning a more consistent effort to reverse the unfavorable trend in the world power situation which it had inadvertently started. To invert Lenin's famous phrase, the Soviet Union had taken two steps backward for each step forward; each effort it had made since 1946 to improve its world position had generated in the West a reaction which threatened still more serious disadvantages. During the next year, the realization of this ironic fact, once absorbed into Soviet thinking, was reflected in the evolution of both its doctrine and its policy.

# VIII

# THE DIPLOMACY OF COEXISTENCE, 1951–1952

T HE year preceding the Nineteenth Party Congress was a particularly important one in the evolution of Soviet foreign policy. Following the defeat of the third Chinese offensive in Korea in the spring of 1951, the Soviet reappraisal of the changing strategic situation began to settle into the form in which it was to be defined at the congress. Although some contradictory tendencies continued to show themselves during this period, Soviet policy was more firmly adapted to the requirements which later were incorporated into the official analysis.

Paradoxically, these requirements were defined, on the one side, by the continued momentum of the Western alliance and, on the other, by the promise of growing Western weaknesses, as well as anticipated increases in Soviet strength. Soviet policy, therefore, in its most immediate aspect was an essentially defensive response to the growth of Western power, but it also represented a turn toward an alternative and more promising form of advance in the longer perspective. It was to be characterized mainly by a selective application of the peaceful-coexistence policy, intended to encourage the relaxation and fragmentation of the Western alliance.

## The Doctrine of "Cracks in the Western Alliance"

Like the flight of a rocket, the Western mobilization continued its upward course during 1951 and early 1952 until, the last stages of impulsion having dropped away, the rocket began to arch downward, responding to the force of gravity. The upward impulsion had come from the successive thrusts of Communist provocation, the last being the Berlin blockade and the attack on Korea. The force of gravity in this case was exerted by the inherent stresses within the Western alliance, which the Communists call "internal contradictions."

Against the rapid strengthening of Western power following the first defeats in Korea, Soviet diplomacy had been fighting a series of ineffective rear-guard actions. Particularly stinging was the inability of the Soviet Union to prevent the signing of the peace and security treaties with Japan, for these steps sanctioned United States military bases in Japan and allied the major industrial nation of the Far East with the Western defense system. Despite Soviet maneuvers and the absence of India, the peace treaty was signed in San Francisco on September 8, 1951, by forty-nine nations, including a substantial representation from Asia. At the same time, the United States also signed a series of defense agreements with Australia, New Zealand, and the Philippines. The net effect of these arrangements was to assure the continued military presence of the United States in the Pacific area.

The ineffectiveness of Deputy Foreign Minister Gromyko at the San Francisco conference seemed to exemplify the helplessness of Soviet diplomacy in the face of an intense period of Western diplomatic activity. Within the same month of September, a conference of the three Western foreign ministers in Washington and a meeting of the North Atlantic Council in Ottawa made further progress toward the rearmament of West Germany. At the latter session, the council also approved the cancellation of the military limitations on Italy under the Italian peace treaty, reduced British and American differences over NATO commands in the Atlantic and the Mediterranean areas, and appointed a subcommittee of "Three Wise Men" (W. Averell Harriman, Jean Monnet, and Hugh Gaitskell, for whom Sir Edwin Plowden served) to study the distribution of the financial burden of rearmament.

In October, American defense preparations moved forward with the creation of the Mutual Security Agency to administer a program of $7.5 billion of foreign military and economic assistance, and with the passage by Congress of a $56.9 billion appropriation for defense during the current fiscal year, to be supplemented by another $1.2 billion in the following month.

At Paris in November, the three Western powers took the initiative at the General Assembly of the United Nations with a concerted proposal for the reduction of armaments, and at Rome a few weeks later the North Atlantic Treaty Council met again to consider a reported demand from General Eisenhower for an increase in NATO's military goals to forty divisions by the end of 1952. During November also, the three Western Foreign Ministers met with Chancellor Adenauer and approved a draft General Agreement on the terms by which the Federal Republic might be included in a European defense community. In the same month, a military-aid agreement was signed between the United States and Yugoslavia. Shortly after the turn of the year, Churchill, once again Prime Minister, assured the American Congress of British support in the Korean truce talks, which had become stalemated. He pledged a "prompt, resolute and effective" British response if a truce agreement should be broken by the Communists.

The climax of this furiously intense round of diplomatic negotiation among the Western powers was still to come within the following four months, but signs of strain had already begun to appear, foreshadowing the difficulties ahead in moving from agreement to realization. At its Lisbon meeting in February 1952, the North Atlantic Council raised its goal to fifty divisions by the end of 1952, to include twelve French divisions and a total of four thousand operational aircraft, approximately doubling the forces then available to NATO. The council reaffirmed its support for the creation of a European army including West German forces and formally declared that West Germany was part of the territory to be defended by NATO. However, as a result of economic strains and unresolved differences on the German problem, the Lisbon goals went unfulfilled. The conviction of the European members as to the imminence of the Soviet military danger had by this time appreciably weakened, and measures which might have been politically manageable under a greater sense of urgency were now too difficult.

Nevertheless, pressure from the United States, which had not yet scaled down its estimate of the Soviet military threat, was still sufficient to clear away some of the remaining obstacles to the incorporation of a nearly sovereign West German state into the Western alliance. On May 26, 1952, the Contractual Agreements between the Federal Republic and the three Western powers were signed at Bonn and the European Defense Treaty at Paris on the following day.

Although, as we shall see, Soviet maneuvers to prevent these steps were ineffective, what Moscow did not do during these months had the effect of hampering the fulfillment of the agreements. Almost two years had passed since the most recent overt Communist aggression, and this was sufficient to relax international tension perceptibly. Early in 1952, Anthony Eden, again British foreign minister, expressed the conviction that the risks of war were less than they had been a year or two years before.[1] Under the balmy influence of this negative attribute of the international situation, differences in the West began to blossom: between people and their governments, between Europe and the United States, between plans and realization.

The $7.9 billion requested by the President in January for foreign economic and military assistance was cut by Congress to $6 billion in July. The $650 to $750 million in military assistance that France had been anticipating from the United States, and on which its own military plans had been based, became $525 million, a reduction which was to lead to charges of bad faith. The British government let it be known in February that its three-year military program was going to be stretched out considerably beyond that length of time. After the Lisbon meeting, the French prime minister, Edgar Faure, had been unable to gain support for the new taxes required to sustain the French contribution to the Lisbon program and had been obliged to resign.

The United States now began to preoccupy itself with a hard-fought presidential election, in which foreign policy was a major issue. The usual reluctance of the administration to undertake financial and other commitments in an election year was compounded by charges of appeasement, bellicosity, and disloyalty. The net effect was to inhibit the United States in its exercise of leadership within the Western alliance and, particularly as a result of the period of McCarthyism in American life, to raise a question in the minds of the Allies about the authority of the United States to claim a position of leadership.[2]

Precarious parliamentary majorities in France and Italy and a slim majority in West Germany made responsible governmental actions in these countries especially difficult. France's burden in Indochina, which absorbed eight divisions of its army, more officers than it was producing, and more financial outlay than it was receiving in aid from the United States, reduced its ability to contribute to the defense of Europe and heightened French national sensitivities. Nationalist sentiments were also inflamed over the issue of the Saar and the prospect of West German ascendancy in Europe. Similar nationalist sensitivities were involved in British, French, and Dutch exasperation with American policies toward colonial territories and in the British demand for the NATO naval command in the Mediterranean. Britain's decision to stay out of the European Defense Community because of its Commonwealth commitments seriously disturbed the French, who feared West German dominance in the EDC.

The neutralist movement in Europe, which had begun in 1950 with an orientation separate from but not inimical to the United States, began in 1951 to assume an increasingly anti-American flavor.[3] This trend reflected a resentment against pressure for an accelerated armament program and a fear that the United States was overly occupied with the military, as against the social and economic, dimensions of the rivalry with the Soviet Union. The European mistrust of American bellicosity was fed, in one notable example, by the appearance in October 1951 of a special issue of *Collier's* magazine describing a future war with the Soviet Union, complete with atomic attacks on Soviet cities and occupation by United States troops under a United Nations banner.[4] The magazine was widely circulated throughout Europe; in view of its roster of distinguished American authors and its claim of having been prepared with the help of "top Washington officials," it was taken to represent American expectations, in contrast to the American proposals for disarmament at the General Assembly of the United Nations which was then in session. In a special issue, the French neutralist weekly, *L'Observateur,* satirized the *Collier's* flight of fancy and derided American claims of peaceful intentions. A Soviet writer claimed that the magazine had "revealed the war plans of the United States' ruling circles."[5] An American Communist writing in a Soviet journal compared the document to *Mein Kampf*.[6]

This combination of neutralism, nationalism, international conflicts, and domestic preoccupations, no longer submerged by Soviet belligerency, increasingly encouraged the Soviet leadership to place its reliance upon the "internal contradictions of the capitalist world" as a promising strategic factor in the changing world situation. The expectation that internal conflicts would set limitations on the Western power position became a central element in the doctrinal declarations of the Soviet regime in this period.

In July 1951, for example, Molotov struck a balance between optimism and pessimism. While warning that the danger of war had been increased by Western rearmament, American bases abroad, and the development of military outposts in West Germany and Japan, he saw a ray of hope in the fact that "in the camp of imperialism, there are growing inner antagonisms in individual countries and, at the same time, sharpening struggle between the ruling cliques of these powers."[7]

The annual anniversary speech, delivered on November 6, 1951, by Lavrenti Beria, though conveying a somewhat listless and defensive account of Soviet policy, nevertheless emphasized Soviet faith in the "internal contradictions within the imperialist camp," including the prospect of an economic crash, colonial struggles, and clashes between the United States and Great Britain. These factors were cited as a basis for reaffirming the Soviet belief in peaceful coexistence and the efficacy of the Peace Movement.[8] Beria, then in charge of atomic-energy development, also significantly stressed the point that a number of "economic and defense" problems had recently been solved, as a result of which, he said, Soviet science now led the world.

By December 1951, the *Pravda* correspondent in Paris, Yuri Zhukov, found conditions much more favorable than they had appeared three months earlier at the Japanese Peace Conference in San Francisco, as a result of "cracks in the Western alliance":

First, the camp of peace has grown and become stronger in this interval. Second, the bulky and shaky structure of the aggressors' bloc is beginning to show cracks, which became noticeable at the Atlantic Alliance Council meeting in Ottawa and increased at the session in Rome. Third, the national liberation movement is rapidy growing and spreading in the countries dependent on the USA, Britain, and France, the UN votes of which Acheson could manipulate as he liked until quite recently.[9]

A few months later, the journal *Bolshevik* provided an ideological underpinning for these reportorial observations:

Naturally, it would be incorrect to underestimate the forces of the imperialist camp. This camp has at its disposal a mighty production machine which is entirely engaged at present in war preparation, building ever-growing armies, stockpiling supplies, etc. The ideologists and propagandists of the war camp lay special stress on this aspect, trying to intimidate the peoples with the "omnipotence" of America and the atom bomb.

But a sober estimate of the situation shows something else. The mere fact that the camp of the imperialists represents an alliance of unequal states dooms it to internal weakness. The compact of the states of West Europe under the aegis of the USA has not eliminated and cannot eliminate the contradictions among them. Behind the outward unity of the imperialist camp of war are concealed ever-deepening internal contradictions, linked above all with the struggle for sources of raw materials, markets, and spheres of capital investment.[10]

Also reflected in Soviet writings of this period was a rising expectation of the approaching general crisis of capitalism in the United States. Soviet writers took up and disputed a current American argument that the economic system of the United States did not correspond to the capitalist model and was therefore exempt from the Marxist laws of decay.[11] In an ostensible answer to questions from readers, *Pravda* saw the current period as one of the intensification of crisis in capitalism, as evidenced by the "tremendous growth of militarism," the "catastrophic drop in the working people's standard of living," a fall in the rate of economic development, and a struggle for spheres of influence among imperialist countries.[12] Generalizing from the steel strikes in the United States during June and July 1952, the *Cominform Bulletin* devoted a lead editorial to "The Rising Strike Movement in Capitalist Countries," and saw in this an opportunity for Communist parties abroad to rally "broad masses in capitalist countries to fight for their immediate and most easily understood demands." [13]

## The Divisive Uses of "Peace"

The Soviet Union, now seeking to relax the atmosphere of international tension, abstained from any overt acts of hostility. During the summer of 1951, an effort was made to encourage speculation that the opening of the Korean truce talks could be followed up by broad settlements with the West, but by autumn this unproductive line was replaced by a selective treatment intended to encourage divisive tendencies among the Western powers. The references to the United States became increasingly harsh, while Great Britain and France were courted.

The summer's peace drive was marked by the appearance of a new English-language magazine in Moscow, *News,* to promote closer understanding with the Anglo-Saxon world. *Izvestiya* gave emphasis and support to the new journal's objective by reprinting its lead article, the main point of which was that there was no basis in history or in current economic and political conditions for strained relations between the Soviet Union and Britain or America.[14] In August 1951, *Pravda* published in full a message to the Russian people from British Foreign Secretary Herbert Morrison. The letter stated an unvarnished British view of Soviet responsibility for existing international tensions. (In publishing the document, however, *Pravda* appended a rebuttal which was somewhat longer than the letter.) Another expression of international amity during the same month came in the form of a letter from Nikolai Shvernik, president of the Presidium of the Supreme Soviet, responding to the McMahon-Ribicoff Resolution of the United States Congress. This resolution, passed in June, had conveyed to the people of the Soviet Union the friendship and peaceful purposes of the American people. Shvernik in reply forwarded a resolution of the Presidium expressing reciprocal sentiments and restating the principal elements of the Soviet claim to a peaceful policy: its advocacy of a reduction in armed forces, a ban on atomic weapons, and a five-power peace pact.[15] An American correspondent in Moscow during this period noted in his diary the unusual freedom with which speculation was being permitted on the question of a change in Soviet foreign policy toward better relations with the West.[16] By September, however, it had become apparent to the Soviet leadership that these atmospheric appeals were having no effect upon the forward momentum of the Western mobilization, and the smile faded from the face of the Soviet press.

A general effort to keep international tension from mounting continued to manifest itself from time to time. When, in October

1951, the Soviet Union exploded its next atomic bomb, Stalin took the occasion of a new *Pravda* interview to calm the "hullabaloo" raised in the foreign press.[17] "There are no grounds whatever for such alarm," he replied to a question concerning the "shouting about a threat to the security of the United States" resulting from the explosion. "The Soviet Union does not contemplate ever attacking the United States or any other country," Stalin declared.

In the spring of 1952, in response to questions submitted from Rome by a group of American journalists, Stalin said he did not believe that a third world war was closer than it had been two or three years before.[18] Asked on what basis the coexistence of capitalism and communism was possible, he replied: "The peaceful coexistence of capitalism and communism is entirely possible given a mutual desire to cooperate, given readiness to carry out commitments assumed, given observance of the principle of equality and noninterference in the internal affairs of other states."

More specifically, the two essential conditions for peaceful coexistence were: first, that the United States abide by the Soviet interpretation of the Potsdam agreement — that is, return to four-power control over Germany; second, that the United States accept the fact of Communist control over the present area of Soviet hegemony. On this basis, the Soviet leader made plain, a stabilization of international relations would be, for the time being at least, possible and desirable.

It was also clear, however, that the Soviet Union entertained no serious hope of persuading the United States to accept either of these conditions. The most that could be expected was that America's allies might be more responsive than the United States itself, thus encouraging a centrifugal tendency within the Western alliance. Toward Britain and France the Soviet Union now spoke in a generally conciliatory voice, but Soviet relations with the United States and Soviet propaganda concerning the United States during this period reflected an increasingly undisguised hostility.

One of the persistent issues on which this hostility centered was alleged American intervention in Eastern Europe. Charges of attempted espionage and subversion in Eastern Europe were formally raised by the Soviet Union in a diplomatic note to the United States in November 1951 and in a draft resolution presented in the United Nations.[19] The specific provocation was the Kersten Amendment to the Mutual Security Act of 1951, which authorized the President to spend up to $100 million in aiding persons "residing in or escapees from" the Soviet Union, the former Baltic states, or the Communist states of Eastern Europe to form military units under NATO or otherwise contribute to the defense of the North Atlantic area or to the security of the United States. Although the United States categorically denied the Soviet allegations, a new Soviet note on January 9, 1952, repeated the charge that the Kersten Amendment stood in violation of the mutual commitment of the two countries under the Soviet-American Agreement of November 16, 1933, to refrain from interference in each other's internal affairs.[20]

A persistent target of Soviet propaganda in Western Europe during this period was the resentment keenly felt in some circles over American barriers against trade with the Soviet Union and Eastern Europe. In the spring of 1952, the Soviet Union organized an International Economic Conference in Moscow; it dramatized the theme of "peaceful coexistence through normalization of trade" and, at the same time, sought to increase Western European pressures against American trade restrictions.

Nominally, the conference was sponsored by the Peace Movement, plans for it having been announced at the Berlin meeting of the World Peace Council in February 1951. A preparatory commission, ostensibly an autonomous international body of individuals interested in trade, met in Copenhagen in February 1952 to organize the details of the conference. A strenuous effort was made to attract non-Communist businessmen, economists, and trade unionists, with a studiously nonpolitical program.

The conference opened on April 2, 1952. The president of the Soviet Chamber of Commerce, M. V. Nesterov, dangled offers of vast opportunities in Soviet markets. He called the attention of the West European countries to the fact that their trade with Eastern Europe was but one third of what it had been before the war, and that their problem of balancing their trade with the dollar area would be less acute if it were not for the Battle Act and other United States restrictions on East-West trade. In order to restore international trade, Nesterov said, it was necessary to do away with all forms of discrimination, including the American trade embargo against Communist China, which he described as a "senseless manifestation of aggressive policy." [21] Although the conference stimulated discussion of large potential trade agreements, in practice little increase in Soviet trade with the West resulted.[22] An unofficial delegation of Japanese parliamentarians on their way home stopped off in Peking where, on June 1, they signed a £60 million "trade agreement." Although the agreement was without force, it was intended to stimulate Japanese resentments against American trade restrictions by dramatizing the exchange that would otherwise be possible between Chinese raw materials and Japanese industrial goods.[23]

### Effect of the Korean Truce Negotiations

In the background of Soviet-American relations in this period where the negotiations at Kaesong, later at Panmunjom, for an armistice in Korea. Once the truce talks had begun in July 1951, and particularly after a line of demarcation had been agreed upon in November 1951, military pressure from the United Nations forces eased, and fighting was limited to minor local engagements. The Communists seemed under no pressure to reach an agreement and the negotiations dragged on for more than two years.[24]

The Soviet Union did not become involved in the negotiations directly and publicly until October 1952, when the issue was raised at the General Assembly of the United Nations. By this time, the principal remaining issue was the Communist insistence that all prisoners of war should be repatriated, as against the United Nations position that no prisoner of war should be forcibly repatriated. This issue was recognized by both sides as one of considerable political significance. The United Nations, and particularly the United States, bore uncomfortably the memory of having returned to the Soviet Union Russian escapees who had sought political asylum in the West at the end of World War II.[25] The senior delegate of the United Nations Command Delegation was not in agreement with the official UN position, fearing that it would jeopardize the return of UN prisoners held by the Communists.[26] From the Communist point of view, the prospect of a substantial number of prisoners opting against a return to China or North Korea would constitute a propaganda disadvantage.

In the course of 1952, the prisoner issue had already become deeply involved in Communist propaganda exploitation. Beginning in February, a series of riots among the prisoners of war on Koje Island in Korea had been organized by the Communists in connection with the screening of prisoners on the question of their repatriation. These were followed by world-wide Communist charges against the United States of atrocities and massacres in the prison camps. This propaganda campaign not only helped to blur the political significance of the prisoners' refusing to return to their Communist homelands, but also furthered the current anti-humanitarian image of the United States which the Soviet Union was then developing through the Peace Movement. The Soviet Union had launched in February a violent campaign against the United States for allegedly having used bacteriological warfare in Korea. This theme was carried forward on a vast scale during the following months by Soviet representatives in the United Nations, by Communist front organizations, and particularly by the World Peace Council. A resolution in the Security Council requesting an investigation of the charges by the Red Cross was vetoed by the Soviet Union.[27]

When in October the impasse on the Korean prisoner issue came before the General Assembly of the United Nations, Vyshinsky remained obdurate. In surprisingly harsh terms, he rebuffed an Indian effort to find a compromise solution. He declared that he was also reflecting the views of the Communist governments of China and North Korea, although the Indian government had been under the impression that its efforts to find a compromise had at least the implied blessing of Peking.[28] By his violent intervention, Vyshinsky provided the "harsh external pressures" which once again averted a serious division among the Western powers, for the United States delegation had indicated reservations about the Indian resolution while the British had strongly supported it. The disparity between the Chinese Communist attitude toward the Indian initiative in direct diplomatic discourse and the harsh rejection by Vyshinsky seemed to indicate the possibility that the Soviet Union was less interested in accepting a compromise on this issue than Peking was.

One factor that may have influenced the Soviet attitude was the American presidential campaign then in full swing. Vyshinsky's rejection of the Indian efforts to perform the role of "honest broker" may have been related to the Soviet judgment of the significance of the Korean issue in the American election. In the same month in which the United Nations debate opened, the Republican candidate announced that he would, if elected, visit Korea and exert his utmost efforts toward ending the war. It may have been the Russian opinion at this time that a Republican administration, being under great popular pressure to bring the war to an end, would make concessions at the conference table at Panmunjom. This possibility is suggested by the Communist press's interpretation of the election campaign.[29]

In the interim, the language used in Communist publications in referring to the United States increased in vehemence. In connection with the alleged American atrocities in Korea, words such as "cannibals," "savagery," and "the extermination of women, children, and the aged" became commonplace. An editorial directive in the *Cominform Bulletin* to the Communist Parties abroad in the spring of 1952 declared: "The peace-loving peoples have no enemy more vicious and more dangerous than sanguinary U. S. imperialism whose every step is marked by the untold sufferings of millions, ruthless enslavement of peoples and by arrogant affronts to their national dignity." [30]

The violence of the language used against the United States approached that which the Soviet Union had directed against the Nazis at the height of the war. Reacting to the mounting "hate campaign," the American ambassador to the Soviet Union, George Kennan, while on a trip outside the Soviet Union, remarked on the similarity of conditions in Moscow to those which he had experienced while interned in Berlin during the early years of the war. He was, as a consequence, declared *persona non grata* by the Soviet government on October 3, and his immediate recall was requested. Whether this action indicated the extreme sensitivity of Soviet feelings over this comparison with the Nazis, a symbolic act of defiance of the United States, or a particular desire to have a noted American specialist on the Soviet Union out of Moscow, the Soviet government in any case left no room for misapprehension regarding its low expectations of a rapprochement with the United States. To the Russians, Kennan was known as the author of the "containment policy." He was often described in the Soviet press as the architect of the cold war. In fact, Kennan's writings urged moderation and an avoidance of bellicosity on the American side, and he had made clear his desire to mitigate the cold war, but this did nothing to moderate the attacks upon him in the Soviet press.[31]

By way of contrast, doubtless not accidental, the new French ambassador to the Soviet Union, Louis Joxe, upon presenting his credentials on August 21, had been granted an extended audience with Stalin, who had received no other Western diplomat during the previous two years, and no French ambassador since 1948. This action immediately gave rise to angry suspicions in the German press and elsewhere of a possible French move toward a private understanding with the Russians on a common approach to the question of German rearmament.[32] This was perhaps the Soviet intention.

### A Soviet Switch on Germany

The main preoccupation of Soviet diplomacy in this period and the central target of its barrage of diplomatic notes was the German issue. In the spring of 1952, the Western powers were striving to reach agreement among themselves on an increased measure of sovereignty for the West German government and its inclusion in a European defense community. The Soviet purpose was to head off this development by playing upon interallied differences, both popular and governmental. The most interesting aspect of Soviet policy in regard to Germany in this period was a dramatic change in position during March 1952 which made it clear that the Soviet Union was less worried about the revival of a German military menace than about the strengthening of the Western alliance.

At the Lisbon conference of the North Atlantic Council in February 1952, and at a meeting in London immediately preceding it between the three Western foreign ministers and Chancellor Adenauer, substantial progress had been made in overcoming obstacles to the European army project. Within West Germany, one of the principal barriers had been the strong pressure from the Social Democrats and other opposition elements on the grounds that this project would make more difficult, if not impossible, the eventual reunification of Germany. Following the Lisbon conference, the Soviet leadership decided to change its position in order to make full use of these nationalist sentiments. Abandoning its previous support of a disarmed Germany, the Soviet Union now proposed, in a note of March 10, 1952, to the three Western powers, discussion of a peace treaty for Germany on the basis of a unified and independent Germany *with a national army,* on condition that Germany be neutralized and all foreign troops withdrawn.[33] This switch created obvious disadvantages elsewhere, particularly in

France, where it undercut the Communist opposition to German rearmament and subjected the French Communist Party to angry and derisive blows at the hands of its critics. The *Cominform Bulletin,* quietly reporting the Soviet note, neglected to mention the fact that it included provision for a German army.[34]

Soviet attention was, however, focused on the internal German opposition. On April 9, the Soviet Union reiterated its proposal, picking up many of the arguments that had been advanced in the meantime by West German opponents of Adenauer.[35] This diplomatic move was supported by a note from Otto Grotewohl to the West Germans demanding prompt action on the Soviet offer of a peace treaty; there were simultaneous efforts on the part of East German leaders to incite strikes and demonstrations in West Germany. These efforts succeeded in complicating and delaying the Western negotiations, but they did not quite succeed in preventing the Western plans from reaching the signature stage. Despite a breakdown in the negotiations over the Saar, and despite a third Soviet note at the very last moment on May 24, the Contractual Agreements were signed at Bonn on May 26 and the European Defense Treaty was signed at Paris on the following day.[36]

Even after the signatures, however, the Soviet note of May 24 continued to have a significant effect. As a direct consequence of the note, the French Council of Ministers on June 11 declared its interest in "a four-power discussion, limited to precise questions immediately concerning the unification of the two Germanies."[37] This response, despite American and West German disapproval, received some support in Britain, where the Labour Party, now in opposition, was taking an increasingly resistant position toward German rearmament. It was almost a month before a reply could be agreed upon among the three Western powers and West Germany and dispatched to the Soviet Union. The reply insisted that a four-power conference could be useful only if there were agreement upon a neutral investigating commission to determine that conditions existed in all of Germany suitable for the holding of free elections, as a precondition for a peace treaty.[38]

To this, the Soviet Union replied with a fourth note on August 23, denouncing the Western proposals and attacking the Western powers for having "entered into a deal with the Adenauer government" while the exchange of notes was going on. However, the Soviet note accepted the plan for a four-power conference "to convene at the earliest time and in any case in October," providing there be an enlargement of the agenda to include: a peace treaty with Germany; the formation of an all-German government; and the "conduct of free all-German elections and a commission for the verification of the existence in Germany of conditions for the conduct of such elections, its composition, functions and powers." [39] The Soviet government also served notice that it intended to raise the question of the withdrawal of occupation troops from Germany and that it desired representatives of both East and West Germany to attend the conference.

A month later, the Western reply accused the Soviet government of evading the essential question of free elections as a first step to the unification of Germany or a peace treaty with a united Germany. It expressed a willingness to meet at a four-power conference in October if the Soviet government were willing to meet on these terms.[40] To this note the Soviet government made no reply, and the seven-month barrage of diplomatic notes came to an end. The Soviet leadership may have been preoccupied with preparations for the Nineteenth Party Congress which was to meet in Moscow shortly. Or the Soviet Union may have observed that neither the French nor the German government appeared confident enough of its political strength to ask its parliament to ratify the European Defense Community treaty. Even without further Soviet intervention, it was apparent that the signing of the EDC treaty did not by any means assure its coming into force. The residual effect of this episode was still being felt ten years later, when opposition elements in West Germany were reported as nourishing the conviction that the Soviet note of March 1952 had represented a genuine opportunity to reunify the country, which was missed because West Germany had not followed a "national policy" in replying.[41] The persistence of this myth testifies to the effectiveness of the move as an appeal to nationalist sentiments in West Germany. The ambiguity of the Soviet note does not offer much support for the interpretation that the Soviet Union seriously entertained the possibility of reunification on any terms. This would have jeopardized the Soviet position in East Germany, where a forced-draft program for the "construction of socialism" was then in preparation, to be proclaimed in May and adopted in July by the Socialist Unity Party.[42]

### Influence of Domestic Factors

In retrospect, the domestic preoccupations of the Soviet regime during this period appear to have been more important than was apparent at the time. Subsequent revelations have clarified some of the domestic economic and political problems, as well as the demands for a period of consolidation within the Communist orbit, which served to reinforce the pressure of external factors toward a foreign policy of low-keyed political maneuver.

On the domestic economic side, the Soviet Union was in an interim period between the Fourth Five-Year Plan, which had concluded in 1950, and the Fifth Five-Year Plan, which was to have covered the years 1951–1955, but which significantly was not presented for public discussion until August 1952. The new plan was central to the Soviet conception of its world strategy, for the basis of future Soviet power rested on the economy — in the repair of its deficiencies, in its support for the development of new military technology, and in the continued growth of the heavy industrial base. That these matters were not beyond dispute within the Soviet hierarchy was indirectly indicated during the Nineteenth Congress, as will be shown later, and was to be even more evident after the death of Stalin. Among the economic deficiencies, the weakness of Soviet agriculture caused deep concern and some differences among Stalin's subordinates, although Stalin himself apparently remained somewhat aloof from these preoccupations.[43] During this time, Andrei Andreyev, the member of the Politburo responsible for agriculture, went into eclipse, and Khrushchev, who took over Andreyev's responsibilities, was publicly repudiated for his suggestion that the amalgamation of collective farms be augmented by the establishment of "agrogorods," or collective-farm towns in the countryside. Later, Khrushchev, in the course of striking back against Malenkov, revealed the astonishing fact that per-capita livestock and grain production in this period had still not reached prerevolutionary levels.[44]

In the political realm, weaknesses in party structure and discipline were seriously troubling the party leadership, as was made evident at the party congress in October. Perhaps of greater importance to foreign policy was the increasing dogmatic rigidity of the aging but all-powerful autocrat.[45] Other problems arose from the rivalry among Stalin's lieutenants to succeed him. In 1952, it appeared that Malenkov had secured the favored position. It was he who was selected to present the report of the Central Committee to the party congress, a task heretofore performed by Stalin. His earlier major rival, Zhdanov, had died in 1948, and Zhdanov's followers had been purged wholesale in early 1949. The temporary decline of Beria, another potential rival for the succession, illustrated the close connection between the political fortunes of the second tier of leaders and developments among the national minorities. A series of disturbances reported among national minorities in Georgia and the Ukraine reflected the complications of centrally directed political purges that were superimposed on situations of local unrest.[46] Similarly, the systematic campaign against Jews in this period involved such charges as nationalist separatism in the "Crimean affair" and embezzlement in the "Kiev affair."[47] Press campaigns calling for heightened vigilance against economic crimes, espionage, and sabotage built up to a tense pre-purge atmosphere in the latter part of 1952.

In Eastern Europe, the Soviet Union was occupied with forcing the pace of industrial development and agricultural collectivization, a task made more difficult by substantial Soviet extractions of resources. In his memorandum intended for the Central Committee of the Hungarian Communist Party, Imre Nagy later wrote: "In the years 1949 to 1952, incorrect evaluation of the international situation, overemphasis on the war danger, and the actions resulting from these assumptions played a very serious part in those grave mistakes that were made by our Party leadership with regard to the economic activities of the people." [48] The effect of the rapidly pushed "socialist construction" brought living standards and political morale in Eastern Europe to their lowest point. [49] This was a period of substantial purges in Poland, Rumania, and especially Czechoslovakia, where the trial of Rudolf Slansky and a number of others broadened the attack from potential "Titoists" to members of Beria's international police apparatus as well as right-wing deviationists; further, it projected on the international plane the anti-Semitic campaign then going on within the Soviet Union itself. [50]

In the Far East, the Soviet Union sought throughout 1952 to resolve a number of problems in its relations with Communist China. During August and September, Chinese Premier and Foreign Minister Chou En-lai was in Moscow for negotiations concerning the control of the Changchun Railway and the naval base at Port Arthur, which, according to the auxiliary agreements in the 1950 treaty, were to have passed to the Chinese upon the conclusion of a peace treaty with Japan or, in any case, not later than the end of 1952. The portions of the agreement publicized by Tass on September 16 indicated the transfer to the Chinese People's Government of all rights in the administration of the Changchun Railway, but stated that Soviet troops would continue to remain in Port Arthur for the time being, on the basis of "joint use" of the facilities. [51] The reason given for the extension of the

Soviet military presence at Port Arthur was the Chinese concern over the Japanese treaty with the United States and the danger of war in the Pacific area. It seems probable that the talks also covered Soviet recognition of Chinese relations with Outer Mongolia, since a delegation from the Mongolian People's Republic, which had been in Moscow during the talks with Chou En-lai, proceeded to Peking where, on October 4, it signed a ten-year economic and cultural agreement with the Chinese government.[52] In October 1954, it was revealed by the Soviet leaders that agreement had also been reached during the Moscow conference among the Soviet Union, Communist China, and the Mongolian People's Republic for the construction of a new strategic rail link through Mongolia to connect the rail systems of the Soviet Union and China.[53] For the Chinese Communists, this was a period in which the energies of the regime were diverted from external military adventures — the war in Korea and the claim to Formosa — to domestic needs. The political position of the regime was consolidated by purges in the party and the bureaucracy, and the foundations for the industrialization and further economic development of the country were advanced by preparations for the nation's first five-year plan, which was to be announced at the end of the year.[54]

All these considerations help to explain the Russians' apparent preoccupation with domestic matters in the period of preparation for the Nineteenth Party Congress. Even more important, however, was the crucial relation of the Fifth Five-Year Plan to the anticipated shift in the balance of military power. From our present vantage point, it is apparent from the unfolding of Soviet military accomplishments during the following years that in 1952 the Soviet leadership felt itself to be on the threshold of a period in which the intensive concentration of resources on scientific and technological research would begin to yield decisive results. After the Soviet atomic test of October 1951, Stalin observed that further tests of atomic bombs "of different calibers" would follow. By August 1953, Malenkov was able to announce that the Western monopoly on the hydrogen bomb had now been overcome, and within a few days the Russians exploded a nuclear device that involved both fission and thermonuclear reactions; two years later, the Russians staged their first air-dropped hydrogen-bomb test, some six months ahead of the United States.[55] In jet aircraft, the Soviet Union had already demonstrated, in the Korean War, its development of jet fighters which compared favorably in many respects with the best the United States had available; by the time of the Nineteenth Party Congress in 1952, the Russians were developing new jet engines for the medium and heavy jet bombers about to make their first public appearance. Meanwhile, techniques of long-range flight refueling were being tested and Arctic bases for aircraft and rockets were being established.[56] Soviet engineers by this time had already tested long-range rockets from submarines in the Baltic, had in large-scale production an improved model of the German V-2 rocket, and would within three years be ready to test-fire their first intermediate-range ballistic missile with a range of 1,500 to 2,000 miles.[57] The first operational test of an intercontinental ballistic missile was only five years away.

In short, it is apparent to the rest of the world now, as it must have been to the Soviet leadership then, that the foundation of the Soviet nuclear, jet, missile, and space advances upon the West in the late fifties and early sixties was being laid in the Fifth Five-Year Plan and earlier. This anticipation of imminent strategic gains helped to focus attention upon economic planning as the key to future power, and served to reinforce both external and internal pressures upon Soviet foreign policy to evolve in the direction of greater flexibility. One mark of this evolution was the growing reliance of Soviet diplomacy on those instruments which could overleap geographical boundaries and manipulate domestic political forces within other societies.

# THE USE OF THE PEACE MOVEMENT
# AND THE FRENCH COMMUNIST
# PARTY, 1951–1952

An account of Soviet foreign policy during 1951 and 1952 would be particularly deficient if it were limited to the plane of conventional diplomatic behavior. While Soviet policy was evolving out of a phase of militant frontal assault and into a phase of political maneuver, the extradiplomatic instrumentalities of Soviet policy played an interesting role and an important one. Apart from its intermittent attention to the German issue, Soviet diplomacy remained relatively quiet in the 1951–1952 period, either because of domestic preoccupations or in a conscious effort to moderate its earlier stimulus to Western mobilization. Meanwhile, however, the Peace Movement and the foreign Communist parties assumed increased significance as instruments capable of reaching into Western societies, playing upon inner vulnerabilities, and thereby seeking to influence the balance of international politics.

The experience of the French Communist Party in this period is particularly illuminating as a clue to the reasoning which lay behind some of the crucial declarations at the Nineteenth Congress of the Soviet party. For example, the familiar "banner of nationalism" argument which was to be enunciated by Stalin at the Moscow congress in October 1952 made its appearance a full year earlier in France, in the experimental strivings of the French party to find, amid conflicting tendencies, the most effective way to support Soviet objectives. Similarly, it is no exaggeration to say that only by taking account of the experiences of the French Communists in getting Jacques Duclos out of jail in June 1952 do the words of Stalin at the Nineteenth Congress, urging Communists abroad to "raise the banner of bourgeois democratic freedoms," take on their full significance. Functionally, the French Communist Party and the Peace Movement were closely intertwined in this period — the latter provided the access to the mass support which the party required but could not itself attract.

### The Broadening of the Peace Movement

For a time in early 1951, the Soviet Union had appeared to contemplate the development of the Peace Movement into an organizational rival of the United Nations. Following the line of Stalin's interview on February 16, 1951, in which he had spoken of the "paramount importance" of the Peace Movement and denounced the United Nations for having become an instrument of the United States in Korea, the World Peace Council at its first meeting in East Berlin a week later condemned the United Nations for its resolution against the Communist Chinese intervention in Korea and demanded that the United Nations return to its proper functions. *Pravda,* on February 24 and again on March 3, further developed this line, insisting that the United Nations choose between accepting the demands of the World Peace Council and sharing the fate of the League of Nations.

Following the defeat of the Chinese troops in Korea during May and the beginning of a softer inflection in Soviet policy, the Cominform sought to adapt the program of the Peace Movement to the changed international situation. An editorial in the *Cominform Bulletin* on July 13 entitled, "Broaden Struggle for Pact of Peace!" described the Malik initiative toward a truce in Korea as "further eloquent testimony of the wise peace policy of the Soviet Union," and insisted that it had been the increasing pressure of world opinion as expressed through the Peace Movement that had forced the United States to agree to the cease-fire. The editorial quoted with fulsome approval a declaration by Jacques Duclos which sought to turn the Malik concession into a propaganda advantage: "If the guns in Korea are silenced, we shall be indebted for this to the Soviet Union. The Soviet proposal corresponds to the will of the peoples, and the U. S. was forced to accept it. This is a blow to the war incendiaries. This is a victory for the peace forces."

The Cominform called attention to the deteriorating international situation and urged the Peace Movement to intensify its efforts in behalf of the campaign for a five-power peace pact as the best means of checking the increase of Western power. Its description of the current international situation constituted a clear directive to exploit nationalist resentments against American policy:

The U. S. imperialists are constantly building new war bases directed against the U.S.S.R. and the People's Democracies. Over 30,000 American soldiers and officers are acting the master in the British Isles; 59 Departments in France are actually occupied by U. S. troops; in Italy, the ports of Augusta, Livorno and Naples are being turned into U. S. military bases; Adenauer, henchman of the U. S. imperialists in West Germany, simultaneously intensifying the repressions against peace champions, has openly declared for the formation of a 350,000-strong army; the American invaders are rapidly arming Japan, seeking to convert it into a base for aggression in the Far East.

A week later, the Peace Movement picked up the cue. The Bureau of the World Peace Council, meeting in Helsinki on July 20–22, 1951, found that, despite the beginning of negotiations in Korea, "the international situation has worsened considerably during recent months." It cited the intensified armament drive, the breaking-off of the deputy foreign ministers' conference, the advancing plans for the Japanese peace treaty, the remilitarization of Germany and Japan, the increasing number of United States bases abroad, the production of more weapons of mass annihilation, and the development of new conflicts in the Near East. The only solution was a peace pact among the five great powers: "Since the United

Nations Organization has failed to achieve its basic task — the preservation of peace — negotiations between the Five Great Powers are at present the sole means of resolving international differences." [1]

In August, the Peace Movement joined in the "atrocity" campaign against the United States. It gave widespread circulation to a report presented at a Sofia meeting of the executive committee of the Women's International Federation, charging the United States with a campaign of extermination against the Korean people and with various atrocities, including the use of banned weapons and the wanton destruction of towns and food supplies.[2] This campaign was the forerunner of the germ-warfare campaign, which the Peace Movement was to bring to its peak in the spring of 1952.

The second session of the World Peace Council, held in Vienna on November 1–7, was closely related in both program and timing to the General Assembly of the United Nations, which began its sessions in Paris on November 8. Perhaps to counter the propaganda effect of the new proposals of the Western powers on disarmament, the Peace Movement set forth a position on disarmament which Vyshinsky picked up and used in the course of the United Nations debates. The council's disarmament proposals were less complex than the Western plan and easier for the world to understand. They called upon the five great powers to conclude a disarmament convention, providing for the absolute prohibition of atomic weapons and all weapons of mass destruction, strict control over declared and suspected weapons and factories, gradual and controlled reduction of every kind of armament, arms reduction amounting by the end of 1952 to between one third and one half of the total arms declared, checked, and discovered, a general census of arms, and an international inspection and control system.[3]

Another significant feature of the Vienna meeting was the growing awareness it disclosed of the need for a broader line, somewhat more detached from the Soviet position in the cold war. The vice-president of the council, Pietro Nenni, gave emphasis in his main report to the growing opportunities for collaboration with neutralist countries in the Middle East and Southeast Asia, particularly India, and with Social Democrats and liberals in Western Europe. He urged the Peace Movement to return to a less political program, in order to draw these new forces into a common front.[4] This concept was to dominate the subsequent thinking of the organization. Laurent Casanova, the *responsable* in the French Communist Party for the Peace Movement, wrote that the hope of the Peace Movement rested upon attracting new elements, especially religious and pacifist circles and the socialist rank and file, away from the socialist leadership.[5]

## The Communist Appeal to Nationalism

This tendency in the Peace Movement corresponded with a significant expansion of the French Communist line on two key ideological issues: nationalism and class relations. The evolution of the French party's position on these points was by no means a smooth and uneventful one. Sharp fluctuations testified to intense clashes within the party, involving both organizational and policy questions. In following the party disputes of this period, it is misleading to chart the conflicting positions on a simple right-left scale, for the alignments often involved the intersection of at least three planes of differences. One of these planes concerned the tension between those who advocated offensive political action against the bourgeoisie, as against those who sought to enlarge the influence of the Party by collaborative action with segments of the bourgeoisie. A second source of conflict arose between those who were primarily concerned about the interests of the French Communist Party, as against those who were willing to subordinate these interests in favor of support for the requirements of Soviet policy. These two sets of considerations were further complicated by a third, which involved complex organizational ties to different groups of the Soviet leadership. There is more than parochial interest, therefore, in following the vicissitudes of the Communist line in France during the months leading up to the Nineteenth Congress, for they offer

an extraordinary glimpse into the processes of policy formation of
an important segment of the international Communist movement.
Moreover, the doctrinal pronouncements of the Nineteenth Congress on nationalism and relations with the bourgeoisie become
more than pale abstractions when they are read in the light of
these experiences.

By the spring of 1951, the ascendant tendency in the French
party toward a broad line of collaboration was being voiced by
Jacques Duclos. In an address on May 17, he stripped the party
program of all doctrinaire economic and ideological elements,
stressing the peace issue as one on which the party should seek
the collaboration of non-Communists in bringing about a change
of government. The issue facing France, he said, was very simple:
"Democracy or Fascism? War or Peace?" "We have no intention,"
he declared, "of ignoring any action that will help to rid France of
the fascist shame and the horrors of war." [6]

Duclos thus sought to reassure the non-Communist intellectuals
of the left, who had been repeatedly rebuffed by the Party in their
advocacy of a restored popular front. His brandishing of the fascist
menace recalled the collaboration of 1936 with the non-Communist
left, without necessarily accepting the exact formula of the popular
front. To the party, Duclos stressed the necessity of "uniting all
French men and women of good will, who may not approve of all
the points contained in the program of the Communist Party, but
who want neither fascism nor war." To this end, he declared that
the party was prepared to participate in, or support, any government
for France that would accept the following principles:

1. Signing of a pact between the five great powers, open to all
countries.
2. Annulment of agreements which trample on national independence
and removal of the American occupationists from French territory.
3. Signing a peace treaty with a demilitarized, united, democratic, and
peace-loving Germany.
4. Peace with Vietnam, the withdrawal of the expeditionary corps
from Vietnam, and the return of French troops from Korea.

5. Adoption of a law banning war propaganda.

6. Prohibition of the atom bomb and all other weapons of mass annihilation.

7. Gradual and controlled reduction of armed forces and armaments.

8. Utilization of the means derived from reducing the armed forces and armaments for economic development of the country, for satisfying the social needs of the people, for improving the living conditions of working people in town and countryside.

9. Defense of democratic liberties against any encroachments on the part of the rebels.

Noticeably missing from the party's electoral program was any reference to the "social transformation of the country." Even the "struggle between capital and labor," recently a point of emphasis, was softened to a demand for improved standards of living for the workers.[7]

In Italy, Togliatti had sounded a similar note in his closing address to the Seventh Congress of the Italian party in April. "Let us do everything possible and take such peaceful measures as will wrest Italy from the front of those who are deliberately preparing another war . . . My view is that, in order to do this, the advent of Communists to power is not even necessary; all that is needed for a policy of peace is to be democratic and healthy-minded. The Communists will not create any difficulties, they will never place any obstacles in the way of a Government that would pursue such a policy." [8]

The Cominform gave its sanction to the formula of an anti-fascist coalition with non-Communist forces of the left and argued that this was what the international situation now required:

Activizing the potential anti-fascist forces, ceaselessly linking the anti-fascist struggle with the struggle of the peoples for peace, proceeding always from the concrete conditions, from the correlation of forces now taking shape, the Communist Parties raise high the banner of anti-fascist struggle. The Communists know that success in this struggle gives a sound basis for developing a broad patriotic popular movement for peace, against the main enemy of peace and democracy — American imperialism.[9]

However, developments on the French political scene soon forced the French Communists to look further to the right for allies than their antifascist slogan had intended. A national election held on June 17 brought important changes in the political complexion of the French parliament. The Gaullists drew 4 million votes from the older parties in the middle of the political spectrum. The Communists lost 400,000 votes, dropping from 28.6 percent in the 1946 election to 26.5 percent. With a total of more than 5 million votes, the Communists still remained the largest party in France, but, because of the new electoral law, their representation dropped from 186 seats (including Communist supporters) to 106. The two extreme parties, the Gaullists and the Communists, accounted for 48 percent of the votes. Only after a ministerial crisis lasting more than a month was it possible to find a viable combination among the remaining center parties.[10]

The effect of the election was to exert a further rightward pull on the Communist program. The gains of the Gaullists, who also opposed the government over the rearming of West Germany, encouraged the Communists to look to them as potential allies under the rubric of nationalism. The Communists muted somewhat, but did not drop altogether, their slogan of antifascism, which had been aimed mainly at the Gaullists, while intensifying their appeal to French patriots on the issue of "national independence." At the same time, they took full advantage of a renewed debate on the church-school issue to seek a common front against the MRP (the Christian-left Mouvement Républicain Populaire), the main support in France of the Western alliance. In August, the Cominform redefined the current objective of the Communist parties in the West as "organizing a broad, national people's front to combat the war danger." [11] The emphasis upon a *national* rather than an *antifascist* keynote meant discarding whatever social content the former alliance may have intended.

A still more explicit development of the broadening tendency emerged from an important session of the Central Committee of

the French party, held on September 7–8 at Ivry-sur-Seine. Foreign
and domestic considerations, as well as the party's internal situation,
combined to encourage a broadening of the line. The Western
alliance at this time seemed to be moving forward steadily. In
France, the new cantonal elections favored a broad electoral appeal
by the party. Within the party, because Thorez had been in Moscow for almost a year, Duclos, the advocate of the broad line, had
retained his dominant position. What had been a steady drift since
the previous fall now became a bold step in the direction of collaboration with other forces in France, forces outside the working
class.

The keynote of Duclos' main report to the Central Committee
was sweeping: "We are ready to struggle together with all those,
regardless of social condition, opinion, or belief, who wish to re-
establish the independence of France . . . to denounce the treaties
which bind it to the chariot of the American imperialists . . ."[12]
To make certain there was no misunderstanding of his meaning,
Duclos added that "employers and workers can perfectly well find
themselves in the same camp for the reconquest of French independence." Just as at the time of liberation, he argued, the French Communist Party defends not just the interests of the working class but
the interests of the whole of France.[13]

Nor should party workers disdain collaboration with any people
who have a common interest in defending France against American
imperialism, even though they disagree with the party on other
matters. "Those Communists who do not take account of such
a situation, and who, by their narrowness and their sectarianism,
rebuff the first steps of those worried people seeking to know, and
let those people think that we consider as irreducible enemies those
who are not in accord with us on all points, give proof of a lack
of political understanding very injurious to the cause that we defend." Communists must work actively in the mass organizations,
he said, including peasant organizations, youth groups, and, above
all, the Peace Movement.

As an earnest of the party's defense of the French national interest, Duclos argued in behalf of the French army and protested against the loss of sovereignty implied in its subordination to a European army. He sympathized with the sense of humiliation that French officers would feel in finding themselves serving under foreign commanders.

Duclos endeavored to show that there was no inconsistency between the party's position as a defender of French national interests and its loyalty to the Soviet Union. "We are, as Frenchmen, firmly attached to the Soviet Union, without which country we would not have been liberated from the Nazi occupation, and we consider that the revival [*remise en vigueur*] of the treaty of alliance between France and the USSR constitutes an imperative in a truly French policy." Attachment to the Soviet Union is, moreover, consistent with the aim of peace. "Soviet initiatives in favor of peace, inspired by the fundamental idea of the coexistence of the two social systems facing each other, and in particular the resounding propositions of Shvernik, contribute powerfully to dissipate the lies of the warmongers."

Another speaker at the September Central Committee meeting made it clear that the party was prepared to subordinate its long-term objectives to the pressing immediate situation: "It is not today a question of socialism. Certainly, and we affirm it aloud, its establishment in France is our purpose . . . but the idea of the necessity of socialism is still subordinate to the ideas we are stressing. And it is for all Frenchmen that we must open up an immediate perspective." [14]

In the *mot d'ordre* of this September 1951 meeting there may be seen a clear foreshadowing of one of the essential points made by Stalin at the Nineteenth Congress a year later: "The sacred task of our French Communist Party is to hold more firmly than ever in our robust hands the banner of the struggle for the independence and the national sovereignty of our country."

Immediately after the Central Committee meeting, the leaders of the Communist trade-union federation translated into action the slogan of "working-class unity" by sending a letter to the leaders of the socialist and the Christian union federations, proposing a meeting to plan joint action against the government's decision on minimum wages.[15] The fact that the letter was sent to the leaders of the other union federations in itself signified that the line had now developed from a united front from below to a united front from above. No reference was made in the letter to political matters, other than to waive them: "Notwithstanding our divergencies on certain problems . . ."

In the National Assembly, some collaboration did result on the wage issue. The combined opposition of the Communists and the Gaullists, reinforced by a government party, the MRP, was sufficient to defeat a socialist bill to tie wage rates to a cost-of-living scale. On political issues, however, the party remained isolated. In particular, it was unable to prevent the ratification of the Schuman Plan in December.

Despite the breadth of its current line, the political isolation of the Communists was starkly illustrated in the cantonal elections. In the first round, held on October 7, the Communists, with 23.8 percent of the votes, led the other parties.[16] The Communists then offered to withdraw their candidates wherever the candidate who polled the most votes would accept publicly a program of eight points, of which the principal one was an endorsement of the five-power peace pact.[17] The Central Committee of the party pleaded for broad alliances in the second round of the cantonal elections on the slogans of "national independence, secular education, social progress, freedom, and peace." The reference to secular education was intended to take advantage of the strong feelings among the non-clerical parties toward the Loi Barrangé regarding church schools, passed by the Assembly in September. However, the other parties, even in some cases including the Gaullists, combined with crushing weight against the Communists, who emerged with 6 percent of the seats. The Communists denounced the election as a bitter illustration of the workings of "bourgeois democracy" and of the perfidy of the socialist leaders, but they pledged a continuation of their efforts for a single front of the working class on wage issues and for a larger union of Frenchmen in behalf of national independence and peace.[18]

The most significant doctrinal justification for the policy of closer cooperation with the middle class can be found in an article published by Duclos in November 1951 in the Cominform newspaper.[19] By virtue of its dissemination in this official journal, it was evident that Duclos was reflecting the views of at least one segment of the Soviet leadership. (In April 1945, Duclos had served as the chosen instrument of Moscow in administering a change of line for the Communist Party of the United States.) The article was a superb illustration of the infinite flexibility of dialectical argument. One of its major tasks was to reconcile the new prevailing slogan of national independence with the long-standing Communist principle of proletarian internationalism.

Duclos began by equating American policy in support of NATO, military alliances, and such supranational developments as the European Community with cosmopolitanism and the destruction of national sentiment in order to "facilitate [its] domination over the enslaved nations." The Soviet Union, on the other hand, was opposed to this and supported national independence and the right of peoples to self-determination. The ruling circles of the Western countries supported American policies, but were increasingly losing the support of their people. The "middle strata," Duclos continued, were beginning to see that the Soviet Union, instead of advocating war and revolution, stood for the five-power peace pact, whereas the ruling groups in Western Europe

are cynically betraying the interests of the national economy (industry, trade, agriculture), shamelessly agreeing to the liquidation of the national character of the army — and all on orders from their American masters.

Meanwhile, all honest people are beginning to see that the Communists, being internationalists, are fighting for the restoration of national independence and, on all issues, at the head of all patriots, are defending the interests of their country, which naturally does not exclude, on the basis of equality, cooperation with all other nations and a policy of international solidarity.

Duclos went on to reassure the middle strata that the advent to power of the working class would not mean the extinction of "all national values and traditions." On the contrary, he said, the examples of the Soviet Union and the Popular Democracies of Eastern Europe showed that "the victory of the working class leads to national regeneration of the homeland and enables every country to make the maximum contribution to the common treasury of civilization." Quoting Marx, Lenin, Stalin, and Thorez on the significance of an alliance between the working class and the "middle strata in town and countryside," Duclos argued that "the present conditions of our struggle" made such an alliance urgently necessary.

From the context of his article, it may be inferred that in referring to "the present conditions of our struggle," Duclos was urging the party to overcome its isolation, in view of the weakness and non-revolutionary temper of the proletariat, by forming an alliance with elements of the bourgeoisie — and in doing so, to acquire additional leverage for the task of moving France away from its present membership in the Western defense system.

Thus, when the Pleven government fell on January 7, 1952, Soviet observers were quick to see this event as evidence of internal contradictions in the Western alliance and of a class-wide nationalist revolt against "American imperialism." The *Izvestiya* correspondent cabled from Paris: "Having compelled Pleven's government to resign, the French people thereby voiced their protest against the country's continued subordination to American imperialism, against the notorious Pleven and Schuman Plans which put the French economy at the mercy of the American and Ruhr magnates who are depriving France of the means for defending its national security at the very time German revanchism is rearing its head in West Germany." [20]

Pleven was succeeded by Edgar Faure, who managed to steer through the National Assembly a much-compromised and much-qualified approval of the draft European army project by a slim majority on the day before the opening of the Lisbon conference of the North Atlantic Council. (In the course of the debate, the Communists on occasion found themselves allied with the Gaullists on proposed reservations to the treaty.) Qualified and compromised though it was, Faure's mandate was sufficient for him to initial the draft at the Lisbon meeting. It was not, however, sturdy enough to face the financial burden of rearmament which the Lisbon goals assigned to France, and on February 29 the Faure cabinet was retired.

The government of Antoine Pinay, a Conservative, who succeeded Faure on March 8, marked an important turning-point in the French political situation. Considerably to the right of previous governments, the Pinay majority covered that part of the spectrum from the middle segment of the MRP to the center group of the Gaullists and depended upon internal divisions in both groups to maintain itself in office. Pinay's conservatism consisted in economic retrenchment and an ambiguous European orientation, which was sufficiently broad and sufficiently vague to keep France moving toward the signature in May of the Contractual Agreements with Germany and the European Defense Treaty without totally committing itself.

Thus it appeared for a time that, despite the rightward movement of the French Communist Party, the governing coalition of France had moved even further and faster. The party's failure by proferring itself to any form of political alliance to check the equivocal drift of France toward support for a European army finally led the party to experiment with an alternative course.

### New Turn to the Left in France

In the spring of 1952 there occurred a curious episode in the history of the French Communist Party, a sharp reversal of course which, as it turned out, was to have disastrous consequences for the party and significance for the entire Communist movement. The evidence suggests that a struggle of factions or tendencies within the party was involved in the shift, although the issue around which the fight raged was the obvious failure of the party to weaken France's adherence to the Western alliance or French support for the rearmament of Germany.

For some months, the party had shown signs of a heightening internal struggle. On February 12, the party had called for a strike in Paris, nominally to celebrate the defeat of the attempted fascist coup in 1934, actually to reactivate the issue of an anti-fascist coalition. The strike was a dismal failure, and the party's post-mortems revealed deep dissensions over the recent trends in policy.

One of the party's secretaries, Étienne Fajon, gave a defensive morning-after explanation which highlighted the party's inability to use its strength among the workers for political goals: "It is more complicated to realize unanimity in a political strike than in a strike on a simple wage issue. The former requires a more highly developed consciousness. That is why it would be false to consider it as a defeat because it did not involve the majority of the workers."[21] At a Central Committee meeting which followed immediately afterward, on February 13–14 at Aubervilliers, another party secretary, Auguste Lecoeur, fought back against militants who had been resisting the recent broadening of the party's line. His position strengthened by a recent visit in Moscow with Maurice Thorez, who sent greetings and presumably instructions through him,[22] Lecoeur defended the necessity of working through the Peace Movement and with elements of the bourgeoisie: "We have devoted comrades, faithful, among the best trainers of men, who hesitated on the signature campaign . . . these comrades think that this is time lost that would be better spent in other forms of struggle against capitalist exploitation and for socialism." [23]

To these comrades, Lecoeur recalled the words of Thorez at the Twelfth Congress of the French party: "In fighting for peace, we are fighting for socialism, for communism." He went on to acknowledge that the broad line sometimes produced ideological confusions:

Taking a position against the Schuman Plan or in favor of commercial relations with the countries of the East and China is not the affair only of the working class and its Communist Party. It is the affair of the most diverse strata, the affair of peasants, shopkeepers, industrialists, and owners of all sorts. The French Communist Party works with them. This leads to some confusion. Some cells have a sacred union with the owners who take a favorable position on these issues, as in the Rhone, the North, the Bouches-du-Rhone, etc. How should we think about these accords? It should be considered a favorable condition. We must be extremely attentive to the development of contradictions among the French capitalists. As we improve our work with the masses, it will increase this disintegration in the camp of the adversary.[24]

A rumble of disagreement with the ascendant broad line was expressed at the time by François Billoux, a leading spokesman of the militant tendency. While not taking issue with the slogan of "unity of action," Billoux pointed out somewhat tartly that nothing in the slogan made it wrong to attack the right-wing socialist leaders.[25] Some people, Billoux implied, were blurring the distinction between a united front from below and that from above.

In March 1952 the party suffered a severe blow. After riding heavily on the slogan of opposition to German rearmament, and attempting to make common cause with French national sentiment on this popular issue, the party was suddenly confronted, on March 10, with the Soviet note to the Western powers proposing a unified, neutralized, *and armed* Germany. To make matters worse, it became evident that the Soviet Union was already building up an East German army. The discomfiture of the French Communists was painfully evident in *L'Humanité*, in which Pierre Courtade elaborately explained how vast was the difference between arming a West Germany that is burning for revenge and arming the whole of a Germany that would be peaceful and democratic. Moreover, said Courtade, the signing of such an agreement would doubtless improve the chances for an international agreement on disarmament.[26] The explanation did not protect Courtade from a twitting at the hands of the socialist newspaper for a "tete-à-queue," and for having been a victim of a Soviet reversal carried out with characteristic disregard for the Communist parties abroad.[27]

More serious for the party were the effects of this reversal upon some of the leaders of the Peace Movement, who were deeply committed, politically and emotionally, to the campaign against German rearmament. When the Peace Movement showed some degree of independence on this issue, as well as a greater sympathy for the neutralists than the party was then ready to accept, its journal, *Action*, was closed down by the Communists as a punishment.[28] Yves Farge, the semi-independent leader of the Peace Movement, in some disfavor with the party, left France for a long visit to China and Korea. (After investigating evidence of the alleged American germ warfare in Korea and reporting on this at the Berlin session of the World Peace Council in July, Farge was killed in an automobile accident in the Soviet Union in 1953.) Despite the Soviet note of March 10 and the pressure of the French Communist Party, the French National Council of the Peace Movement continued to describe its objective as a "demilitarized" Germany, although its principal efforts were deflected to other issues, such as the Big Five peace pact, germ warfare, and East-West trade.

In April and May of 1952, a bizarre sequence of events transformed the life of the French Communist Party. Normally, the party was accustomed to fairly slack lines of control from Moscow, mainly based on an anticipatory reading of the Soviet press, with intermittent leads through Cominform channels. In April, however, explicit instructions arrived from Moscow which required an abrupt change in line. The instructions came in the person of Billoux, the member of the politburo who had just visited Thorez in Moscow; he was therefore understood to have behind him the authority of Thorez and of a significant segment of the Soviet leadership, for the new line was accepted by the top levels of the French party without argument. The personal notebook of Duclos, which subsequently became publicly accessible through circumstances which will be explained in a moment, records a series of three meetings of the politburo, on April 11, April 17, and May 16, and a number of meetings of the party secretariat, at which Billoux' reversal of the current line was received by the leadership of the French party with disciplined obedience.[29] The famous "Billoux theses" were then published in the Communist press in early May,[30] in a form which corresponds closely to the references recorded in Duclos' notebook. Despite the desire of the party leadership to avoid any public appearance of a turnabout, the Billoux theses were instantly recognized in France as a significant shift in the party's policy.[31]

The Billoux article ordered an abrupt hardening of the party's line. The goal of ending France's support of the Western alliance remained the same, but, so Billoux argued, the Duclos policy of trying to achieve this by class collaboration had failed.[32] What was now called for was a renewal of the class struggle in France, an intensification of the anticolonial theme, and "concrete actions" to weaken the French army by encouraging refusals to manufacture or transport war matériel and insubordination or mutiny among the French soldiers in Indochina, Tunisia, and Korea. Billoux also ordered the Peace Movement, as well as labor and women's and youth organizations under Communist control, to be directed to organize active demonstrations along these lines, as well as against the "American occupation."

Significantly, Billoux began his article by referring to "the lamented Comrade Zhdanov" and his two-camp analysis, for the spirit of his approach recalled the militancy of Zhdanov in 1947 and reviewed the hard line taken by Suslov at the 1949 meeting of the Cominform. From here, Billoux took up Duclos' recent efforts to "enlarge" the party's approach in the November 1951 Cominform article, and rebutted each argument in turn. Where Duclos had talked of making common cause with the middle classes, and even with elements of the upper bourgeoisie, in defense of French national independence, Billoux took a position of uncompromising hostility. The French bourgeoisie, he argued, was not the victim of American imperialism but its willing servant. "The reconquest of national independence is only possible by the defeat of the French bourgeoisie which, being a class whose interests are contrary to those of the nation, organizes and directs national treason."

Whereas Duclos had talked, in his closing speech at the September 1951 meeting of the Central Committee, of the possibility of employers' and workers' finding themselves in the same camp in the fight for French independence, Billoux replied sharply that "the defense of French industry cannot be undertaken in a 'national union' of workers, middle classes, and industrialists, the latter taken as a group. This would only be a union of traitors . . ." Where Duclos had appealed to the national pride of the army in the struggle against being subordinated to a European army, Billoux argued that the army was nothing but an instrument of the French bourgeoisie and that the party must work for its defeat in Korea, Indochina, and North Africa. Where Duclos had seen possibilities of collaboration in parliament with the Gaullists against the European army project and the rearmament of West Germany, Billoux replied scornfully that each French government had been further to the right than the previous one, each more repressive than its predecessor, and that "the fascist RPF [Rassemblement du Peuple Français, the Gaullist party] is in collusion with the police, the government, and the men of the various sections of the bourgeoisie."

Billoux was also critical of the September 10, 1951, letter to the leaders of the non-Communist union federations for common action; only "unity of action from below," he insisted, could be effective. The party should stress, rather than conceal, its ideological differences with the socialists and others. Defending the political strike of February 12, he drew from it several significant lessons: political strikes should always be related to some economic objective; "the spontaneity of the masses" had to be carefully planned and organized; diverse forms of action were required to take account of the different levels of readiness of the workers.

In the Billoux article, and in the Politburo discussions reported in the Duclos notebooks, some interesting inflections in the party's attitude toward the Peace Movement are indicated. The party leaders are chided for having fallen into a dilemma: in allowing the Peace Movement a measure of independence in order to attract non-Communists, they had suffered it to become something of a political compromise. The Duclos notes revealed that this included more than the matter of the Peace Movement's reluctance to follow the line of the Soviet note on the German rearmament issue.[33] Pierre Cot and a number of Communist doctors had apparently been indicating some skepticism in regard to the germ-warfare campaign. In another place, Duclos makes a note to send Casanova, the party's overseer of intellectuals and the Peace Movement, to take firmly in hand the Abbé Boulier for his reaction to recent insults in the Communist press against the "worker-priest" movement. While credit is given the Peace Movement for its successful use of such devices as the Stockholm signature campaign, the party leaders are mentioned as indicating determination to tighten their control over the movement.

In the period immediately following Billoux' return, the party, the Peace Movement, the Communist trade-union federation, the Communist youth groups, and the women's organizations were whipped into militant action. Incidents involving American soldiers were seized upon and magnified, film showings by the United States Information Service in France were violently interrupted,

American leaflets were burned, ships on which American ammunition was shipped were seized, trains were stopped, ammunition was dumped, work stoppages were organized at munition factories, demonstrations were mounted against conscription. But the climax of the drive came quickly and, as it turned out, disastrously in what came to be called the "Ridgway riot." Early in May, it had been announced that General Matthew Ridgway would arrive in France toward the end of the month to replace Eisenhower as Supreme Commander of SHAPE. Immediately, both the Communist Party and the Peace Movement announced plans for a massive protest demonstration.[34] The call for a demonstration was almost an automatic response to an occasion which could hardly be ignored by the party, and it provided an immediate application of Billoux' call to militant action. Ridgway's arrival fell on May 28, one day after the signing of the EDC treaty in Paris, two days after the signing of the Contractual Agreements in Bonn. He was not only a symbol of the American military presence in Europe, but had also been developed in Communist propaganda as a symbol of the Korean conflict and had been the principal target of the Communist germ-warfare campaign. From the end of March, at the meeting of the executive committee of the World Peace Council at Oslo, the germ-warfare issue, which had been mentioned occasionally with other atrocity charges during the previous year, was blown up into a major campaign.

However, the Ridgway riot turned into a catastrophe for the party. On May 27, General Ridgway was conducted through the heart of Paris and to a public ceremony in his honor at the Arc de Triomphe, without impediment. On the next day, although the expected mass uprising did not materialize, there were street fights. Party militants clashed with the police. Two persons lost their lives, and many were wounded. The police were fully prepared and acted with firmness. A ban on the demonstration had been proclaimed in advance, and André Stil, editor of *L'Humanité,* had been arrested two days before as a consequence of his inflammatory appeals. On the evening of the demonstration, Jacques Duclos, ignoring the party's planned security arrangements,[35] appeared at the site of the riot and was arrested, under humiliating circumstances. In his possession were found a radio transmitter, a revolver, carrier pigeons, and a 135-page notebook in which he had kept a record of the proceedings of the politburo and the secretariat of the party for the period of April and May 1952.[36] (It was later judicially ruled that the birds found in Duclos' possession were of a type fit only for eating, rather than for carrying messages.)

Two consequences of the Ridgway demonstration made it a disaster from the Communist point of view. Once again it had been made painfully clear that the Communist Party, the CGT, and the Peace Movement could summon up their cadres, but all three together were not capable of evoking a mass response. In addition, the event led to swift action by the police which caught the party by surprise and left it for a time disorganized and demoralized.[37]

Four tons of documents were seized by the police in raids on the party headquarters in Paris, Toulon, and elsewhere. For a time, none of the higher leaders of the party dared sleep in his own bed. Duclos, Stil, Lucien Molino, and André Tollet were in jail; Benoît Franchon, the party's *responsable* for the CGT, was in hiding; and, according to Marty, Lecoeur took over the presidency of the polit-buro. Marty himself became secretary general of the party in the interim, despite the fact that serious charges had been introduced against him in the politburo only a few days earlier.[38]

The weakness of the party was further revealed by its effort to fight back against the arrest of Duclos, who was being held on a charge of plotting against the internal security of the state. A strike called by the CGT to begin on June 4 and to be followed forty-eight hours later by a strike in the provinces as a massive protest against the detention of Duclos turned out to be a dismal fiasco.[39] Despite appeals by the politburo for a world-wide movement of protest, an intensive development of the issue in the *Cominform Bulletin,* and protest meetings held in the Popular Democracies, Duclos remained in jail until July 2, when a grand jury ruled that he had not been caught *in flagrante delicto* and was therefore protected by his parliamentary immunity. The Soviet press, which had not echoed the hard line advocated by Billoux, did react strongly to the police action following the Ridgway riot and the arrest of Duclos. It saw in these events evidence of the effort of the United States "to set up fascist regimes in its satellites as it has done at home, to prepare the 'home front' for war." [40]

In quick succession, the government carried out further arrests of leaders of the Party, the CGT and Communist youth organizations and conducted raids on Party headquarters, front organizations, and the bank which handled the Party's funds (the Banque Commerciale pour l'Europe du Nord). Four months later, in October, Minister of Defense Pleven asked the National Assembly for a waiver of the parliamentary immunity of five Communist deputies — Jacques Duclos, François Billoux, Étienne Fajon, Raymond Guyot, and André Marty — in order to prosecute them for demoralization of the army and the nation and for plotting against the territorial integrity of France.[41] Accompanying his request was an extensive brief, documenting the party's activities against the army from the Duclos notebook and materials gathered in recent raids.[42] The request, which led to prolonged and in the end fruitless debates on the touchy issue of parliamentary immunity, served to publicize the government's evidence on what came to be called "the Communist conspiracy," but it was not acted upon by the Assembly.

## The Reascendancy of the Broad-Front Policy

The efforts of the French Communist Party to recover from this brief and damaging excursion to the left gave an impetus to another emergence of the broad-front policy in the international Communist movement. The first step for the French Communists was to deny that any change in the line had taken place. On June 6, Auguste Lecoeur, then in temporary command of the politburo, referred indignantly to "assertions in the bourgeois press" that there had been a "turning point" in the party's policy, as evidenced by the Ridgway riot, the article by Billoux and another by Jeannette Vermeersch calling for a "hardening," and appeals to direct action.[43] It was not the party that had changed, Lecoeur argued, but the policy of the Pinay government that had grown more aggressive; the party was simply responding to a changed situation. Its line was still as defined by Thorez at the Twelfth Party Congress in April 1950. All the Vermeersch and Billoux articles in the May issue of *Cahiers du communisme* had intended to do, he said, was to call attention to the changed external situation.

As *L'Observateur* quickly pointed out, Lecoeur was performing a sleight-of-hand in claiming a consistency of line since the Thorez speech. Billoux had also claimed the same authority for his appeal to a harder line, and with more justification. The status quo ante to which the Party was seeking to return, after the disaster of the Ridgway riot, was the broad line introduced by Duclos at the end of 1951 and the beginning of 1952.

After the strike for the liberation of Duclos had made painfully apparent the impotence of the party to "fill the streets," Lecoeur drew still more explicitly the lesson that the party could only be effective if it could enlist the support of others, and this clearly required a broader line: "To enlarge the protest of the masses must be the dominant concern. *It is necessary to open the doors and the windows, to banish all sectarianism, to put aside everything which could be prejudicial to unity and to action against war and fascism and in favor of economic issues."* [44]

Support for this tactical line was immediately forthcoming from the *Cominform Bulletin.* Despite the increasing violence of its language toward the United States, the Cominform newspaper generalized the experience of the French and other Communist parties and urged a policy of collaboration with nonparty masses:

The experience of the Communist Parties in France and Italy, in West Germany and Japan, in India and Brazil and other capitalist, colonial and dependent countries testifies that the creation of a united national front of struggle for peace, for the vital interests of the peoples, against imperialist reaction, is possible only by means of establishing the closest possible contact with all patriotic sections of the population affiliated to the different parties and with non-Party people, with the middle strata in the towns, the millionfold masses of the peasantry and with the intelligentsia, ready to uphold peace and the independence of their countries from encroachments by the United States imperialists.[45]

The significant document in the French party's final acceptance of the broader formulation which was to become the basic line of the entire international Communist movement was a report by Étienne Fajon at a meeting of the Central Committee of the party on June 18 at Gennevilliers.[46] Fajon carried the weight of Cominform authority behind him, since he was one of the links between the French Communist Party and that organization. Following his definitive declaration, it was now understood within the party that the militant tendency, the appeal to class struggle, to "direct action," to uncompromising noncollaboration, to sectarianism, as it was called pejoratively, was no longer to be allowed to contend with the broader line in the upper councils of the party. These conflicting tendencies cannot, of course, be understood as utter opposites; they appear, rather, as differences in emphasis. But great weight was placed upon these nuances, and the distinctions were of more than academic interest to the individual leaders whose fate was tied to one tendency or the other.

It is interesting in this connection to observe the delicacy with which Fajon carried out his repudiation of the Billoux line. In a party in which castigation had been developed to a fine art, Fajon chose to treat the matter as a mere misunderstanding. Billoux had only been trying to correct some "opportunist errors," he said; the entire politburo had been responsible for misinterpreting Billoux as seeming to favor a sectarian course. The delicacy testified to Fajon's recognition that Billoux had been speaking for Thorez and for at least a segment of the Soviet leadership.

Among the sectarian errors dissected by Fajon was the party's contemptuous dismissal of the neutralists, and in dealing with this point Fajon gave an interesting exposition of the party's changing attitude toward neutralism. He took as an example a recent article by Pierre Courtade which had attacked an editorial in *Le Monde* signed "Sirius." [47] The position taken by Sirius, said Fajon,

illustrates the existence of contradictions among the French bourgeoisie over such important questions as the American domination, the war in Vietnam, the remilitarization of Germany, in short, war or peace. For reasons which are obviously not the same as ours, a part of the French bourgeoisie has reservations about the policy of slavery and of war followed by our government. It is these reservations which the Sirius article expressed.

It goes without saying that the cause of peace cannot but gain by this opposition, however timid it may be, on the part of certain circles of the bourgeoisie, to the aggressive plans of the American imperialists. We can therefore only congratulate ourselves when articles appear like this one of Sirius. Such articles should confirm us in our preoccupation against separating ourselves from anyone in the battle for peace, on account of divergencies of opinion or differences in social condition.

Instead of that, the article of Courtade drives Sirius back into class solidarity with the instigators of war.

The quotation clearly illustrates the essential element of the emerging strategy: its reaffirmation of significant differentiations within the bourgeoisie, a part of which can be brought into an alliance with the Communists, while the class struggle is held in abeyance.

The immediate objective of the party, Fajon indicated, must be to get Duclos out of jail. All democrats without exception must be enlisted for this cause, on the issue of the defense of civil liberty and respect for the Constitution. Beyond this, the party's objective remained the same: to bring about a change of government in France, in favor of a "government of broad democratic union."

There was a touch of irony in Duclos' situation. Having gone to prison at a time when his position in the party was under a cloud, and having been arrested under particularly ignominious circumstances, he now found himself in a stronger position in the party than ever before. The campaign to "liberate Jacques Duclos" became the entire focus of the party's activities. His photograph was everywhere; his name was on the lips of every party orator. Even his critic, Billoux, paid homage to his stature by referring to the "Party of Maurice Thorez and of Jacques Duclos." [48] The party's effort to enlist prominent non-Communists in the campaign against Duclos' imprisonment on the basis of constitutionality and civil rights had some success.[49] When, on July 1, Duclos was released, the party took this as confirmation of the efficacy of its broad line. In an interview upon his release, Duclos gave thanks "to all those, socialists, democrats of various kinds, Catholics, and others, who, in rising against this governmental repression, have helped to show the efficacy of the united action of the masses in barring the way to fascism and to war." [50] The experience helps to explain Stalin's instructions to the foreign Communist parties at the Nineteenth Congress to raise "the banner of bourgeois democratic freedoms."

An editorial in the *Cominform Bulletin* on the following day made clear its belief that the episode demonstrated that the French Communist Party was now on the right track. The campaign for the release of Duclos and the decision of the court to release him gave further testimony, in the judgment of the Cominform, "to the contradictions and differences among the ruling classes, to the growing opposition among some sections of the bourgeoisie to the policy of servile groveling before the U.S. imperialists." The release also was cited as confirmation of the correctness of the party's effort to unite into a "single national front all French patriots determined to fight for peace and for the independence of the country, irrespective of political and religious beliefs and social status." [51]

This new formulation, the "single national front," went much further than the party had gone before. The nuance which separates this formula from the previous conception of a "united front" of the working class, within a "broad democratic front," is of considerable ideological and practical significance. The national coalition was understood as extending far beyond the democratic alliance of the center and the left; its reach goes clear across the political spectrum, totally obliterating for the time being any considerations of class.

This new formula had first made its appearance in one of the many letters written from prison by the indefatigable Duclos sometime in late June. The hesitant manner in which the party had handled Duclos' tentative extension of the line indicated a feeling of uncertainty about how far the party could safely go in broadening its appeal. *L'Humanité* made no mention of the letter except for a small advertisement which appeared toward the end of June, announcing that a letter of Duclos to one of the members of the Central Committee would appear in the forthcoming issue of *France nouvelle,* the Central Committee's weekly newspaper, where it was in fact published on July 5, 1952, after Duclos' release. Significantly, the letter was given international circulation by the *Cominform Bulletin* at the same time.[52]

Duclos' letter compared the Pinay government with that of Laval in 1935. He argued that, just as the mass political struggle under the popular front brought about Laval's downfall, a mass political struggle must now be organized, on the basis of "the largest possible union," to bring down the Pinay government. Socialist and Catholic workers have to be brought into the struggle and also "increasingly wider nonproletarian masses." This was a delicate euphemism for the bourgeoisie, calculated not to offend and arouse militant Party sensibilities.

The first step, wrote Duclos, was to "unite the working class in action" and then, around this nucleus, to build a broader union of all national and democratic energies in a "powerful United National Front [un puissant Front National Uni] against the government of national betrayal, war, impoverishment, and fascism, with a view to saving the peace and imposing a policy of social progress."[53] Duclos' formula, a "powerful United National Front," was conceived as a 1952 equivalent of the popular front of the 1930s, but it was broader in scope, emphasizing the "national" theme rather than the social content of the early popular front; this also had the advantage of not requiring any programmatic concessions to the socialists.

For a time, the new slogan hung suspended in uncertainty, while the higher party councils weighed the political compromises implied in the national appeal. Then, within a month, there appeared a sign that the broad formula had won acceptance. According to a frequent Communist practice, the endorsement of the new line came from the very man who might have been expected to oppose it most strongly, François Billoux, thus demonstrating to the party his obedient solidarity and to the outside world the "unshakeable unity of the party." To the August issue of *Cahiers du communisme,* Billoux contributed the lead editorial, entitled "Toward a United National Front of All the Patriots of France." [54] Billoux made it clear that he accepted and endorsed the Duclos line, the Fajon criticism at the June Central Committee meeting, and the validity of the analysis which emphasized internal contradictions among the bourgeoisie.

Billoux also stressed another element essential to the broad strategy: that the Peace Movement was conceived by the Communists as playing an essential role in reaching the nonproletarian classes. Correlated with the broadening of the line of the foreign Communist parties, a corresponding series of actions was taken by the Peace Movement to enlarge its constituency. The Moscow Economic Conference in April, which it had originated, had been designed to find a common meeting ground with elements of the Western bourgeoisie. The germ-warfare campaign, which it had launched at the Oslo meeting of its executive committee on March 29–April 1, 1952, had been primarily intended to enlist the support of European and Asian neutralists and to give the neutralist movement an anti-American orientation. The Stockholm Appeal for the banning of the atomic bomb and the appeal for a Big Five peace pact were calculated to give the Peace Movement a mass base in the hundreds of millions of signatures which served as a minimum token association with the movement. However, the sponsorship of the Ridgway demonstration by the French branch of the Peace Movement had turned out to be a militant deviation, one which cost the movement the confidence of the party because of its failure and the support of many non-Communists because of its violence. In its subsequent concentration of energies upon the campaign to block the ratification of the Paris and Bonn agreements, the Peace Movement once again sought to attract non-Communist support. The primary instrument upon which the Peace Movement relied in seeking to prevent the ratification of the Bonn and Paris treaties was the appeal for general popular pressure in behalf of immediate negotiations among the five great powers.

Called into extraordinary session at Berlin on July 1-6, the World Peace Council condemned the continuation of the war in Korea, the use of bacteriological warfare and other alleged American atrocities in Korea, the Japanese peace treaty, the Paris and Bonn treaties, and in all respects followed the general line of current Soviet policy objectives. The council also announced that it would hold a third "Congress of the Peoples for Peace" at Vienna in December and that it would particularly welcome to the Vienna congress persons of varied opinions who did not necessarily belong to the Peace Movement, but who were interested in helping to end the cold war.

While the World Peace Council was thus engaged in trying to mobilize popular pressures to block the military association of West Germany with the Western alliance, the Chinese Communists at approximately the same time were organizing an Asian People's Peace Conference to prevent the Japanese peace treaty and Japanese-United States security treaty from coming into force. The Asian Peace Conference, which met in early October, attracted delegates from forty countries; against its major target — American imperialism — its principal themes were peace, trade, peaceful coexistence, and a five-power peace pact.[55]

By midsummer 1952, however, it may have become apparent to

the Soviet Union, the foreign Communist parties, and the Peace Movement that the Western alliance had passed its apogee with the signing of the Contractual Agreements and the European Defense Treaty in May. Since that time, signs of internal weaknesses within the Western alliance had continued to mount. Internal political dissension in both France and West Germany made it clear that ratification of the European Defense Treaty was not, at any rate, an immediate prospect. This may have strengthened the further movement of the Communist instruments abroad during the late summer and early fall toward a more clearly defined broad-front policy. The fundamental presumption of that policy was that there were fissures within the bourgeoisie to be exploited in collaboration with part of the bourgeoisie.[56]

### The French Party Anticipates the Nineteenth Congress

The political implications of this analysis were stated most explicitly in a report by Jacques Duclos at the decisive meeting of the Central Committee of the French Communist Party, held at Montreuil on September 3–4, 1952. The report, entitled "The Action of the French Communist Party in Rallying the Masses for the Defense of Peace," [57] is an important document in the study of Soviet policy, for it foreshadows the essential elements of the analysis and the policies to be presented a month later at the Nineteenth Congress in Moscow. This is not intended to suggest that the ideas necessarily originated in France. Stalin's essay on the "Economic Problems of Socialism," in which the emphasis on the internal contradictions of capitalism was further developed, was published in October but was composed of letters written in February, April, May, and September of 1952, the substance of which could probably have become known to the French party leadership through Cominform or informal party channels.

The Duclos report placed its principal emphasis upon the conflicts within capitalist countries and among them. The Pinay government, which was "pursuing a policy of national betrayal," leading to fascism and the suppression of French national interests, had "underestimated the contradictions within the French bourgeoisie, contradictions which are becoming sharper." Duclos related these contradictions in turn to the Marxist theory of the decline of capitalism and the Leninist theory of imperialism. "Glaring contradictions" had also developed, said Duclos, between the United States and Great Britain and between the United States and France, in the Far East, the Near East, and Africa, where the imperialists are "both accomplices and rivals": "The Washington government has decided to assign to West Germany the main role in the Atlantic coalition in Europe. However, the revival of German militarism, to which the French bourgeoisie agreed, motivated by class selfishness which is counterposed to the national interests, gives rise to serious contradictions in the camp of the imperialists."

This pointed to the main immediate task before the party: to mobilize "strong pressure by the masses" to persuade the deputies not to ratify the European army project and to bring about a change of governmental policy. To do this, Duclos declared, the Party must attract into a

United National Front the great mass of French men and women determined to fight for the peace and independence of the homeland, irrespective of political conviction, religious belief, and social status . . .
The struggle of the masses can lead not only to a change of government (which would yield nothing should the new government pursue the old policy), but also, and this is important, to a change in policy.

The inner core of a United National Front, Duclos insisted, is working-class unity, which does not mean a cessation of attacks upon the socialist leaders, who "are playing into the hands of Pinay." The lower levels of the socialist organizations must be approached with specific proposals for joint action. In other words, as far as the working-class core of the United National Front was concerned, it was to have the familiar characteristics of a united front from below.

Built around this inner core of working-class unity, the United

National Front was to draw its real strength from other classes, attracted by a broad program of common interests:

Undoubtedly at the present moment many French men and women do not agree with a number of points in the program of the Communist Party which we ourselves regard as the sole program fully corresponding both to the present and the future needs and interests of our country. However, many of these French men and women agree with us on certain points and can form a powerful United National Front which would chart the political and economic aims corresponding to the demands of the present moment.

The United National Front, uniting men and women of all convictions, all beliefs and social status could, of course, on the basis of common consent, set itself the tasks of regaining the independence of France, of breaking with the "Schuman Plan," of resolute resistance to the remilitarization of West Germany, of struggle for a peaceful settlement of the German problem and for an end to the war in Vietnam.

The United National Front could also, on the basis of common consent, set itself the task of conducting an economic, financial, and social policy which, within the framework of a peaceful economy, would ensure an upsurge in the industry and agriculture of France, satisfaction of the immediate demands of the working masses, the development of mutually beneficial trade relations with all countries, and large-scale housing construction. Relying on the unanimous support of French men and women, the United National Front could also set itself the task of safeguarding democratic freedoms against all attacks by reaction and fascism . . .

Here, in this collection of appeals to all interests, and in the signal to continue the attacks upon the socialist leaders, Duclos made it clear that the United National Front was not to be a popular front. The latter, at least at its inception, had been built around a program of working-class reforms to be carried out in collaboration with the socialists and under Socialist leadership. The United National Front, as the title of Duclos' report indicates, was to be a "rally," a political force without positive content, built around a collection of disaffected interests for the negative purpose of voting the existing government out of office.

To appreciate how far the Communist attitude toward the bourgeoisie had evolved, it is interesting to observe the changed inflection in the party's discussion of the Schuman Plan. Whereas at the time it was first proposed, in May 1950, the Communists treated the Schuman Plan as a plot devised by the French bourgeoisie, now Duclos addressed the bourgeoisie as the victims of the plan and therefore as potential allies.

> The German trusts will be the first to benefit from the "Schuman Plan," which signifies the betrayal of the interests of France, while French factories . . . are doomed to close down with resultant increases in unemployment and a further weakening of France.
>
> Thus our country is reduced to the status of a junior partner, which will give rise to discontent not only in the ranks of the working class but also among those bourgeois circles whose interests are affected.

Part of the price of this extension of the appeal across class lines — and a price particularly troublesome to party militants — was the playing down of two standard planks in the party's platform: aggressive support for higher wages and vigorous anticolonialism. Both remained on the books, but in muted form. An appeal to elements of the bourgeoisie implied an offer of an industrial truce at home, as in the halcyon days of the Franco-Soviet Treaty of 1944. Also, a line of "revolutionary defeatism" in Indochina, Algeria, or Tunisia could hardly be reconciled with the appeal to nationalist sentiments against the revival of the Wehrmacht or against the alleged American trampling upon French sovereignty.

In its relations with the Peace Movement, Duclos urged the party to be active but to retain the freedom to follow a more militant peace program if necessary, particularly if the People's Congress for Peace scheduled for Vienna in December should succeed in attracting a larger proportion of non-Communists:

> Thus, together with men and women of good will, of all convictions and beliefs, the Communists must be active members of the Peace Movement. They must be in the front ranks of organizers of peace committees in the factories and in the localities. Active participation by the organizations and members of the Party in the work of the masses pre-

paring for the People's Congress of Peace must, under no circumstances, prevent us from calling on the working people for a struggle against war on the basis of the slogans of the Party which may not necessarily be the slogans of the Peace Movement.

Finally, Duclos urged each member to study the draft of the Soviet Fifth Five-Year Plan and the proposed changes in the rules of the Communist Party of the Soviet Union, which had been published a fortnight before in preparation for the Nineteenth Congress. Duclos added significantly that the rule changes, which had been presented by Khrushchev, contained "valuable lessons" for the French party as well.

### The Marty-Tillon Affair

One valuable lesson hinted at by Duclos concerned the need for "unshakeable unity" within the party. Behind the scenes, the French Communist Party was in the midst of its most serious postwar leadership purge. Only after it had been revealed to the rank and file through the non-Communist press did *L'Humanité*, two weeks later, inform its readers that the Central Committee, along with its other business, had taken action against two prominent leaders of the party: André Marty and Charles Tillon.[58] Marty had been dropped as one of the four party secretaries, but was to remain for the time being a member of the politburo. Tillon had been dropped from the politburo, but remained on the Central Committee. Further action was to follow: in December and January, Marty was expelled from the party by his local branch at the insistence of the Central Committee; Tillon was dropped from all party positions but remained a member of the party.

There are many interesting aspects of "L'Affaire Marty-Tillon" that have since come to light, and many others that remain obscure. Whatever else may have been involved, the episode is germane to any study of the evolution of the party's line during this period.

The charges leveled against Marty and Tillon were involved and contradictory.[59] Marty was accused of "bourgeois nationalism," of "minimizing the role of the Soviet Union in the liberation of France," of having concealed his inner opposition to the party line, of having met secretly with Tillon after the latter had fallen into disfavor in April 1951 (for having sought to transform the Peace Movement into a mass political organization), and finally of failing to make an adequate "self-criticism." After the final blow in December, Tillon remained silent.[60] Marty, stung by charges of having been a police agent,[61] replied with a series of letters hotly denying them. When the party refused to print his letters, Marty published his own version in book form.[62]

When the highly polemic language is stripped away from the exchange, it seems evident that these two party leaders, both men of revolutionary temperament and experience, had found it increasingly difficult to accept Moscow's requirements for a broadening of the party line. An instigator of the Black Sea Mutiny, an emissary whose brutal role in the Spanish Civil War was portrayed by Ernest Hemingway in *For Whom the Bell Tolls,* Marty had been a leader in the resistance, tough, "sectarian," uncompromising. Tillon had been one of the most popular and effective leaders of the resistance forces.[63] From 1944 on, both men believed in the revolutionary possibilities of the French situation.[64] They were undoubtedly far from being disloyal to the Soviet Union, but they were reluctant to let supposed considerations of Soviet foreign policy stand in the way of exploiting the opportunity they felt was present for more vigorous, more truly proletarian, more revolutionary action within France.

According to Marty's account, his troubles with the party had begun on February 13, 1952, when he was scheduled to present a report to the Central Committee on the liberation movement in colonial territories.[65] (It is interesting to observe that the left wing of the French party consistently emphasized the theme of anti-colonialism, which was logically related to an emphasis upon a renewal of the class struggle against the bourgeoisie and an anti-nationalist orientation.) When he appealed to the Central Committee "to break with its parliamentary policy in order to return to a class policy whose revolutionary perspectives alone could effectively defend the interests of the workers," he ran into trouble. Marty despised the notion that collecting signatures would change the course of history. "This is not to say that the signatures are useless; to get them, one has to persuade, but to count on the simple accumulation of signatures to stop the war in Vietnam is a deceit, it is a poultice on a wooden leg." [66]

As for the Peace Movement, Marty was equally outspoken:

It doesn't serve any purpose to hide the truth, and the truth is this: Joliot-Curie, president of the World Peace Movement, asked in his report to the World Congress at Vienna in 1953 that the Peace Movement be made into a true mass movement. Now, there wasn't any such movement; of course, they published many communiqués with the signature of Sartre, for example, but what do such personalities represent? They don't bring anyone with them. What do these departmental or national "rallies" represent? One sees there almost always the same faces, that is to say, an immense majority of Communist militants or sympathizers, plus some "personalities." How many socialist sections or trade-union sections, whether from the F.O., or autonomous, or others, are en bloc in the Peace Movement? None . . .

The Peace Committees are purely formal; in any case, they are composed of "personalities" and of designated Communist militants, but the mass of the people are not in it. [67]

On May 26, 1952, according to Marty, the first accusation was leveled against him within the party's secretariat by Léon Mauvais, a member of the politburo and chairman of the political control commission. During the disarray following the Ridgway riot and the Duclos arrest, the case against Marty and Tillon was not pressed further until the September meeting of the Central Committee. In the end, Marty believed, he and Tillon had been sacrificed at the altar of the United National Front:

The secretariat of the C.P. launched the Marty-Tillon Affair at the meetings on September 3 and 4 of the Central Committee of the French C.P., at which Duclos' report set forth the necessity for realizing the

"United National Front," that is, the union of the workers with their exploiters, with their enemies (or what was called "the Sacred Union" during the war of 1914–1918).

The campaign and the measures taken against Tillon and against myself were, obviously, the necessary complement for the realization of the United National Front.[68]

The challenge raised by Marty bears some structural resemblance to the argument of the Left Opposition against Stalin in the twenties and to the argument of the Chinese Communists against alleged Soviet revisionism in the late fifties and early sixties; essentially, it is the response of fundamental orthodoxy to expediential flexibility. To what extent the argument was a determining factor in the Marty-Tillon affair, as against essentially organizational questions, it is still difficult to judge. In any case, the alignments are clearly not sufficiently explained by a simple right-left dichotomy, for the essential separations came on the issue of French considerations versus subordination to Moscow,[69] as had been the case thirty years earlier in the fight which had led to the resignation of L.-O. Frossard, the party's secretary general, over the question of the establishment of a united front. However, to the extent that issues of policy were involved in the dispute, the argument for the broadening of the party line, which Marty was resisting, depended on two major points: first, the Soviet situation required broad political action whose primary purpose was to bring about a change in the orientation of French foreign policy; and, second, within France the growing ripeness of the neutralists, the pacifists, and the non-Communist left created opportunities for effective political collaboration to this end.

Some signs of this ripeness were at hand. Like Jean-Marie Domenach, the editor of the Catholic left-wing journal, *L'Esprit,* many Frenchmen felt that the existing system was becoming less and less capable of domestic reform, less and less capable of asserting France's independence from both blocs in world politics. To those who shared this position, and there were many who did at this

PEACE PARTISANS AND THE FRENCH PARTY          237

time, the expulsion of Marty and Tillon was taken as a sign that "the French Communists prefer, more clearly than ever, 'unconditional support for the Soviet Union' as against whatever revolutionary possibilities the French situation might offer." [70] But, given the situation of France between the two great power blocs, Domenach continued, this line appeared to have significant possibilities, particularly in light of Stalin's *Bolshevik* article, which had just been published:

> From this point of view, the importance of Stalin's article in *Bolshevik* is considerable. Whereas, in recent years, the Communists have tried to represent the countries of West Europe as American satellites, the accent is now going to be on the possibilities of conflicts between these countries and the United States, conflicts which appear to Stalin as more likely than a collision between the two blocs.
>
> It is in this light that the "United National Front" makes sense, and one can be pleased with this new Communist orientation even if he does not believe it will be successful. The Communists have waited a long time before understanding that a European emancipation would be the best chance for peace, too long to hope today to be able to take the leadership of it. Defensive agreements with them may be necessary; they are, today, in France . . . At least the new Communist attitude will lead many minds to challenge the validity of the division of the world into two blocs, which has tended to replace the flexibilities of the Leninist dialectic.

These words by a man of independent spirit outside the party well illustrate the state of mind of a large number of Frenchmen in the year 1952. It was to this state of mind that the Communists had to address themselves if they desired the weakening of popular support for the Western alliance and the defeat of the European army project. This was the whole meaning and purpose of the United National Front in France, and it was but a local application of a general strategic outlook to be spelled out more fully at the Nineteenth Party Congress in Moscow.

# X

# THE NINETEENTH PARTY CONGRESS

So many spectacular developments have occurred in the Communist world since the Nineteenth Congress of the Communist Party of the Soviet Union in October 1952 that this event has not received the attention and analysis it deserves. It is true that, compared to the dramatic tensions of the Twentieth and Twenty-Second Congresses, there is a stage-managed dullness about the Nineteenth; its proceedings regurgitate the same stale platitudes over and over again. Still, when the congress is re-examined with the benefit of our subsequent knowledge, and as a culmination of the experiences which have been analyzed in the preceding chapters, it becomes evident that behind its ponderous formulations the congress signaled some significant departures in Communist thought and practice.

In retrospect, it is more clearly apparent than it was at the time that the congress served to articulate and sanction lines of thought and action which had been emerging during the previous four years of experimentation. The nuances of the congress take on a fuller significance when viewed in this light; the doctrinal formulations evoke memories of successes and defeats in practice; the new departures stand out despite the appearance of consistency. Most important of all, a reappraisal of the Nineteenth Congress confirms the impression that the Soviet leadership had in this period further developed its estimate of the strategic position of the Soviet Union and had accepted the necessity for a more flexible policy to deal with the changing balance of forces in the world.

The decision to convoke the Nineteenth Congress was announced on August 20, 1952.[1] Thirteen years had passed since the previous congress — years of war, reconstruction, and renewed concentration upon industrial and military growth. Five years had passed since Malenkov had mentioned, at the founding meeting of the Cominform, that a congress was in preparation. Through all the preparatory meetings of regional congresses and conferences, and in the Party's announcement, it was clear that the primary business of the congress was intended to be domestic: to approve the Fifth Five-Year Plan and the new party statutes. The war's decimation and subsequent engorgement of the party had weakened the discipline and efficiency of the party mechanism, which is crucial to the Soviet system of government. The two main elements of the program were both aspects of a domestic consolidation: the new party statutes, presented by Khrushchev, were intended to intensify ideological pressure against slackness and corruption in the economic bureaucracy. The Fifth Five-Year Plan, presented by Maxim Z. Saburov, chairman of the State Planning Commission, was being offered for approval almost two years after it was scheduled to have begun, a delay that may have been related to difficulties experienced in various sectors of the economy.

These domestic preoccupations, however, were integrally related to the Soviet leadership's assessment of the world situation. The fundamental perspective of the congress was one of vulnerability in the face of the growth of Western power but also one of future strength, stemming from divisive forces within the Western alliance and the expected growth of Soviet industrial and military power. Therefore, while Soviet foreign policy was directed to thwart Western mobilization and to play upon Western "contradictions," the main task was to repair weaknesses in the Soviet economy, raise industrial output, and hasten the development of the scientific-military complex.

## *"Economic Problems of Socialism"*

The most interesting feature of the congress is the indirect evidence it offers that this view of the domestic economic priorities was by no means universally shared in the upper levels of the party. Beneath the outward appearance of monolithic conformity, incipient "revisionist" pressures were challenging Stalin's scale of priorities and economic methods. In a sense, Stalin's foreign policy had been moving in an essentially revisionist direction, in that it had increasingly accepted the nonrevolutionary state of the proletariat of the advanced industrial countries and the consequent necessity of a balance-of-power policy within the international system of nation-states. But in domestic affairs, and particularly as they affected the crucial question of the priority of heavy industry, Stalin raised a mailed fist within a glove of turgid prose against any suggestion of the slightest relaxation.

Three days before the congress opened, Stalin published a collection of comments on a draft of a new textbook on political economy. Written in February, April, May, and September of 1952, these comments appeared in *Bolshevik, Pravda,* and in tens of millions of pamphlet reprints under the title, "Economic Problems of Socialism in the USSR." [2] Hailed as Stalin's testamentary contribution to Marxist theory, the essay sketched the essential conditions for "the gradual transition from socialism to communism," which was to become the keynote of the congress. Speaker after speaker praised the profundity of the essay and stayed safely within the bounds it defined. (Mikoyan, who was to criticize the essay as "hardly correct" at the 1956 congress and as "vulgarly simplified" at the 1961 congress, described it at the Nineteenth Congress as "brilliant," a "treasure house of ideas.") Repeatedly in his essay Stalin took issue with "some comrades," who were guilty of one or another mistaken view, as well as a number of named economists who had submitted variant ideas to the conference engaged in drafting the new textbook. In retrospect, it is clear that "some comrades" was far from being a purely rhetorical device, that it referred to specific Communist leaders, foremost among whom was Nikolai Voznesensky, former deputy premier and chief of the State Planning Commission. Despite the fact that Voznesensky was known to have been deposed three years before and (what was not to become known until later) had been put to death at least two years earlier, one of the major functions of Stalin's essay was to dispose of the persistent influence of some of the ideas advanced by Voznesensky in his book on the war economy written in 1947. Although Voznesensky was not identified by name, much of the essay consisted of a point-by-point refutation of arguments which had appeared in his book.[3] (Two months later, Suslov explicitly identified Voznesensky as the target and organized a large-scale recantation by economists and administrators of earlier support for his views.[4])

Behind such cloudy phrases as "the objective laws of political economy under socialism" and the proper application of the "law of value" under socialism, what Stalin mainly appeared to be attacking in Voznesensky was his appeal for greater economic rationality, a more rational pricing system for producer goods, and a balanced development of the economy that would give greater attention to light industry and consumer goods. In fact what Stalin was defending in the name of "objective economic laws" was the right of the party leadership to determine priorities for the allocation of resources on the basis of essentially political considerations, however painful to the economic planners might be the consequent dislocations. The policy of continued high priorities for heavy industry was cynically represented at the congress as part of a "gradual transition to communism," and Stalin officially defined the basic law of socialism as "the securing of the maximum satisfaction of the constantly rising material and cultural requirements of the whole of society through the continuous expansion and perfection of socialist production on the basis of higher techniques." A further analysis of these differences, in the light of subsequent revisionist

developments in Soviet economics, would without doubt be reward-
ing, but it lies outside the scope of our present concern with the
foreign-policy implications of Stalin's essay.[5] It is worth noting,
however, that another economist who was among the "some comrades" criticized in the Stalin essay appeared to be Eugene Varga
and that, despite the attack of Voznesensky upon Varga in 1948,
there appeared to be no necessary incompatibility between their
views. Apparently, Varga's analysis of the adaptive capabilities of
capitalism and Voznesensky's emphasis upon economic rationality
at home continued to attract persistent but unexpressed (or at least
unprinted) support, for Stalin felt it necessary to dispose with fi-
nality of these departures from his orthodoxy. (In November, Varga
appeared before an augmented meeting of the Learned Council of the
Institute of Economics to acknowledge his errors in the light of
Stalin's new "work of genius." [6])

The substance of the party leadership's argument concerning
world affairs and Soviet foreign policy is to be found in three documents, of which Stalin's essay is the most important. The second
basic document was the report of the Central Committee, delivered
by Malenkov, the first third of which was devoted to "The International Situation of the Soviet Union." Finally, there was a brief
but significant closing speech delivered by Stalin to the delegates of
the foreign Communist parties.[7] Taken together, these three documents convey an analysis of the current international situation and
policy guidances for the Soviet Union, the foreign Communist parties, and the Peace Movement.

The analysis begins with a reaffirmation of the two-camp doctrine. As a result of the Second World War, the "peace-loving,
democratic camp" headed by the Soviet Union had been greatly
strengthened by the accession of the states of Eastern Europe and
China and by the "surge of the national liberation struggle" in
colonial and dependent territories. The other camp, the "aggressive, antidemocratic camp headed by the United States," on the
other hand, had been weakened by the war and its aftereffects.

This was in part an anticipatory judgment, Stalin indicated in answer to those who were overimpressed by Western strength; the United States appeared to have been strengthened at the moment, but the signs were clear that its weaknesses would soon make themselves felt:

Outwardly, everything would seem to be "going well": the U.S.A. has put Western Europe, Japan and other capitalist countries on rations; Germany (western), Britain, France, Italy and Japan have fallen into the clutches of the U.S.A. and are meekly obeying its commands. But it would be mistaken to think that things can continue to "go well" for "all eternity," that these countries will tolerate the domination and oppression of the United States endlessly, that they will not endeavor to tear loose from American bondage and take the path of independent development.[8]

The theoretical underpinnings for this sanguine hope were derived from Marx's analysis of the dynamics of capitalism and Lenin's theory of imperialism, with some adaptations. As a consequence of the Second World War and the "disintegration of the single, all-embracing world market," the capitalist system had entered the second stage of its deepening general crisis.[9] The United States, which "expected to raise its production fourfold or fivefold after Germany and Japan were put out of action" in the war, had only doubled it and "is now tumbling downhill toward economic crisis." [10] Lenin's thesis that capitalism, though doomed, was still in a growing phase was no longer valid.[11] Nor, asserted Stalin, was capitalism to be regarded any longer as being in a period of temporary relative stabilization, as he had proclaimed it to be in 1925.[12] Therefore, the anticipated strengthening of the socialist camp and the collapse of the capitalist camp would produce a balance of forces more favorable to the Soviet Union than currently existed.

Malenkov developed the point further. Economic difficulties had driven American capitalism to war in Korea, he said. This had been accompanied by a militarization of American industry; and this in turn had led to inflation and increases in taxes and would reduce purchasing power and thereby precipitate the crisis.[13] American capitalism had now entered the stage of imperialism described by Lenin, in which a struggle for markets and for raw materials was leading to war among the capitalist countries.

This was indeed the main point. "Contradictions" between the United States and the other industrial nations, Britain, France, West Germany, and Japan, had reached the point where war was now more likely among the capitalist states than between the capitalist states and the Soviet Union. The United States, in its drive for world domination, would have preferred to attack the Soviet Union, but it did not dare to do so because this would "put into question the existence of capitalism itself." [14] "There is every reason to believe," Malenkov declared, "that a third world war would cause the collapse of the world capitalist system." [15] Another factor deterring the United States from attacking the Soviet Union, he argued, was the resistance of the "peace-loving democratic forces" in the West.[16]

Therefore, this curious situation resulted: although the contradictions between capitalism and socialism theoretically were even greater, war was more likely among the capitalist states themselves. "Some comrades," said Stalin, thought that "wars between capitalist countries have ceased to be inevitable . . . These comrades are mistaken. They see the outward phenomena that come and go on the surface, *but they do not see those profound forces which, although they are so far operating imperceptibly, will nevertheless determine the course of developments.*" [17] "Capitalist Britain, and, after her, capitalist France, will be compelled in the end to break from the embrace of the U.S.A. and enter into conflict with it in order to secure an independent position and, of course, high profits." As for West Germany and Japan, "to think that these countries will not try to get on their feet again, will not try to smash U. S. domination and force their way to independent development, is to believe in miracles."

Both Stalin and Malenkov made it clear that these frictions

among capitalist states were not merely on the level of political or economic difficulties: they meant war. This was stated as an inevitability by Stalin[18] and as a possibility by Malenkov.[19]

## Guidelines for Policy

For the Soviet Union, peace was both a political tool and "in present historical circumstances" a genuine necessity. As a slogan, "peace" was one of the levers with which to move the broad masses (democratic or progressive or peace-loving) of the Western nations whose support was imperative and the "anti-imperialist" masses in Asia. Another essential lever for bringing about a reversal of course by the Western governments was the reduction of international tension. For this purpose, the doctrine of peaceful coexistence was reaffirmed as the order of the day. As it was used here, peaceful coexistence implied no prospect of settlement with the West, but a temporary stabilization of the international situation based on a Soviet desistance from harsh provocation and an acceptance by the West of the Potsdam terms for Germany and Soviet hegemony in Eastern Europe: "The Soviet policy of peace and security for nations is based on [the premise] that the peaceful coexistence of capitalism and communism and cooperation are quite possible, given a mutual desire to cooperate, readiness to carry out commitments undertaken, and observance of the principle of equality and non-interference in the internal affairs of other states." [20]

Even a war among the capitalist states, foretold as inevitable by Stalin,[21] was potentially dangerous from the Soviet point of view, in Malenkov's judgment. Apart from the manipulative possibilities of the peace issue, Malenkov made it clear, by reference to such elliptical explanations as "in present historical circumstances," that the avoidance of any major war was genuinely felt to be a requirement of Soviet interests at that time. Malenkov went on to argue that an enlargement of East-West trade would relieve the capitalist economies of their dependence upon armaments. He foresaw the peaceful victory of the Soviet system, and expressed confidence that in peaceful competition with capitalism the socialist economic system would prove its superiority "more and more strikingly with each passing year." In the meantime, he said, the Soviet Union had no intention of forcing its system upon anyone else; "the export of revolution," he said, citing Stalin, "is nonsense." [22]

In this connection, the policy directives of the congress bearing upon the Peace Movement are pointed and revealing. Both Stalin and Malenkov emphasized (perhaps against such efforts as Tillon was alleged to have made) that the Peace Movement is not to be regarded as an instrument of revolution; its aims are more limited so that its reach may be broader. In the following passages, Stalin defined with remarkable candor the functions and the limitations of the Peace Movement:

The object of the present-day Peace Movement is to rouse the masses of the people to fight for the preservation of peace and for the prevention of another World War. Consequently, the aim of this movement is not to overthrow capitalism and establish socialism — it confines itself to the democratic aim of preserving peace. In this respect, the present-day Peace Movement differs from the movement of the time of the First World War for the conversion of the imperialist war into civil war, since the latter movement went further and pursued socialist ends.

It is possible that in a definite conjuncture of circumstances, the fight for peace will develop here or there into a fight for socialism. But then it will no longer be the present-day Peace Movement; it will be a movement for the overthrow of capitalism.

What is most likely is that the present-day Peace Movement, as a movement for the preservation of peace, will, if it succeeds, result in preventing a *particular* war, in its temporary postponement, in the temporary preservation of a *particular* peace, in the resignation of a bellicose government and its supersession by another that is prepared temporarily to keep the peace. That, of course, will be good. Even very good. But, all the same, it will not be enough to eliminate the inevitability of wars between capitalist countries generally. It will not be enough because, for all the successes of the peace movement, imperialism will remain, continue in force — and, consequently, the inevitability of wars will also continue in force.

To eliminate the inevitability of war, it is necessary to abolish imperialism.[23]

Malenkov in his turn developed the point in language which suggested a directive to party militants to avoid "overpoliticizing" the Peace Movement and to accept the necessity for its broad multiclass base. He described the movement as

an anti-war coalition . . . of various classes and social strata . . . [It] does not pursue the aim of abolishing capitalism, for it is not a socialist movement but a democratic movement of hundreds of millions of people. The peace partisans are advancing demands and proposals for the preservation of peace and prevention of a new war. In the present historical circumstances, attainment of this end would be a tremendous triumph for the cause of democracy and peace . . . The task now is to increase the activity of the masses of the people, to improve the organization of the peace partisans . . . to curb and isolate the adventurers of the imperialist aggressors' camp . . .[24]

In other words, Stalin and Malenkov were saying to the party militants abroad, like Marty, who had been expressing impatience with the idea of a working-class revolutionary movement nursemaiding a conglomeration of bourgeois pacifists: the Peace Movement can, in present historical circumstances, perform an objectively progressive role. It can be used to bring about changes of government and policies in the capitalist countries. It can inhibit the freedom of action of the bourgeois governments, so that the Soviet Union would not be obliged to "fight the wrong war in the wrong place and at the wrong time." For this purpose, it must include elements of the bourgeoisie, and to do this its program must be broader than the program of the party.

The climax of this directive to the Communist movement was reached in two striking paragraphs of Stalin's closing address to the delegates of the foreign parties:

The banner of bourgeois democratic freedoms has been cast overboard. I think that it is up to you, the representatives of the Communist and democratic parties, to lift this banner and carry it forward if you wish to gather the majority of the people around you . . .

The banner of national independence and national sovereignty has been cast overboard. There is no doubt that it is up to you, the representatives of the Communist and democratic parties, to lift this banner and carry it forward if you wish to be patriots of your country, if you wish to become the leading force of the nation.[25]

To the French party, as we have seen, these exhortations came as a confirmation of their own experience. The appeal to bourgeois democratic freedoms had not only protected the party leadership from legal prosecution, but had shown the promise of winning support from non-Communist liberal elements in common opposition to the French government. The slogan was also seen as an aid in inhibiting Western mobilization, which, according to the Soviet argument, was leading to fascist trends in Western societies.

Similarly, the trial-and-error experience of the French party had led it, more than a year earlier, to the conception of "raising the banner of national independence," and it was expressed in the same figure of speech. The French party had known its greatest isolation when it had defied French nationalism (at the time of the Thorez declaration of support for the Red Army in February 1949); conversely, it had had the best chance of breaking out of isolation and becoming politically effective when it followed a patriotic line (the resistance, the liberation, opposition to German rearmament). Now the leader of world Communism was telling them that if they wished to gather the majority of the people around them — that is, if the parties abroad were to function not as revolutionaries, but as political levers for influencing the orientation of their countries — then they must follow a nationalist line. Moreover, they must use the slogans of democratic liberalism as a shield against the legal repression of their activities.

Both Stalin and Malenkov had been careful, despite the extreme violence of their attacks upon the capitalist warmongers ("fascist," "Hitler-like"), not to indict the bourgeoisie as a class and to avoid references to the existence of a class struggle in the West. The "ruling circles," the "billionaires," and the "imperialist bourgeoisie" were the carefully specified targets of the indictment. Malenkov made it clear, however, that no alliance with the socialist leaders was intended:

Direct responsibility for this international policy of the ruling circles is borne also by the right-wing Social-Democrats, primarily by the hierarchy of the British Labor Party, French Socialist Party and Social-Democratic Party of Western Germany. The right-wing socialists of Sweden, Denmark, Norway, Finland, Austria and other countries are following in the footsteps of their colleagues and during the whole period since the second World War have been furiously fighting the peace-loving and democratic forces of the peoples. The present-day right-wing Social-Democrats, in addition to the old role of flunkeys of the national bourgeoisie, have turned into agents of foreign, American imperialism and are performing its dirtiest assignments in the preparation of war and in the struggle against their own peoples.[26]

The climate of attack upon the socialists was so strong, it may be noted, that Thorez, in delivering greetings from the French Communist Party, did violence to history in describing his party's innovation of the popular front before World War II as part of a struggle against Social Democracy, "the main pillar of the bourgeoisie." [27]

The task of the foreign Communist parties, therefore, was to "weld together a powerful democratic anti-war front." This time, unlike the popular front with the socialists in the thirties, it was to be composed of a series of national fronts. The socialist leaders, now wary as a result of their experience with the earlier united-front period, were regarded as the principal obstacle to the creation of the broad coalition desired by the Communists. The new alliance was therefore to burrow under the socialist leaders by appealing to the rank and file and to extend as far to the right as possible, on the basis of an appeal to nationalist and patriotic sentiments. The strategic purpose of this slogan of "peace and national independence" for the Western European countries was to reduce American influence on the continent and thus reduce the cohesion and the military development of the Western alliance.

Malenkov implied that the Soviet Union would recognize a neutral status for those countries that broke away from American hegemony and followed an independent policy:

the more sober-minded and progressive politicians in the European and other capitalist countries, those who are not blinded by anti-Soviet animus, distinctly see the abyss into which the reckless American adventurers are dragging them, and they are beginning to take a stand against war. It is to be presumed that in the countries condemned to the role of obedient pawns of the American dictators there will be found genuinely peace-loving democratic forces which will pursue an independent peace policy and will find a way out of the impasse into which the American dictators have driven them. Taking this new path, European and other countries will meet complete understanding on the part of all the peace-loving countries.[28]

This implied invitation to disaffected elements of the bourgeoisie in the West to follow a course independent of the United States epitomizes a central strategic conception of the Nineteenth Congress. To check the further development of the Western alliance, now the prime Soviet requirement, the Soviet Union sought to take into its hands the levers by which it could assist in the fragmentation of that alliance. This meant the use of nationalism, the peace issue, neutralism, trade, and other forms of collaboration with elements of the middle class.

### The Significance for Foreign Policy

When due allowance is made for rhetorical and ideological language, what the foreign-policy analysis presented at the Nineteenth Congress comes down to is an essentially defensive strategic outlook in response to the adverse trend in world power developments in the postwar period, combined with an anticipated favorable shift in the balance of power within the coming decade. Since 1946, the militancy by which the Soviet Union sought to consolidate its hold on the territories that came under its control in the course of the war had greatly increased Western military superiority. The United States, far from having withdrawn from Europe as expected, was now deeply involved, militarily and economically, up to the Elbe River and West Berlin. For the present at least, the United States Strategic Air Force, with its stockpile of atomic weapons and its overseas-base system, was *the* decisive strategic weapon. Western military appropriations were continuing to rise astronomically, and the Western alliance was in the process of absorbing the important industrial areas of West Germany and Japan.

At the same time, the Soviet leadership perceived underlying trends in the situation which it believed would reverse the power relationships. Some of its perceptions were based upon an ideologically shaped pattern of thought; others were rooted in a hard assessment of the changes in military technology. It was anticipated that the Western power structure would be weakened by capitalist economic crises, mounting unemployment, sharpened competitive interests among the Western countries, disintegration of the colonial system, and popular sentiment for peace. The decisive factor, however, was seen as the growth of Soviet industrial and military power. Not much was said explicitly at the congress about the concentration of resources on weapon development, but several speakers[29] recalled and confirmed Stalin's February 1946 projection of three postwar five-year plans which would be necessary to strengthen the Soviet Union for "any eventuality." This perspective was implied in Stalin's firm insistence upon the continued priority of heavy industry and his rejection of pressures for a greater proportionate increase in consumer goods. At this point, the Soviet leadership was within sight of the fruition of these policies: the first Soviet hydrogen bomb was to be announced in less than a year, the first Soviet intermediate-range missiles were ready to be tested within two years, and the first Soviet intercontinental missiles and space satellites were only five years away.

The foreign policy stemming from this analysis was neither right nor left in the pure sense of these terms, but a new amalgam which grew out of the experimentation of the preceding period. What made it confusing to many observers, including the French Communist Party, was that it did not seem new. The new strategy made limited use of certain traditional right-wing forms, for purposes which were defensive in an immediate sense but which were intended also to weaken the adversary, in the way that a boxer uses a left jab to gain time, to hold off and harry a temporarily stronger opponent. The immediate defensive requirement of damping down international tensions and reducing the stimulus to Western mobilization and cohesion was met by an acceptance of the policy of peaceful coexistence, which had been intermittently tried in the preceding period. The concept of peaceful coexistence has always had a variety of meanings, both before and after Stalin. In the sense in which it was used at the Nineteenth Congress, it implied no conciliation with the West, no prospect of settlements, no soft words for the Western leaders. On the contrary, the language used against the "imperialist warmongers" was violent in the extreme, attributing to the ruling circles of the United States the intention of seeking to avoid economic crises by precipitating general war and thereby driving for world domination. The Western leaders were, in a frequent Soviet formulation, "following in the footsteps of Hitler." In the face of this comparison, peaceful coexistence could have but a limited application. (It was not until the period immediately following Stalin's death that the Soviet leadership, in its uncertainty regarding Western intentions during the succession crisis, explicitly broadened the formula to imply the possibility of specific settlements with the United States.) At this point the formula implied a limited detente, a surcease of the "harsh external pressures" which had driven on the Western advance, and an offer to the West of temporary stabilization in exchange for formal and practical acceptance of the Communist position in Eastern Europe and China and, if possible, a return to four-power control over Germany.

"Peaceful coexistence" involved political action to bring about changes in the policies of the Western governments and thereby weaken the Western bloc in relation to the Soviet bloc. Thus, the Nineteenth Congress approach clearly rejected any revolutionary policy in the West (there had been no prospect for revolutionary action by the Western proletariat since the end of the war) in favor of power-bloc politics. The directives to the foreign Communist parties called for a broad national line, avoiding for the present any emphasis upon the class struggle or other revolutionary slogans in the interest of soliciting political support among sections of the bourgeoisie, without, however, any intention of seeking alliances with the leaders of the socialist or bourgeois parties. The general trans-class appeal which had in earlier periods been sought by a popular front or other right-wing tactics was now to be the primary function of the Peace Movement, which could carry the "struggle for peace" into the ranks of the bourgeoisie without compromising and diluting the programs of the Communist parties. The general purpose of this quasi-right strategy[30] was to weaken the Western power bloc. Meanwhile, an essentially left emphasis characterized Soviet policy at home and within Eastern Europe, marked by campaigns for ideological tightening, conformity, purges, and shrill vigilance against Western espionage and subversion.

The foreign policy laid down at the congress was no more than a holding action, which might be described as "what to do until the deterrent comes." Whether or not the Soviet leaders believed that the West intended to precipitate a general war, they clearly felt vulnerable[31] and in any case wanted to minimize the political advantages which the West might claim as the fruits of its current military superiority. The center of Soviet attention in this period was turned inward, on the political and economic consolidation of its new empire and on the scientific and industrial foundation for its future power position.

Whether the Russians anticipated that, after the balance of power had been changed in their favor, the Soviet Union would then

return to a policy of direct revolutionary advance can only be conjectured. To the extent that this question was resolved in the minds
of the Soviet leaders, the assumption may have been that Soviet
supremacy would roughly coincide with the economic collapse of
the capitalist countries and the disintegration of the colonial system;
the consequence would be a more or less automatic rise of the
Soviet Union to a position of world dominance. This, however, was
not a matter of discussion, nor did it seem a question of immediate
urgency, at the Nineteenth Party Congress.

It is worth underlining the point that the foundations for the
anticipated shift in world power were laid during the years of
Stalin's leadership. Subsequent developments were to affect the way
in which these policies were applied, but it should not be forgotten
that the change in outlook had its origins during the latter years of
Stalin's rule and that it involved a large degree of responsiveness to
changes in world power relationships. Our understanding of Soviet
foreign policy suffers if we overlook this.

# XI

# THE EVOLUTION OF SOVIET POLICY

T HE assertion that the Soviet leadership changed its outlook in 1949–1952 rests in large measure upon aprioristic reasoning, but it is not without some confirmation from an authoritative Soviet source. A course of study on Soviet foreign policy, prepared in 1957 at the Institute of Advanced Studies of the Communist Party of the Soviet Union, emphasizes a distinction between the strategic character of the period from 1945 to 1949 and the period from 1950 to 1953. Indeed, the head of the Department of International Relations and Soviet Foreign Policy of the institute took strong exception to a "periodization" of Soviet foreign policy which combined the years from the end of the war to 1953, on the grounds that it ignored the significance of the change which had taken place in 1949–1950.[1]

The curriculum of the party's program of study of Soviet foreign policy, not surprisingly, attributed this change to the aggressiveness of its adversaries. It divides the postwar years into three phases; in the first, up to 1949, "the Socialist system was being transformed into a world system." The essential features of this period included:

The radical changes in the international situation as a result of the Second World War. The struggle of the USSR and the People's Democracies for a democratic organization of the post-war world, against the imperialist "negotiation from strength" policy.[2]

The second of the three periods specified in the curriculum lasted from 1950 to 1953 and was characterized by:

The aggravation of international tensions as a result of the aggressive actions of the imperialist states. The struggle of the USSR and other peace-loving peoples against imperialist aggression and for preservation and strengthening of peace.

The third period, from 1953 to 1957 (when the curriculum was prepared), was mainly identified as:

The struggle of the Socialist camp, led by the USSR, and other peace-loving peoples for a *détente,* peaceful coexistence, and the cooperation of states with different systems, for friendship among the peoples.

Thus, although the party curriculum puts the beginning of the current Soviet emphasis upon peaceful coexistence at 1953 (the year in which Stalin died and a new leadership took over — a factor not mentioned in the curriculum), it discerns a significant change in 1949, characterized by defensive Soviet efforts to deal with the rise in international tensions. This view is shared by some other Soviet specialists in international affairs but is by no means unanimous. The publication of these extracts from the party's curriculum occurred in the course of a controversy over "the periodization of the history of Soviet foreign policy" in the pages of the Soviet journal, *International Affairs,* during 1958. The controversy aroused a lively correspondence from readers of the journal.[3] Some readers were even more explicit than the party curriculum in defining 1949 as a major turning point, as can be seen from this proposed "periodization":

1945–1949: Soviet foreign policy in the period of the emergence and strengthening of the world Socialist system;
1949-onwards: the struggle of the Soviet Union to ensure stable and lasting peace in the current period.[4]

A summation of the discussion in authoritative terms by a senior member of the editorial board of the journal emphasizes 1953 as the "important milestone" because of "the tremendous impact of the Soviet peace policy after 1953 and the extension of the Soviet peace effort," but he finds justification for the establishment of a sub-division at the year 1949.[5] However, the development which he emphasizes in using the 1949 date is that the victory of the Chinese Communists in that year "completed the process of Socialism's emergence as a world system."

In a book which grew out of the periodization controversy, the acknowledgment of a qualitative change in the international situation in the last years under Stalin is explicitly accepted: "The years 1950–1953 represent a definite, independent stage in the history of international relations and of the foreign policy of the USSR." [6] In the minds of the authors, the main factor which gives this period its distinctive character is the growth of the Soviet economy, which helped to strengthen the "struggle for peace," to avert the danger of a new war's arising out of the "adventurist plans of the imperialists," and to relax international tensions. [7]

It should be added that the controversy over periodization, apart from the partial confirmation it offers for the argument regarding a change in Soviet strategic outlook in the period preceding the Nineteenth Congress, is also of general significance. The controversy reflects a serious effort by Soviet scholars to recognize and characterize the successive phases of Soviet foreign policy and particularly to grapple with the delicate problem of the interrelation of domestic and external factors in the determination of that policy. [8] This approach to periodization, in contrast to the simplified polemic writings which claimed an unvarying consistency of policy, implies an attempt to analyze the determinants of Soviet policy from one period to the next and, despite differences of terminology and viewpoint, makes it possible to compare Soviet and Western perceptions of the main features of international politics. There is some common ground to be found in the fact that most of the Soviet contributors to the discussion recognize a well-defined separation between the fluid power situation of the immediate postwar years and the later period of provisional stabilization in Europe, beginning around 1949 or 1950. From the point of view of a non-Soviet observer, the character of these periods might be summarized in the following terms.

*1946–1949.* The main character of this period was established by two fundamental conditions. One was the breakdown of the great-power network which had previously defined the boundaries of Soviet control in Europe. The serious weakening of the British and French positions in Central and Eastern Europe and the destruction of German and Eastern European power led to a period of active probing by the Soviet Union to establish the outer periphery of its new sphere of control. The militancy with which this was done in the early Cominform period created the impression in the West that this constituted the revival of a world revolutionary drive. This impression was probably mistaken, for the key to the action now appears to have been the consolidation of Soviet control over territories gained since 1939 and an essentially reactive response to ward off an anticipated effort by the West to recover these territories. To make the point as plainly as possible: the aggressiveness of such actions as the satellization of Eastern Europe, the blockade of Berlin, and the violent actions of the West European Communist parties, while consistent with a long-term commitment to the ultimate dominance of Soviet power, in the immediate context reflected the intention to hold positions gained by the Red Army as far to the West as feasible, against the threat to these positions perceived in the United States' involvement in Western Europe.

This point is closely related to the second fundamental condition: the emergence of the United States as the chief rival to the Soviet Union in a new bipolar power configuration. The rival was so formidable because of its highly developed industrial base, its decisive superiority in nuclear weapons and aircraft delivery system, and its growing interest in Western Europe; it was, further, assumed to be inherently hostile as a consequence of the ingrained Russian interpretation of the dynamics of American society. The result of this perception was Stalin's determination, as expressed in his February 1946 election speech and elsewhere, to drive his nation to build up its heavy industry and to concentrate resources in the research and development of the new military technology. This gearing of Soviet society to maximum effort, in the face of natural tendencies toward relaxation after the war, was at least partly responsible for the repression at home.

*1949–1952.* With the failure of the Berlin blockade, it became clear that a provisional stabilization had been established in Europe and that the aggressive militancy of the first postwar period of Soviet policy had resulted in an interreacting spiral of international tension and a growth of Western military power. The prime need in Soviet policy, therefore, was to check the adverse trend by relaxing international tension and by playing upon Western divergencies. The essential characteristic of the strategy which began to emerge experimentally and unevenly in this period was the elongation of time perspective and the increasing emphasis upon the manipulation of political forces. This meant concerting political and economic means in order to deny the West those non-European areas vital to its economy or strategy and also to turn European industrial countries away from the United States and hopefully toward the Soviet bloc. This quasi-Right strategy was invoked to minimize the disadvantages of an adverse power relationship while the foundations were being laid for a later and more favorable concatenation of forces. Pending the maturing missile and nuclear capabilities then in the research and development stage, and the further consolidation of political and economic conditions within the new Soviet sphere, the Soviet leadership felt obliged to use its foreign policy as a deterrent against general war during the interim period of vulnerability and to weaken the political base of Western power. By restraint in the use of overt acts of provocation after the Korean attack, and by encouraging the development of neutralism, nationalism, the Peace Movement, and anticolonial agitation, Soviet policy was intended to achieve such specific purposes as the weakening of the structure of American strategic airbases abroad (which had been growing rapidly since 1948), as well as such general purposes as undermining the cohesion and momentum of the Western alliance.

## The Distracting Question of Stalin's Sanity

The swirl of complex domestic developments in the months immediately following the Nineteenth Congress has tended to obscure the significance of the evolution in strategic outlook reflected at the congress. Within weeks after the congress, a tense pre-purge atmosphere gripped the country. Ominous political shufflings at the top level of the party, according to Khrushchev's later testimony, created the impression that Stalin was preparing to purge Beria, Voroshilov, Molotov, Mikoyan, and perhaps other members of the old Politburo.[9] The press was filled with campaigns stressing vigilance against the danger of war, espionage, and ideological deviation. Mass recantations by economists and administrators were organized to exorcise any remaining influence of Varga or Voznesensky. The Kiev Case,[10] the Slansky trial, and the Doctors' Plot — directed against bourgeois nationalism, the Jews, Western influence, or the pervasiveness of treason — contributed to the nightmarish anticipations of another Great Purge. The five months from the close of the Nineteenth Congress to the death of Stalin saw tension and fear spreading — party officials, government bureaucrats, doctors, Jews, economists, foreigners, lawyers, philosophers, historians, foreign Communists — one after the other watched the signs and waited for the next blow to strike. These events, whose terrifying brutality has been freshly recalled in Khrushchev's de-Stalinization campaign, have etched deeply the impression of Stalin's pathological behavior, encouraging the view that Soviet foreign policy during this period was no more than the projection of Stalin's paranoia on a wider stage. "Stalin's last years were ones of increasing madness and sterility," writes one historian.[11] "His thoughts on foreign policy tended to the reliving of old situations and to the re-employment of old devices rather than to the recognition of the realities of a new day."

It reflects no desire to salvage Stalin's reputation if one questions whether this assessment adequately characterizes Soviet foreign policy in the latter years of Stalin's life. First of all, even on the domestic side of Stalin's behavior, there is a lingering uncertainty over the extent to which Stalin was paranoid rather than cynical in the employment of grotesque charges against his associates and subordinates.[12] Brutality, savagery, cynicism, irascibility, arbitrariness — all these qualities are evident, but the case for insanity rests upon the testimony of a subordinate, and one who was not a disinterested witness. Moreover, as some Italian Communists have argued, one may question how far "the system" can be absolved of responsibility for Stalinism, whatever may have been the condition of Stalin himself. In any case, however one explains the domestic repressions of this period, there is no necessary inconsistency between a harsh and repressive phase of domestic politics and a foreign policy of qualified retrenchment and maneuver. (This had been the case in the late thirties.) In fact, as it has been argued earlier, the continued emphasis upon heavy industry and the urgent concentration of resources upon science and technology may have been responsible at least in part for the domestic rigors.

Whether Stalin's mind was less disordered than has been pictured, or whether his aberrations were heightened in matters of domestic intrigue, it seems evident that Soviet foreign policy in this period did not lack a "recognition of the realities of a new day." Perhaps "the system" bore the main brunt of policy formation.[13] It is reasonable to suppose that, even in a dictatorial society, much of what is done in the name of a leader is necessarily the product of a bureaucracy, and may imply any degree of responsibility from his active guidance to his inattention. Be that as it may, despite the bizarre domestic developments of this period, despite even the apparent ineffectiveness of Soviet diplomacy, the fact is that the analysis of policies at the Nineteenth Congress, in conjunction with the foundations then being laid for a new relationship of forces in the world, reflected a calculated appreciation of the implications of the new military technology and of its effects upon international politics.

Another factor which has tended to blur the appreciation of this

fundamental change of outlook is that the outward behavior of the
Soviet Union in the period following the Nineteenth Congress appeared ambiguous and inconsistent until after the death of Stalin —
then it displayed greater verve and style. The political line defined
at the congress, which sought something of a relaxation in international tensions while continuing to belch smoke at intervals, did
not have much of an impact. Though some official commentaries
on the congress stressed the "hard" inflection of the peaceful-coexistence line as a form of unremitting struggle,[14] Stalin underlined
the implied invitation to a détente in several interviews with foreigners. In responding to a series of questions submitted by James
Reston of the *New York Times*, Stalin hinted to the newly elected
Eisenhower administration that he would be receptive to a new
effort to bring the fighting in Korea to an end [15] and to the possibility of a personal meeting with the new President to ease world
tensions. Again, in an interview with two Indian diplomats a fortnight before his death, Stalin was quoted as expressing his deep
concern about the consequences of another war for the Soviet Union
and as accepting with equanimity the prospect that each country
would follow its own path of economic and political development.[16]

In the period immediately following Stalin's death, the peaceful-
coexistence line was given a broader and less ambiguous application.
For a time, references to the United States in the Soviet press were
subdued, coincident with an impression of a sharp break with the
past in domestic affairs. Although their peaceful-coexistence line has
experienced some vicissitudes since those halcyon days, the Russians
have continued to apply it with greater subtlety and flexibility than
in the past and have capitalized on its apparent disassociation from
Stalin. After 1957, when Stalin's successors, emboldened by missile
and space achievements, began to claim that the balance of power
was shifting in the Soviet favor, peaceful coexistence began to reveal its offensive potentialities. Against the backdrop of the finally
realized accomplishments of Soviet science, technology, and heavy
industry in developing a modern weapon system and space satellites,

this policy was seen as the means of securing the ascendancy of the Soviet system — moreover, it was argued, it was the only safe means of doing so, given the change in the destructiveness of modern warfare.

The continuing chain explosion of the anticolonial movement also caused an evolution in the application of the political line. Perceiving the possibilities of the newly independent nations as a favorable factor in international politics, the Soviet leaders reshaped their bipolar conception of the world into the image of a troika. The neutral bloc, described as a "zone of peace," was seen as a potential ally of the Soviet bloc in a loose coalition against the West under the broad rubric of "peace and anti-imperialism." The obverse side of this alliance, of course, was the further postponement of a revolutionary program in favor of a prolonged collaboration with the "bourgeois nationalists."

In the circumstances, the greater flexibility of the peaceful-coexistence policy — with its creation of tension and the easement of tension, its adaptation to the political uses of the underdeveloped areas, and its promise of a peaceful victory under the protection of a favorable relationship of forces in the world — represented not so much a departure from the policies of the late Stalin era as the fruition of those policies. Although it is doubtful that Stalin would have been capable of administering the later policy with equal deftness and flexibility, it is clear that what evolved in the late fifties was the harvest, for better or for worse, of the insistence in the Stalin period on the fundamental importance of concentrating resources on the development of economic and military power.

### Steps in a Process of Adaptation

One needs only to back away a few paces from the details of the changes we have been examining to become aware that the pattern of these events includes more than certain recurrent features. There have also been some secular changes, in the sense in which economists use the adjective — that is, changes representing long-term

evolutionary modifications in the character of the Communist movement. The separate elements of what I have here called the quasi-
Right strategy — the use of détente, of divisive action, nationalism,
the peace sentiment, and anti-imperialism, an indirect policy of
maneuver to strengthen the Soviet bloc and weaken the Western
bloc, in place of a direct advance toward social revolution — have
all appeared before as tactical expedients, but the emergence of this
combination in the late Stalin period, and its further development
in the post-Stalin period, reflects a qualitative change in the direction
of Soviet policy. In this fundamental sense, the changes which have
been attacked as "revisionism" and defended as "creative Marxism"
represent a process of adaptation of the Communist movement to
the great transformations in the character of international politics
since the Second World War.

The reality to which the Communists have been obliged to adapt
has been shaped not by the revolution of Marx and Lenin, but by
the revolutions of military and nonmilitary technology and of nationalism. In the advanced industrial societies of the West, it has
been increasingly difficult to maintain the Marxist theory of the
pauperization of the working class. The expectation that the proletariat of the industrialized countries would provide the dynamic
source of revolutionary energy has been a source of repeated disappointment. Instead, the continuing modernization of Western
societies has transformed the attitudes and conditions of life of the
wage earners, evoking not only a new sense of participation in
society but even an outright embourgeoisement. In describing the
difficulty of the French Communists in dealing with the political
and social effects of modernization, a French scholar writes: "Yester-
day's proletariat living on the edge of society was replaced by a
progressively Americanized class of wage-earners, integrated into
and transforming social life." [17]

One consequence of this development can be seen in the movement of European Social Democratic parties toward non-Marxist
ameliorative programs, which has its counterpart in the essentially

conservative trend to be observed within the Communist parties of both Italy and France in recent years. A relevant occurrence may be the current efforts of Soviet economists to redefine their ideological "theses" on capitalism, in the face of the economic growth and integration in Western Europe.[18] Despite such continuing problems as recessions and unemployment, the adaptive capacity of capitalist economies has made it increasingly difficult for Soviet analysts to place their reliance upon competitive conflicts within the Western camp.

Another consequence, which was more readily perceived by Stalin, is the knowledge that no Communist Party can be expected to come to power through the ripening revolutionary temper of its own working class. It can hope to prevail only through the intervention of the Red Army. This lesson was, of course, reinforced by the experience of the states of Eastern Europe, as Stalin bluntly reminded Tito in the correspondence preceding their break.

A further consequence of the new adaptation to reality concerns the necessity of collaborating with, rather than fighting, the bourgeoisie, or at least large segments of it. When the Communist parties are directed to put aside for the time being the objective of attaining power and to strive instead to influence the orientation of their governments in accordance with the requirements of Soviet foreign policy, they are obliged in one way or another to come to terms with the bourgeois parties. Even in Italy and France, where the Communist parties still command a large popular vote and have a strong position in the trade unions, it has been possible for the Communists to be politically effective only to the extent that they could overcome their political isolation and enter into coalitions with non-working-class parties.

This adjustment has required in turn a muting of the class struggle, the distinctive and critical element of the Communist ideology which has enabled it to claim a link with the traditional militant working-class movement and which has set it off from the "reformist" Marxist parties. How long a foreign Communist Party can maintain the élan of its cadres under this inhibition is a question that has been raised repeatedly by restive militants. A related question which has arisen in the polemic exchanges with the Chinese Communists is whether the acceptance by the Soviet leadership of the postponement of revolutionary expectations in the capitalist countries may not contribute to the devitalization of both the ideology and the Communist movement itself. Soviet ideologists have sought a dialectical resolution to this dilemma, by arguing that the class struggle is carried forward on a higher plane in conditions of peaceful coexistence. A recent major reassessment of "the laws governing modern international life" declares:

The course and outcome of the class struggle in any country have never been so dependent on the general correlation of class forces and the state of international relations as in our epoch . . . In conditions of coexistence and competition between the two systems, the ruling classes in the imperialist countries are forced to make concessions and carry out reforms where in the past they resorted to arms.[19]

The content of peaceful coexistence has continued to evolve, this authoritative Soviet work acknowledges, and in the present period it is no longer to be regarded as a purely defensive policy: "Peaceful coexistence not only does not preclude, but, on the contrary, presupposes revolutionary changes in society, accelerates the revolutionary process, and intensifies the decline and collapse of imperialism." However the Soviet ideologists, under pressure from the Chinese champions of orthodoxy, are obliged to redefine revolutionary changes and the class struggle, it is apparent that these words no longer mean what they did in the Soviet usage, primarily as a result of the fact that social changes in the advanced industrial societies of the West have rendered the conceptions of orthodox Marxism more and more irrelevant.

Another development which has also required profound adaptations in Soviet practice has been the unexpected strength of nationalism in the contemporary period. The most dramatic expression of nationalist sentiment has been seen in the underdeveloped areas, but the continued potency of this force in the advanced industrial nations has also been an important political factor. The Communists have been rediscovering what the Second International learned to its sorrow at the outset of World War I, that the allegiances of the working class are still primarily vertical and not horizontal — that the *Marseillaise* still stirs more pulses than the *Internationale*. As we have seen, the experience of the Thorez declaration of support for the Red Army in February 1949, which marked the furthest development of the antinational position of the world Communist movement, quickly taught the Communists that nationalism was still a major political force in Europe. Soviet policy was quick to adapt to this realization. Within a few months, the Communists had returned to the slogan of "national independence" and were seeking a "government of democratic national union." Within two years, the "united national front" had become the watchword. Within three years, Stalin had exhorted the foreign Communists to lift high "the banner of national independence and national sovereignty . . . if you wish to be patriots of your country, if you wish to become the leading force of the nation."

Thus, at a time when the United States was committed to a supranational policy for Europe — the economic integration of Europe as one of the objectives of the European Recovery Program, the European Defense Community as a means of adding the military contribution of West Germany to the Western alliance — the Soviet Union was hitching its policy in Western Europe to the dynamics of nationalism. In placing national independence first in its propaganda, the Soviet Union was endeavoring to use the force of nationalism in Western Europe as an anticoagulant against "the pseudo-theories of cosmopolitanism, of national nihilism, which are the ideological weapons of the USA in its struggle for world domination." [20] This has continued to be the line of attack against the integration of Western Europe in the late fifties, although Soviet theorists have now begun to respond by modifying their conceptions of capitalism as well as their view of nationalism in advanced societies.[21]

Of course, the same nationalism when expressed within the Communist sphere — in the Ukraine, in Yugoslavia, or elsewhere in Eastern Europe, and even in the ranks of the Western European Communist parties — represented a mortal danger and was excoriated as bourgeois nationalism, national deviationism, or homeless cosmopolitanism. This was, however, only one of several contradictions in the use of nationalist motivation by the Communists, and it required dialectical dexterity. The distinction between proletarian internationalism — which meant loyalty to the Soviet Union — and national independence — which meant independence from the United States — was one which required clarification at intervals. The simultaneous encouragement by the Communists of French nationalist resistance to a new Wehrmacht and of German nationalist support for German reunification, and (after March 1952) a German army, created certain operational difficulties. Similarly, Communist appeals to nationalist sentiments in the metropolitan powers tended to offset Communist support of nationalist movements in colonial territories and Communist use of the slogan of "revolutionary defeatism" and exhortations to mutiny among the troops of the colonial powers. Despite such difficulties, and the awkwardness created by the gathering of unaccustomed allies under the banner of national independence, the power of national feelings undoubtedly strengthened whatever cause could identify itself with it, as was to be shown in the defeat of the European Defense Community in 1954.

Although the explosion of nationalism in the underdeveloped world was not unforeseen in Soviet thinking, the forms through which this force has expressed itself have not corresponded to Soviet anticipations. The Russians have been obliged to reckon with what has been in effect a temporary stabilization of the anticolonial movements at the nationalist stage of development. Far from showing any readiness to follow the Soviet model of social transformation, the new nations have shown a disposition toward forms of socialism which bear little resemblance to the Soviet use of the word; there has been no evidence of internal social or political forces to match the power of raw nationalism. This fact, when taken together with the priority in Soviet foreign policy for weakening the Western bloc by denying it markets, sources of raw materials, and military bases in the underdeveloped areas, has resulted in an extended period of collaboration with the "national bourgeoisie," at the expense of support for social and political revolution in these countries. Although the full awareness of the useful potentialities of a neutral bloc did not develop until 1954–1955, when the zone-of-peace conception began to take shape as a third pole in the world power configuration, the process of adaptation centered on the previously developed "struggle for peace." The twin issues of peace and anti-imperialism were developed as the principal instruments in the effort to organize the new nations into an auxiliary bloc in international politics. The significant point is that here, too, the process of adaptation has led the Soviet Union toward a prolongation of a power-bloc policy and a further postponement of a policy of revolutionary social transformation.

It is apparent that the enormous developments in the technology of communications and transportation have been essential in giving the Soviet Union the physical means of operating with ease on a world-wide scale. The Soviet presence in distant continents, the instantaneous coordination of political action in the remote reaches of the Communist apparatus, the by-passing of previous geographical barriers to military, economic, or political operations, all have contributed not only to changing the instrumentalities of international politics, but also to qualifying the basic conceptions of national power and the international system. Perhaps the most profound effects in this direction, however, were those resulting from the changes in military technology.

The single-minded concentration of scientific and technological resources on the development of a modern weapon capability was, as we have seen, the dominant characteristic of the late Stalin period. Although its first intention may have been to overcome an acutely felt vulnerability and to attain a dominant power position, the military emphasis had unforeseen effects upon the very nature of international politics. The growing awareness of these implications has been recorded in the successive modifications of the doctrine of the inevitability of war and in the insistent long-term prolongation of the policy of peaceful coexistence — now treated as a vital and indefinite necessity. The mounting inhibition against the actual employment of nuclear weapons did not, however, make their possession irrelevant or lead to thoughts of stabilizing the military aspect of the confrontation with the West; if anything, this inhibition has had the effect of heightening the Soviet consciousness of the political effect of the military balance. What impelled the Soviet Union to concentrate all efforts on weapons and space achievements — and what appeared to determine its priorities within these fields — was the conviction that the relationship of forces was the crucial backdrop of political and diplomatic action. (As early as 1945 or 1946, according to an unconfirmed report, Stalin is said to have expressed to his technical staffs working on the intercontinental ballistic missile the belief that its development would give him decisive leverage against Truman at the conference table.[22]) Despite a conservative approach toward the hazards of a general nuclear war, the Soviet leadership has made clear its belief that superior weight in the balance of power represents the ultimate sanction in international politics which can produce political gains in specific local situations. In this way, the Russians anticipate that military capabilities can be translated into political advances without general war.

This tendency, which is consistent with the Soviet propensity to project capabilities in all fields — economic growth, space achievements, cultural developments, and so on — onto a plane of political effect, serves to reinforce the priority of Soviet policy upon power-bloc politics, as against the ever more distant goal of revolution.

The elongation of what began as an expedient effort to manipulate political forces in order to weaken the Western bloc has sometimes been described as the ascendancy of a balance-of-power policy on the part of the Soviet Union. It is not, strictly speaking, a *balance-of-power* policy, since it is not directed toward an equilibrium in the international system. Despite the significant ideological modifications concerning the nature of capitalism and the requirements of the present period, there remains an essential element in Soviet anticipations that is profoundly hostile to international stability. In the course of adapting itself to fundamental changes in world politics, the Soviet conception of revolution has changed greatly: not only has it receded in time, but it has evolved from a specific action program into an interacting process involving complex historical forces. To put the matter in another way, the mode by which peaceful coexistence is intended to achieve the ultimate purposes of the Revolution is through the conjuncture of a number of factors: an acceptance of Soviet military ascendancy, a demonstrated superiority of the Soviet economic system as a mode of organizing human and material resources, the detachment of the underdeveloped areas from the Western bloc, the inadequacies of the capitalist economic and social systems. The end result would be the voluntary and peaceable acceptance of a new political unity in the world under Soviet leadership. Only when this has been achieved can the Soviet system regard its security as assured, given the character of modern weapons and its fundamental assumptions about the nature of non-Soviet societies. In these circumstances, stabilization in the international system seems remote, but, if events persuade the next generation of Soviet leaders that history offers more variety than their predecessors anticipated, one basic source of conflict may be diminished.

BIBLIOGRAPHY
NOTES
INDEX

# BIBLIOGRAPHY

Since this book deals with events of the past decade and a half, for sources of information it has relied chiefly upon Communist and non-Communist newspapers, magazines, and pamphlets, as well as yearbooks and interviews.

For the Soviet outlook in this period, *Pravda*, the daily newspaper published by the Communist Party, and *Izvestiya*, the daily newspaper published by the government, are of course the standard sources. Particularly helpful for the Soviet official view of developments in Eastern and Western Europe in this period is the newspaper of the Communist Information Bureau, *For a Lasting Peace, For a People's Democracy!* (referred to by the short title, *Cominform Bulletin*), first issued in Belgrade on November 1, 1947, and transferred to Bucharest after the Tito-Cominform break in 1948. Published fortnightly and later weekly in a varying number of foreign languages, including English, the newspaper remained under Soviet editorial direction until its suspension in April 1956.

Basic background data on developments in the non-Communist world and texts of speeches and diplomatic notes were derived from the *New York Times* for the period 1947–1952, and from the following yearbooks: *L'Année politique, 1949–1952*, edited by André Siegfried and others (Paris, Éditions du Grand Siècle, 1950–1953); Royal Institute of International Affairs, *Survey of International Affairs, 1947–1948, 1949–1950, 1951*, and *1952*, edited by Peter Calvocoressi and others, and the corresponding volumes, *Documents on International Affairs*, both series published in London by Oxford University Press between the years 1952 and 1955; and Council of Foreign Relations, *The United States in World Affairs, 1947–1948, 1948–1949*, edited by John C. Campbell, and *1949, 1950, 1951*, and *1952*, edited by Richard P. Stebbins (New York: Harper and Brothers, 1948–1953).

On developments within the French Communist Party for the period 1947–1952, three publications of the Central Committee of the party were worthy of detailed consultation: *L'Humanité*, a daily newspaper (on Sunday it is issued as *L'Humanité dimanche*) in which are to be found the current party preoccupations as well as directives and exhortations addressed to the rank-and-file members by the leadership; *France nouvelle,* a weekly newspaper for the guidance of local party leaders; and *Cahiers du communisme,* a monthly review which deals with theoretical and political problems and through which is made available to the party cadres texts of resolutions, speeches, and other documents clarifying the position of the Politburo or the Central Committee.

Among the other periodicals consulted for specific points as indicated in the notes were the following: *Bolshevik, Le Figaro, Literaturnaya gazeta, Le Monde, Novoe vremya, Planovoe khozyaistvo, Le Populaire, Trud, Voprosy ekonomiki,* and *Voprosy istorii.*

Interviews with more than forty-five persons in France during the summer of 1954 were invaluable in obtaining information not available in printed sources and in suggesting insights into the complex relationships involved. Among the persons interviewed were Raymond Aron, Marcel Baufrère, Père Henri Chambre, Michel Collinet, Jean-Marie Domenach, François Goguel, Georges Lassère, Guy Lemmonier, Daniel Mayer, Pierre Naville, A. Rossi, Jean Rous, and several members of the French Communist Party and the Peace Movement who prefer not to be identified. Two former officials of the French party, Pierre Hervé and Auguste Lecoeur, were interviewed in 1959.

Other works cited or consulted include the following:

Acheson, Dean G., press conference, October 25, 1950, United States Department of State Bulletin, November 6, 1950.

—— *Sketches from Life of Men I Have Known* (New York: Harper, 1961).

Airapetyan, Mikhail E. and Grigori A. Deborin, *Etapi vneshnei politiki SSSR* (Stages in the Foreign Policy of the USSR; Moscow, 1961).

*The Anti-Stalin Campaign and International Communism,* Russian Institute, ed. (New York: Columbia University Press, 1956).

Armstrong, Hamilton Fish, *Tito and Goliath* (New York: Macmillan, 1951).

Beloff, Max, *The Foreign Policy of Soviet Russia,* I (London: Oxford, 1947).

Bergson, Abram, James H. Blackman, and Alexander Erlich, "Postwar Economic Reconstruction and Development in the U.S.S.R.," *Annals of the American Academy of Political and Social Science,* special issue: "The Soviet Union Since World War II," CCLXIII (May 1949), 52–72.

Boffa, Guiseppe, *Inside the Khrushchev Era* (New York: Marzani and Munsell, 1959).

Borkenau, Franz, *European Communism* (London: Faber, 1953).

Brayance, Alain, *Anatomie du parti communiste français* (Paris: Denoel, 1952).

Brzezinski, Zbigniew, "The Pattern of Political Purges," *Annals of the American Academy of Political and Social Science,* special issue: "The Satellites in Eastern Europe" CCCXVII (May 1958), 79–87.

———— *The Soviet Bloc, Unity and Conflict* (Cambridge: Harvard University Press, 1960).

Casanova, Laurent, *Le Parti communiste, les intellectuels et la nation* (Paris: Éditions Sociales, 1948; 2nd ed., 1950).

Chambre, Père Henri, "Le P.C.F. durant les six premiers mois de 1949," *Travaux de l'action populaire* (Paris: Éditions Spes, September-October 1949), pp. 612–614. Also, "Le P.C.F. depuis la libération," in the same journal for December 1948, p. 745.

Conquest, Robert, *Power and Policy in the USSR* (New York: St. Martin's Press, 1961).

*Current Digest of the Soviet Press,* published weekly by the Joint Committee on Slavic Studies, containing translations of selected articles in the Soviet press, in full or in condensed form. Began in 1949.

Davison, W. Phillips, *The Berlin Blockade* (Princeton: Princeton University Press, 1958).

Dedijer, Vladimir, *Tito* (New York: Simon and Schuster, 1953).

Degras, Jane, ed., *The Communist International, 1919–1943, Documents, Vol. I (1919–1922)* (London: Oxford University Press for Royal Institute of International Affairs, 1956), pp. 323–326.

———— *Soviet Documents on Foreign Policy, Vol. I, 1917–1924* (London: Royal Institute of International Affairs, 1951).

Dinerstein, Herbert S., *War and the Soviet Union* (New York: Praeger, 1959).

Djilas, Milovan, *Conversations with Stalin* (New York: Harcourt, Brace and World, 1962).

Domenach, Jean-Marie, "The French Communist Party," in Mario Einaudi, ed., *Communism in Western Europe* (Ithaca: Cornell University Press, 1951).

—— "Tillon-Marty et le 'Front National Uni,'" *Esprit*, November 1952, pp. 731–734.

Duclos, Jacques, *Écrits de la Prison* (Paris: Éditions Sociales, 1952).

—— Notebook in *Journal officiel*, no. 4415, October 21, 1952, supplement; *La signification politique du cahier de Jacques Duclos* (Paris, July 1952).

Duverger, Maurice, *Les Partis politiques* (Paris: Colin, 1951).

Ehrmann, Henry W., "The French Peasant and Communism," *American Political Science Review*, XXVI (March 1952), 19–43.

*Est & Ouest*, no. 168, "Le Communisme européen depuis la morte de Staline," February 16–28, 1957 (Paris: Associations d'Études et d'Information Politiques Internationales).

Fainsod, Merle, "Postwar Role of the Communist Party," *Annals of the American Academy of Political and Social Science*, special issue: "The Soviet Union Since World War II," CCLXIII (May 1949), 20–32.

—— *How Russia Is Ruled* (Cambridge, Harvard University Press, 1953; rev. ed., 1963).

Farge, Yves, "Report on the Bacteriological War, the War in Korea and Their International Consequences," at the Extraordinary Session of the World Council of Peace, Berlin, July 3, 1952 (Brochure, no date, no identification of publisher).

Fauvet, Jacques, *Les Forces politiques en France*, 2nd ed. (Paris: Editions Le Monde, 1951).

Feis, Herbert, *Churchill, Roosevelt, Stalin* (Princeton: Princeton University Press, 1957).

F[itzgerald], C. P., "The Chinese Revolution," *The World Today*, VI (London: Royal Institute of International Affairs, June 1950).

Garthoff, Raymond L., *Soviet Strategy in the Nuclear Age* (New York: Praeger, 1958).

George, Alexander L., "American Policy-Making and the North Korean Aggression," *World Politics*, VII (January 1955), 209–232.

Goguel, François, *France Under the Fourth Republic* (Ithaca: Cornell University Press, 1952).

—— *Géographie de Élections Françaises, de 1870 à 1951*, no. 27 in *Cahiers de la Fondation Nationale des Sciences Politiques* (Paris: Colin, 1951), pp. 116–117.

—— "Le Parti communiste français," in *Encyclopédie Politique de la France et du Monde*, I, 2nd ed. (Paris: 1950).

Goodrich, Leland M., *Korea: A Study of U. S. Policy in the United Nations* (New York: Council on Foreign Relations, 1956).

Gruliow, Leo, ed., *Current Soviet Policies: The Documentary Record of the Nineteenth Party Congress and the Reorganization after Stalin's Death* (New York: Praeger, 1953).

Guerard, Albert, "The French Bourgeoisie and Communism," *The Yale Review*, XXVII (March 1938), 557–567.

Herriot, Eduard, "France Looks Ahead," *Foreign Affairs*, XXVII (April 1949), 403–412.

Hervé, Pierre, *La Révolution et les Fétiches* (Paris: Table Ronde, 1956).

——— *Lettre à Sartre* (Paris: Table Ronde, 1956).

H.G.L., "The European Defense Community," *The World Today*, VIII (June 1952), 236–248.

Hsieh, Alice Langley, "The Strategy and Tactics of Communist China's Foreign Policy towards Japan" (MS), September 1956, RAND Corporation, Santa Monica, California.

Institut National de la Statistique et des Études Économiques, *Études et Conjoncture: Économie Française*, VI (May-June 1951).

Ivashin, I. V., "The Periodization of the History of Soviet Foreign Policy," *International Affairs* (Moscow), no. 7 (July 1958), pp. 59–63.

Joy, C. Turner, *How Communists Negotiate* (New York: Macmillan, 1955).

Kautsky, John, *Moscow and the Communist Party of India* (New York: Technology Press of Massachusetts Institute of Technology and John Wiley, 1956).

Kennan, George F., *Russia and the West under Lenin and Stalin* (Boston: Atlantic, Little, Brown, 1961).

Kershaw, Joseph A., "Recent Trends in the Soviet Economy," *Annals of the American Academy of Social and Political Science*, special issue: "Russia Since Stalin, Old Trends and New Problems," CCCIII (January 1956), 37–49.

Kramish, Arnold, *Atomic Energy in the Soviet Union* (Stanford: Stanford University Press, 1959).

Labedz, Leopold, ed., *Revisionism: Essays on the History of Marxist Ideas* (London: Allen and Unwin, 1962).

Lecoeur, Auguste, *L'Autocritique attendue* (St. Cloud: Éditions Girault, 1955).

Lee, Asher, *The Soviet Air Force* (New York: John Day, 1962).

Lenin, V. I., speech to a meeting of Moscow Communist Party secretaries, November 27, 1920, in Jane Degras, ed., *Soviet Documents on Foreign Policy*, I (London, 1951), 221–224.

Leonhard, Wolfgang, *Child of the Revolution*, trans. C. M. Woodhouse [originally published as *Die Revolution Entlasst Ihre Kinder*] (Chicago: Henry Regnery, 1958).

———— *The Kremlin since Stalin,* trans. Elizabeth Wiskemann and Marian Jackson [originally published as *Kreml Ohne Stalin*] (New York: Praeger, 1962).

Lorwin, Val R., *The French Labor Movement* (Cambridge: Harvard University Press, 1954).

*Lumière et vie,* XXVIII (July 1956): "Où en est le communisme français."

Marcus, John T., *Neutralism and Nationalism in France* (New York: Bookman Associates, 1958).

Marshall, George C., Report to the American People on Fifth Meeting of Council of Foreign Ministers, United States Department of State, *Bulletin,* XVII (December 28, 1947), 1247.

Martinet, Gilles, articles on French Communist Party in *L'Observateur,* June 12, 1952, June 26, 1952.

Marty, André, *L'Affaire Marty* (Paris: Deux-Rives, 1955).

Matthews, Ronald, *The Death of the Fourth Republic* (New York: Praeger, 1954).

Micaud, Charles, "Organization and Leadership of the French Communist Party," *World Politics,* IV (April 1952), 318–355.

Millis, Walter, ed., *The Forrestal Diaries* (New York: Viking, 1951).

Mosely, Philip E., "The Kremlin's Foreign Policy Since Stalin," *Foreign Affairs,* XXXII (October 1953), pp. 20–33.

———— "The Nineteenth Party Congress," *Foreign Affairs,* XXXI (January 1953), 238–256.

———— "Soviet Policy in the Two-World Conflict," *Journal of International Affairs,* VIII (1954), 107–113.

Nagy, Imre, *On Communism* (New York: Praeger, 1957).

*Nationalism: Report by a Study Group of Members of the Royal Institute of International Affairs* (London: Oxford University Press, 1939).

Nikolić, Mirko, "Defeat of the Cominform Policy in France," *Medjunarodni Problemi* (Belgrade), January-March 1953.

Nove, Alec, "Recent Developments in Economic Ideas," *Survey,* no. 21–22 (November-December 1957), pp. 19–26.

Ostrovitianov, K. V., D. T. Shepilov, and others, *Politicheskaya ekonomiya, Uchebnik* (Political Economy, A Textbook; Moscow, 1954).

Pickles, Dorothy M., "France's Prospects for 1950," *The World Today,* VI (February 1950), 55–63.

—————— *French Politics* (London: Royal Institute of International Affairs, 1953).

Pokrovsky, G. I., *Science and Technology in Contemporary War,* trans. Raymond L. Garthoff (New York: Praeger, 1959).

"Polycentrism," special issue of *Survey,* no. 42, June 1962.

Reale, Eugenio, *Avec Jacques Duclos au banc des accusés: À la réunion constitutive du kominform à Szklarska Poreba (22–27 Septembre 1947),* trans. Pierre Bonuzzi (Paris: Librairie Plon, 1958).

Reitzel, William, Morton A. Kaplan, and Constance G. Coblenz, *United States Foreign Policy, 1945–1955* (Washington: Brookings Institution, 1956).

Rieber, Alfred J., *Stalin and the French Communist Party, 1941–1947* (New York: Columbia University Press, 1962).

Roche, Emile, "The Retreat of the Communists in France," *L'Information* (Paris: February 27, 1951).

"Russia and Germany," special issue of *Survey,* no. 44–45, October 1962.

Salisbury, Harrison E., *Moscow Journal* (Chicago: University of Chicago Press, 1961).

Schapiro, Leonard, *The Communist Party of the Soviet Union* (New York: Random House, 1960).

Schilling, Warner, "The H-Bomb Decision — How to Decide Without Actually Choosing," *Political Science Quarterly,* LXXVI (March 1961).

Shulman, Marshall D., "Changing Appreciation of the Soviet Problem," *World Politics,* X (July 1958), 499–511.

*Sondages: Revue française de l'opinion publique,* XIV (1952): "Le Parti communiste français et ses électeurs."

Stalin, Joseph V., *Economic Problems of Socialism in the U.S.S.R.* (New York: International Publishers, 1952).

—————— Report to the Tenth Congress of the Russian Communist Party (Bolshevik) on the Immediate Tasks of the Party in the National Question, March 10, 1921, *Sochineniya* (Works), V (Moscow: Foreign Languages Publishing House, 1953), 41–42.

Taurer, Bernard, "Stalin's Last Thesis," *Foreign Affairs,* XXXI (April 1953), 365–381.

Taylor, O. R., *The Fourth Republic of France: Constitution and Political Parties* (London: Royal Institute of International Affairs, 1951).

Thomson, David, *Democracy in France,* 2nd ed. (London: Oxford University Press, 1952).

Truman, Harry S., Text of Order to Armed Forces of the United States on the Fighting in Korea, June 27, 1950, United States Department of State, *Bulletin,* July 3, 1950, p. 5.

United Nations, Department of Economic Affairs, *World Economic Report, 1949–1950* (E/1910/Rev. 1, ST/ECA/9, March 16, 1951; New York, 1951), pp. 5, 13–20.

——— Economic Commission for Europe, Research and Planning Division, *Economic Survey of Europe in 1948* (E/ECE/91, Rev. 1, May 12, 1949; Geneva), p. 211.

United States Department of State, *Moscow's European Satellites,* Publication No. 5914 (Washington: Government Printing Office, 1954).

Varga, Eugene S., *Izmeneniya v ekonomike kapitalizma v itoge vtoroi mirovoi voiny* (Changes in the Economy of Capitalism Resulting from the Second World War; Moscow, 1946).

Vatcher, William H., Jr., *Panmunjom: The Story of the Korean Military Armistice Negotiations* (New York: Praeger, 1958).

Voznesensky, Nikolai, *The War Economy of the U.S.S.R. During the Patriotic War* (Moscow, 1948).

Walter, Gerard, *Histoire du parti communiste français* (Paris: Somogy, 1948), pp. 77–123.

Whiting, Allen S., *China Crosses the Yalu: The Decision to Enter the Korean War* (New York: Macmillan, 1960).

Williams, Philip, *Politics in Post-War France* (London: Longmans Green, 1954).

Wright, Gordon, *The Reshaping of French Democracy* (New York: Reynal and Hitchcock, 1948).

# NOTES

## I. INTRODUCTION TO THE ARGUMENT

1. That some form of alternation may not be a singular characteristic of the Russians is suggested by Frank L. Klingberg in "The Historical Alternations of Moods in American Foreign Policy," *World Politics*, IV (January 1952), 237–273. See also Arthur M. Schlesinger, "Tides of American Politics," *Yale Review*, XXIX (December 1939), 217–230.

2. I am especially indebted to Paul Kecskemeti for his help with the discussion in this paragraph.

3. Alfred J. Rieber, *Stalin and the French Communist Party, 1941–1947* (New York, 1962).

## II. THE VIEW FROM MOSCOW IN THE SPRING OF 1949

1. Speech at Massachusetts Institute of Technology, Cambridge, Mass., March 31, 1949. *New York Times,* April 1, 1949, p. 10.

2. Election speech by J. V. Stalin, February 9, 1946, *Pravda,* February 10, 1946, pp. 1–2. Andrei Zhdanov, speech on the twenty-ninth anniversary of the revolution, *Pravda,* November 7, 1946, and in *Bolshevik,* no. 21 (November 1946), pp. 1–13.

3. For example, at Churchill's discussion with Stalin in Moscow on October 9, 1944, of the respective interests of the Soviet Union and the West in the Balkans, expressed in percentages. Winston S. Churchill, *The Second World War,* VI: *Triumph and Tragedy* (Boston, 1953), pp. 227–228. Djilas quotes Stalin as saying in April 1945: "This war is not as in the past; whoever occupies a territory also imposes on it his own social system. Everyone imposes his own system as far as his army can reach. It cannot be otherwise." Milovan Djilas, *Conversations with Stalin,* trans. Michael B. Petrovich (New York, 1962), p. 114.

4. In the case of the Greek civil war, it appears probable in retrospect that this venture owed its support mainly to the Yugoslavs in spite of Stalin's opposition, which seems to have been based on the understanding that the West had claimed a dominant influence in Greece (see previous note) and would not allow its lifeline to the eastern Mediterranean to be broken. Djilas, p. 182.

5. That the published records of this meeting were carefully edited to conceal its real purposes is disclosed by the published notes of an Italian par-

ticipant, who left the Party in 1956 — Eugenio Reale, *Avec Jacques Duclos au banc des accusés,* trans. Pierre Bonuzzi (Paris, 1958), p. 18. The Cominform established a newspaper, entitled *For a Lasting Peace, For a People's Democracy!* (cited hereafter as *Cominform Bulletin*). Reale says that he protested the ungainly title, but was told by Zhdanov that it had been chosen by Stalin and telephoned to the meeting (p. 48). Djilas confirms this and adds that Stalin thought the Western press would have to repeat the slogan whenever it quoted from the newspaper (p. 129).

6. Maurice Thorez, in an interview with *The Times* of London, November 18, 1946, reprinted in *Cahiers du communisme,* November 1946, pp. 1014–1016, declared: "The progress of democracy around the world, in spite of rare exceptions which prove the rule, makes it possible to visualize the march toward socialism by other paths than those followed by the Russian Communists. In any case, the path is necessarily different for each country . . . The French Workers' Party that we propose to constitute by fusing the Communists and the Socialists would be the guide to our new and popular democracy."

7. Rieber, *Stalin and the French Communist Party,* p. 124.

8. Stalin is quoted by Djilas as saying to Tito in April 1945: "Today socialism is possible even under the English monarchy. Revolution is no longer necessary everywhere" (p. 113).

9. Although Reale quotes Edvard Kardelj as saying, several years later, that Zhdanov and Malenkov had assigned and helped prepare the principal roles at the conference (p. 34), Djilas indicates that the line he expressed genuinely represented his criticism of the French Communists (p. 127). At that time, the Yugoslavs, flushed with the success of their revolution, were even more militant than the Russians in their international orientation. Gomulka, who had not been enthusiastic about the establishment of the Cominform, was given the assignment of reproaching the French and Italian Communists for not having seized power after the war. This corresponds to the position taken by the militant wing of the French Communist Party headed by André Marty and was apparently shared by Zhdanov, implying a criticism of the previous policy of the Soviet leadership.

10. Val R. Lorwin, *The French Labor Movement* (Cambridge, Mass., 1954), pp. 120–130.

11. *Cahiers du communisme,* October 1948, pp. 1173–1174.

12. United Nations, Economic Commission for Europe, Research and Planning Division, *Economic Survey of Europe in 1948* (Geneva, 1949), p. 211.

13. For example, a telegram from General Lucius D. Clay to Army Intelligence, March 5, 1948, speaks of "a feeling that [war] may come with dramatic suddenness." Walter Millis, ed., *The Forrestal Diaries* (New York, 1951), p. 387.

14. Djilas, p. 153.

15. For example, Evelyn Anderson, "East Germany," *Survey,* no. 42 (June 1962), pp. 96–97; Walter Laqueur, "Thoughts at the Wall," *Encounter,* XIX (August 1962), 63–67; *Survey,* issue on "Russia and Germany," no. 44–45 (October 1962).

16. Stalin's concern about American power and Soviet vulnerability is implied in the following quotation attributed to him by Djilas, in the course of a reproach to the Yugoslavs in February 1948 concerning the Greek civil war: "What do you think, that Great Britain and the United States — the United States, the most powerful state in the world — will permit you to break their line of communication in the Mediterranean Sea! Nonsense. And we have no navy. The uprising in Greece must be stopped, and as quickly as possible" (p. 182). On an earlier occasion, Djilas reports Molotov as cautioning the Yugoslavs against shooting down any more American aircraft (p. 131).

17. "On July 24 I casually mentioned to Stalin that we had a new weapon of unusual destructive force. The Russian Premier showed no special interest. All he said was that he was glad to hear it and hoped we would make 'good use of it against the Japanese.'" Harry S. Truman, *Memoirs,* I: *Years of Decisions* (Garden City, 1955), p. 416.

18. For example, Stalin's interview with Alexander Werth, in *Pravda,* September 25, 1946.

19. Raymond L. Garthoff, *Soviet Strategy in the Nuclear Age* (New York, 1958), p. 64.

20. Djilas, p. 153.

21. Arnold Kramish, *Atomic Energy in the Soviet Union* (Stanford, 1959), p. 114.

22. It is striking to observe that in the four industrial categories specifically mentioned by Stalin, Soviet figures for 1961 show that his 1946 projections were fulfilled and, in the case of oil, almost trebled.

|  | Stalin's projections for 1961 | 1961 actual fulfillment |
| --- | --- | --- |
| Pig iron | 50 mill. tons | 50.9 mill. tons |
| Steel | 60 | 70.7 |
| Coal | 500 | 510 |
| Oil | 60 | 166 |

Stalin's goals are from the text of his speech, *Pravda,* February 10, 1946, pp. 1–2. Figures for 1961 are from *Izvestiya,* January 24, 1962, p. 1.

23. Djilas, pp. 114–115.

24. Malcolm Mackintosh, "Disarmament and Soviet Military Policy," in Louis Henkin, ed., *Arms Control* (Englewood Cliffs, 1961), pp. 143–144.

One study of published sources concludes that the rapid advance of Soviet ground forces across Europe in the event of war is still an essential part of Soviet military strategy — see Herbert S. Dinerstein, *War and the Soviet Union* (New York, 1959), p. 25.

25. Mackintosh, p. 144.

26. Garthoff, p. 177.

27. *Pravda*, February 10, 1946.

28. *Cominform Bulletin*, December 1, 1947, p. 1.

29. Kramish, pp. 97–120.

30. *Pravda*, November 7, 1947, pp. 1–4.

31. Kramish, pp. 114–115.

32. G. I. Pokrovsky, *Science and Technology in Contemporary War*, trans. Raymond L. Garthoff (New York, 1959), pp. vi–vii.

33. *Soviet Space Programs: Organization, Plans, Goals, and International Implications*, staff report prepared for the Committee on Aeronautical and Space Sciences, United States Senate, 87th Congress, 2nd sess. (Washington, May 31, 1962), p. 64.

34. Garthoff, p. 178.

35. *New York Times*, April 10, 1949, p. 26.

36. *New York Times*, February 13, 1949, p. 16.

37. Mackintosh, p. 145; also Brigadier General (USA) Edwin L. Sibert, "Armies of the World," *Britannica Book of the Year, 1949* (Encyclopedia Britannica, Chicago), pp. 68–75.

38. *Pravda*, January 15, 1960, p. 1.

39. These figures include all expenditures for the military functions of the Department of Defense, military assistance and defense support under the Mutual Security Program, and the Atomic Energy Commission, as well as stockpiling and defense-production expansion. *United States Budget for Fiscal Year 1958*, p. 1149.

40. James Forrestal, Secretary of Defense, speaking February 1, 1949, at the National Press Club in Washington. Forrestal defended the Joint Chiefs' request as not having been ill advised at the time "if you project yourself back to last summer and to the conditions that flowed from the events of the spring." *New York Times*, February 2, 1949, p. 1.

41. *New York Times*, March 31, 1949, p. 4.

42. Herbert Feis, *Churchill, Roosevelt, Stalin* (Princeton, 1957), p. 531.

43. Kenneth C. Royall, Secretary of the Army, in testimony before a closed session of the House Appropriations Committee, *New York Times*, April 11, 1949, p. 1.

44. Henry Wallace's letter in *New York Times*, May 12, 1948. Stalin's reply in *Documents on International Affairs, 1947–48*, Royal Institute of International Affairs (Oxford, 1952), pp. 163–164.

45. Jay Franklin (John Franklin Carter), "Harry Truman's Foreign Policy," *Life*, January 10, 1949, pp. 28–29.

46. *New York Times*, January 21, 1949, p. 6.

47. *Ismeneniya v ekonomike kapitalizma v itoge vtoroi mirovoi voiny* (Changes in the Economy of Capitalism Resulting from the Second World War; Moscow, 1946). A summary of the contents of Varga's book may be

found in Frederick C. Barghoorn, "The Varga Discussion and Its Significance," *American Slavic and East European Review,* III (October 1948), 214–236.

48. A verbatim report of the discussion was published as a supplement to *Mirovoe khozyaystvo i mirovaya politika,* no. 11, November 1947. An English translation is available under the title, *Soviet Views on the Post-War World Economy, An Official Critique of Eugene Varga's "Changes in the Economy of Capitalism Resulting from the Second World War,"* trans. Leo Gruliow (Washington, 1948).

49. An economic discussion of the issue may be found in Evsey D. Domar, "The Varga Controversy," *American Economic Review,* XL (March 1950), 132–151. A comment on the article by Paul M. Sweezy and a reply by Domar may be found in the same journal, June 1950, pp. 405–407.

50. It may be significant that Varga had collaborated with Trotsky in drafting the theses at the Third Comintern Congress in July 1921. These theses also emphasized the temporary stabilization of capitalism during this "breathing spell" period in Soviet and Communist international policies. Jane Degras, ed., *The Communist International, 1919–1943, Documents, Vol. 1, 1919–1922* (Oxford, 1956), p. 229.

51. For example, *Bolshevik,* no. 17 (September 15, 1947), pp. 57–64, and no. 5 (March 15, 1948), pp. 74–80; *Planovoe khozyaystvo,* no. 2 (March-April 1948), pp. 50–69; *Voprosy ekonomiki,* no. 6 (June 1948), pp. 106–119; and particularly *Pravda,* January 26, 1948, pp. 3–4.

52. Proceedings reported in *Voprosy ekonomiki,* no. 8 (1948), pp. 65–110; no. 9 (1948), pp. 52–116. An English translation is available in *Current Digest of the Soviet Press,* I (March 8, 1949), 2–11; April 12, 1949, pp. 2–23; April 19, 1949, pp. 3–28.

53. *Voprosy ekonomiki,* no. 9 (1948), p. 57.

54. No. 3 (1949), pp. 79–88; English translation in *Current Digest of the Soviet Press,* I (June 7, 1949), 3–9.

55. March 16, 1949, p. 6; English translation in *Current Digest of the Soviet Press,* I (April 5, 1949), 45.

56. United Nations, Department of Economic Affairs, *World Economic Report, 1949–1950* (New York, 1951), pp. 5, 13–20.

57. *Bolshevik* on July 15, 1949, reaffirmed "the deepening of the general crisis of capitalism" and described "the beginnings of a new economic crisis of overproduction in the capitalist world" (no. 13, pub. August 23, 1949, pp. 46–56). For another example among fifty or more along the same lines in the Soviet and Communist press of this period, see P. Todorov, "Capitalist Countries on the Eve of Crisis," *Cominform Bulletin,* August 15, 1949, p. 4.

58. *World Economic Report, 1949–1950.*

59. M. Marinin, "On the International Situation," *Cominform Bulletin,* July 1, 1949, p. 5.

60. Vladimir Dedijer, *Tito Speaks* (London, 1953), pp. 391–394; Djilas,

*Conversations with Stalin,* pp. 142–161. Khrushchev, in his secret speech of February 25, 1956, quotes Stalin as saying: "I will shake my little finger — and there will be no more Tito. He will fall." *The Anti-Stalin Campaign and International Communism, A Selection of Documents,* Russian Institute, Columbia University, ed. (New York, 1956), p. 62.

61. For a fuller discussion of these events, see Zbigniew Brzezinski, "The Pattern of Political Purges," *Annals of the American Academy of Political and Social Science,* CCCXVII (May 1959: "The Satellites in Eastern Europe"), 79–87. For a tabular reference to these developments, see Department of State Publication 5914, *Moscow's European Satellites* (Washington, 1954).

62. Zbigniew Brzezinski, *The Soviet Bloc, Unity and Conflict* (Cambridge, Mass., 1960), p. 92.

63. Wolfgang Leonhard, *The Kremlin Since Stalin,* trans. Elizabeth Wiskemann and Marian Jackson (originally published as *Kreml Ohne Stalin,* Cologne, 1959), revised (New York, 1962), p. 196.

64. Nicolas Spulber, *The Economics of Communist Eastern Europe* (New York, 1957), pp. 425–432.

65. *New York Times,* May 10 and 11, 1949.

66. Merle Fainsod, *How Russia is Ruled* (Cambridge, Mass., 1953), p. 232.

67. Merle Fainsod, "Postwar Role of the Communist Party," *Annals of the American Academy of Political and Social Science,* CCLXIII (May 1949), 26.

68. *New York Times,* March 5, 1949, p. 1.

69. Interview with Anne O'Hare McCormick, *New York Times,* March 7, 1949, p. 20.

70. *New York Times,* March 8, 1949, p. 2.

71. Djilas, p. 149.

72. Yuri Pavlov, *Pravda,* April 7, 1949.

73. Harry Schwartz, *New York Times,* March 31, 1949, p. 11; May 7, 1943, p. 3.

74. Abram Bergson, James R. Blackman, and Alexander Erlich, "Post-war Economic Reconstruction and Development in the USSR," *Annals of the American Academy of Political and Social Science,* CCLXIII (May 1949: "The Soviet Union Since World War II"), 52–72.

75. Leonard Schapiro, *The Communist Party of the Soviet Union* (New York, 1960), pp. 511–517.

76. Joseph A. Kershaw, "Recent Trends in the Soviet Economy," *Annals of the American Academy of Social and Political Science,* XXXIII (January 1956: "Russia Since Stalin"), 43.

77. *World Economic Report, 1949–1950,* p. 214.

78. Alfred Zauberman, "Revisionism in Soviet Economics," in Leopold Labedz, ed., *Revisionism: Essays on the History of Marxist Ideas* (London, 1962), pp. 268–280. Also Alec Nove, "Recent Developments in Economic Ideas," in *Survey,* no. 21–22 (November-December 1957), pp. 19–26.

79. Nikolai A. Voznesensky, *Voyennaya ekonomika SSSR v period otechestvennoi voiny* (The War Economy of the USSR in the Period of the Patriotic War; Moscow, 1947). Published in English as *The Economy of the USSR During World War II,* by the Russian Translation Program of the American Council of Learned Societies (Washington, 1948). There was also a Soviet-sponsored edition in English.

80. Schapiro, p. 442.

81. *The Anti-Stalin Campaign,* p. 58.

82. Djilas, pp. 149–150, 156.

83. On January 1, 1949, wholesale prices of producer goods were steeply increased to take account of actual costs plus a small profit, for the purpose of eliminating hidden subsidies to industries. In 1950, this policy was reversed. In February 1949 retail prices on food, clothing, and other consumer goods were reduced from 10 to 30 percent.

84. *The Anti-Stalin Campaign,* p. 58.

85. The traces of this rivalry are detailed in Schapiro, p. 507ff, and in Robert Conquest, *Power and Policy in the USSR* (New York, 1961), pp. 79–94.

86. The circumstances of Zhdanov's death have never been made clear. In the Doctor's Plot of 1953, he was alleged to have been the victim of a medical murder, but the entire plot was later dismissed as a fabrication. Djilas reports Zhdanov as explaining his nonindulgence in alcohol at a dinner in January 1948 on the grounds that he had a bad heart and might die at any moment. Djilas, p. 155.

87. The following account draws upon Conquest, pp. 95–111, and Schapiro, pp. 507–508.

88. *Pravda,* July 7, 1957, pp. 1–2.

89. Conquest, pp. 101–102.

90. Brzezinski, *The Soviet Bloc,* p. 92.

91. In a report unconfirmed from Soviet sources, Khrushchev was quoted as saying, in Sofia in the summer of 1955, that Stalin had had Voznesensky shot for advocating some relaxation of overcentralized planning and for certain NEP-style measures to restore the economy. Richard Lowenthal, *The New Leader,* February 9, 1959, quoted in Leonhard, p. 177.

92. Conquest, pp. 97–100.

III. PEACEFUL COEXISTENCE, SWEET AND SOUR

1. Eddy Gilmore, reported in *Pravda,* March 23, 1946; Elliott Roosevelt, published February 4, 1947, in *Look*; Harold E. Stassen, in *Pravda,* May 8, 1947, and *New York Times,* May 4, 1947.

2. *Cominform Bulletin,* November 10, 1947, p. 2 (Zhdanov); and December 1, 1947, p. 3 (Malenkov).

3. *Pravda,* October 29, 1948, p. 1.

4. *Pravda,* November 7, 1948, p. 1.

5. *Pravda* and *Izvestiya,* January 29, 1949.

6. *L'Année politique, 1949* (Paris, 1950), pp. 2–3.

7. Speech at Bologna, January 15, 1949, reported in *New York Times,* January 17, 1949, p. 1.

8. Victor Michaut, "Lenin, Stalin, and Peace," *Cahiers du communisme,* January 1949, pp. 56–58.

9. *Pravda,* January 22, 1949; also *Cominform Bulletin,* February 1, 1949.

10. *Cahiers du communisme,* October 1948, pp. 1173–1174.

11. "The enemies of the people, thinking to embarrass us, pose the following question: 'What would you do if the Red Army occupied Paris?' Here is our reply:

"1. The Soviet Union is never found and never could be found in the position of being an aggressor toward any other country. The country of socialism could not, by definition, practice a policy of aggression and of war as do the imperialist powers . . .

"2. We take a position on facts and not on hypotheses. The present facts are: the active collaboration of the French government with the aggressive policy of the imperialist Anglo-Saxons, the presence of a foreign general staff at Fontainebleau, the transformation of our country and the French territories overseas into bases of aggression against the USSR and the countries of Popular Democracy.

"3. Since the question is put to us, let us say clearly this: if the common efforts of all Frenchmen devoted to liberty and peace do not succeed in bringing our country back into the camp of democracy and peace, if later our people should be dragged against their will into an anti-Soviet war, and if under these conditions the Soviet Army, defending the cause of the people, the cause of socialism, should be brought to pursue the aggressors onto our soil, could the workers and the people of France act toward the Soviet Army otherwise than did the workers and the people of Poland, of Rumania, of Yugoslavia, etc.?" *L'Humanité,* February 23, 1949, p. 1.

12. February 23, 1949, p. 1.

13. *L'Année politique, 1949,* pp. 24–26; *New York Times,* February 25, 1949, p. 1.

14. *New York Times,* February 28, 1949, p. 1.

15. A student of French politics, presenting a number of reasons for the Communist decline of influence in France during these years, made the following observation: "although the leaders of the Party appear to follow Moscow's orders unquestioningly, the overwhelming majority of the rank and file have never had the slightest intention of being disloyal to France, and if forced to choose between France and the Soviet Union would unhesitatingly choose France. The statement by M. Thorez in February 1949 implying that the workers would not defend France against Russia came as a shock to many people, even though M. Thorez was careful to add that the Soviet Union would never fight an aggressive war." Dorothy M. Pickles, *French Politics* (London, 1953), pp. 272–273.

16. Wolfgang Leonhard, at that time a Communist official in East Germany, wrote in describing this period of tightening control in East Europe as a result of the Soviet drive against possible Titoist influence: "the Communist Parties of Western Europe were spared nothing: at the end of February, 1949, their leaders were required to declare publicly that in the event of military conflict their Parties would support the troops of the Soviet Union. On 2nd March, 1949, the *politburo* of the S.E.D. also made an announcement to this effect. Thus the last pretense of independence was abandoned, and the Party openly declared itself to be an auxiliary of the Soviet Army." *Child of the Revolution,* trans. C. M. Woodhouse (Chicago, 1958), p. 513.

17. Reported in *New York Times* from London monitors, March 21, 1949, p. 4.

18. *New York Times,* March 28, 1949.

19. April 7, 1949.

20. Harrison E. Salisbury, *Moscow Journal* (Chicago, 1961), p. 28.

21. Edouard Herriot, "France Looks Ahead," *Foreign Affairs,* XXVII (April 1949), 403–412.

22. *New York Times,* April 9, 1949.

23. *New York Times,* April 26, 1949.

24. *New York Times,* April 9, 1949.

25. W. Phillips Davison, *The Berlin Blockade* (Princeton, 1958), pp. 264–268, 275, 277. *New York Times,* May 5, 1949.

26. Figures reported by General Clay, *New York Times,* April 26, 1949.

27. *New York Times,* May 18, 1949.

28. *New York Times,* April 17, 1949, p. 1.

29. *New York Times,* April 7, 1949.

30. *New York Times,* April 8, 1949, p. 3. The story reports that Paul Reynaud, who as French premier in June 1940 had appealed in vain to Roosevelt for "clouds of planes," expressed his confidence that if another such emergency arose the planes would come quickly. He was convinced, he said, that the United States would not let the Russians seize Europe.

31. *New York Times,* April 9, 1949, p. 4.

32. *New York Times,* April 14, 1949, p. 1.

33. Pertinax, April 28, 1949, to the North American Newspaper Alliance, *New York Times,* April 30, 1949.

34. *New York Times,* May 15, 1949, pp. 1, 3.

35. Davison, pp. 254–256.

36. *Pravda,* January 31, 1949.

37. *Pravda,* February 3, 1949.

38. *New York Times,* April 26 and 27, 1949.

39. The *Times* correspondent in Berlin on April 19 quoted "reliable Allied sources" as saying that the Soviet military administration had told the German Economic Commission in the Soviet zone that the barriers would be lifted by midyear. *New York Times,* April 20, 1949.

40. *New York Times,* April 20, 1949. In February, Polish representatives in Berlin were reported as telling the Western military governments: "This time the Soviet peace offensive is meant seriously." *New York Times,* March 2, 1949, p. 13.

41. Harold Callender, *New York Times,* February 5, 1949, p. 3.

42. *New York Times,* May 11, 1949, p. 19.

43. Djilas, p. 181.

44. *New York Times,* May 5, 1949.

45. Anne O'Hare McCormick, *New York Times,* May 28, 1949, p. 14.

46. *Novoe vremya* (New Times), May 18, 1949, p. 1.

47. U. S. Department of State, *Bulletin,* XVII (December 28, 1947), 1247.

48. A mark of the confidence of the three Western ministers was their decision to break off the conference if the Soviet Union did not immediately settle a strike on the Russian-operated railway which had once again brought rail traffic into Berlin to a standstill. At first refusing, Vyshinsky reversed himself when it became clear that the conference would otherwise be ended at once. Dean G. Acheson, *Sketches from Life of Men I Have Known* (New York, 1961), pp. 13–14.

49. Acheson, pp. 14–16.

50. *Pravda,* August 12, 1949, p. 3.

51. *New York Times,* September 18, 1949, p. 1.

52. *New York Times,* September 28, 1949, p. 5.

53. *New York Times,* September 23, 1949.

54. Text in *New York Times,* September 24, 1949, p. 4.

IV. THE PEACE MOVEMENT AS AN INSTRUMENT OF DIPLOMACY

1. This comment and much of the material in this chapter on the origins of the Peace Movement in France are drawn from interviews with persons who were in a position to know of these matters at firsthand and who wished to remain anonymous.

2. Guiseppe Boffa, *Inside the Khrushchev Era* (originally published in Italy under the title, *La Grande svolta*) trans. Carl Marzani (New York, 1959), p. 77. Boffa, now foreign editor of the Italian Communist newspaper, *L'Unità,* was its chief correspondent in Moscow from 1953 to 1958.

3. E. H. Carr, Note E, "The Marxist Attitude towards War," *The Bolshevik Revolution, 1917–1923* (New York, 1953), pp. 549–566, contains a useful summary of the Communist attitude on this issue.

4. "Decrees on Peace, Passed by the Second All-Russian Congress of Soviets of Workers', Soldiers' and Peasants' Deputies," November 8, 1917 [new style], in Jane Degras ed., *Soviet Documents on Foreign Policy, Vol. I, 1917–1924* (London, 1951), pp. 1–3.

5. *Za pyat let* (After Five Years), 1922, p. 60. Quoted in Carr, p. 12.

6. March 22, 1946, Stalin interview with Eddy Gilmore, in *Pravda,* March 23, 1946.

7. Interview with Alexander Werth, in *Pravda,* September 25, 1946.

8. *Pravda,* November 7, 1946, and *Bolshevik,* no. 21 (November 1946), pp. 1–13.

9. *Cominform Bulletin,* November 10, 1947, p. 4.

10. V. M. Molotov, Report to the Moscow Soviet, November 6, 1947. *Documents on International Affairs, 1947–48,* Royal Institute of International Affairs [RIIA] (London, 1952), p. 142.

11. Farge is generally regarded as not having been a member of the Communist Party, although one British newspaperman has described him as having been a secret member. Ronald Matthews, *The Death of the Fourth Republic* (New York, 1954), p. 151.

12. *Cominform Bulletin,* April 1, 1948, p. 3.

13. Emilio Sereni, "Congress in Wroclaw: Battle for Peace and Culture," *Cominform Bulletin,* September 15, 1948, p. 2.

14. September 15, 1948, p. 1.

15. Jean-Marie Domenach, "The French Communist Party," in Mario Einaudi, ed., *Communism in Western Europe* (Ithaca, 1951), pp. 110–111. In 1950, Domenach was expelled from the peace organization by Casanova for having visited Yugoslavia. In 1961, Casanova was expelled from the Central Committee of the party.

16. "French Communist Party and Intelligentsia," *Cominform Bulletin,* November 1, 1948, p. 8. In February 1948 the article was republished as part of a book by Casanova entitled *Le Parti communiste, les intellectuels et la nation* (Paris). In December 1950 the book was republished in a second edition, somewhat edited and considerably enlarged, including material on the Peace Movement, which had developed in the meantime.

17. Père Henri Chambre, "Le PCF durant les six premiers mois de 1949," *Travaux de l'action populaire,* September-October 1949, pp. 612–614.

18. *Cominform Bulletin,* December 15, 1948, p. 8.

19. *Cahiers du communisme,* December 1948, p. 1335.

20. December 15, 1948, p. 8.

21. "The Miners' Strike in France and After," *Cominform Bulletin,* December 15, 1948, p. 2.

22. *Cominform Bulletin,* December 15, 1948.

23. *L'Humanité,* February 25, 1949, pp. 1, 5.

24. *New York Times,* March 28, 1949, p. 3.

25. E. Rubinin, in *Trud,* March 16, 1949, p. 4.

26. *Cominform Bulletin,* April 15, 1949.

27. *Cominform Bulletin,* April 1, 1949.

28. *New York Times,* April 3, 1949, p. 6.

29. April 12, 1949, p. 1.

30. *Cahiers du communisme,* May 9, 1949, pp. 623–646.

31. Alain Brayance, *Anatomie du parti communiste français* (Paris, 1952), p. 112.

32. *New York Times,* April 21, 1949, p. 1.

33. *Cominform Bulletin,* May 1, 1949, p. 1.

34. Full text of the manifesto and resolutions may be found in *L'Humanité,* April 27, 1949, and of the manifesto in *Cominform Bulletin,* May 1, 1949.

35. *New York Times,* April 26, 1949, p. 7.

36. *Cominform Bulletin,* June 1, 1949, p. 1.

37. *New York Times,* April 25, 1949, p. 3.

38. April 24, 1949, p. 1.

39. March 1, 1949.

40. March 2, 1949, p. 1.

41. Aimé Cesaire, "French Intellectuals and the Cause of Peace," *Cominform Bulletin,* May 1, 1949, p. 5.

42. *Cominform Bulletin,* July 15, 1949, p. 3, and September 30, 1949, p. 1. *New York Times,* May 18, 1949, pp. 1, 3.

43. August 1, 1949, p. 3.

44. *Cahiers du communisme,* August 1949, p. 1053.

45. Raymond Guyot, in *Cominform Bulletin,* September 1, 1949, p. 4.

### V. EFFECTS OF THE CHANGING POWER BALANCE

1. James Reston, *New York Times,* September 25, 1949, p. 3.

2. *New York Times,* September 25, 1949, pp. 1, 5.

3. In July 1949, a prominent Soviet poet had eulogized the blasting of a granite mountain in Siberia with an explosive "more powerful than dynamite" —Y. A. Dolmatovsky, "Vasha sila" (Your Strength), *Novy mir,* July 1949, p. 170; see also Arnold Kramish, *Atomic Energy in the Soviet Union* (Stanford, 1959), pp. 133–135. An American correspondent's dispatch on this published poem was killed by the Soviet censor (Salisbury, *Moscow Journal,* p. 47). On November 10, Vyshinsky created a stir in the United Nations by using the present tense in referring to Soviet uses of atomic energy to "blast mountains and change the flow of rivers." *Pravda*'s account of the Vyshinsky speech, on November 17, reported these achievements only as matters of future intent.

4. *New York Times,* January 29, 1949, pp. 1, 3; February 14, 1949, p. 1.

5. C. L. Sulzberger, *New York Times,* February 14, 1949, p. 10.

6. Djilas, p. 182. See also Vladimir Dedijer, *Tito* (New York, 1953), p. 322.

7. C. P. F[itzgerald], "The Chinese Revolution," *The World Today* (RIIA, London), VI, June 1950.

8. *Cominform Bulletin,* May 1, 1949, pp. 1, 3.

9. I. Sergeyev, "Military-Political Situation in China," *Cominform Bulletin,* June 15, 1949, p. 6.

10. Djilas, p. 183.

11. Schapiro, pp. 528, 534–538.

12. *Pravda* and *Izvestiya,* November 7, 1949. English translations may be found in *Cominform Bulletin,* November 11, 1949, pp. 1–2, and in *Current Digest of the Soviet Press,* I (November 22, 1949), 3–10.

13. *Pravda,* September 25, 1946.

14. Telegram to Pieck and Grotewohl of October 13, 1949, *Documents on International Affairs, 1949–1950,* RIIA (London, 1953), pp. 383–384.

15. Salisbury, pp. 113–115.

16. Peter Calvocoressi, *Survey of International Affairs, 1949–1950* (Oxford, 1953), pp. 10, 16–17.

17. A. Leontiev, "O mirnom sosushchestvovanii dvukh sistem" (On Peaceful Coexistence of Two Systems), *Pravda,* March 28, 1950, p. 3.

18. B. Ponomarev, "K 30-letniyi raboti V. I. Lenina, 'Detskaya bolezn levizni v kommunizme'" (On the Thirtieth Anniversary of V. I. Lenin's Work, "Left-Wing Communism, An Infantile Disorder"), *Pravda,* April 27, 1950, pp. 2–3. *Current Digest of the Soviet Press,* II (June 10, 1950), 38–40.

19. *Pravda* and *Izvestiya,* March 11, 1950, p. 2. Condensed text in *Current Digest of the Soviet Press,* II (April 29, 1950), 6–9.

20. Suslov had been promoted to the post of chief of the Agitprop Department by Zhdanov in 1947 to replace one of Malenkov's associates, G. F. Aleksandrov, during the Zhdanov purge of Soviet intellectuals and artists. Schapiro, p. 508.

21. Press accounts speculated that the meeting was held on November 15–21 at a resort hotel in the Matra Mountains, some sixty miles northeast of Budapest. *New York Times,* November 30, 1949, p. 1; *Neue Zurcher Zeitung,* December 1, 1949 (quoted in *Survey of International Affairs, 1949–1950,* p. 55).

22. The full text of the communiqué and resolutions was simultaneously published in the *Cominform Bulletin, Pravda,* and *L'Humanité* for November 29, 1949. Quotations used here are from the *Cominform Bulletin.*

23. Warner Schilling, "The H-Bomb Decision — How to Decide Without Actually Choosing," *Political Science Quarterly,* LXXVI (March 1961), 24.

24. Full text of the Togliatti and Suslov reports may be found in the *Cominform Bulletin,* December 2, 1949, pp. 2–6. A report by the Rumanian Gheorghe Gheorghiu-Dej, renewing the attack on Tito, was also presented.

25. November 30, 1949, p. 1.

26. *Documents on International Affairs, 1949–1950,* pp. 541–547.

27. *New York Times,* November 15, 1949, p. 10.

28. *L'Humanité,* December 13, 1949, pp. 3–4; excerpts in *Cominform Bulletin,* December 14, 1949, p. 2.

29. *L'Humanité,* December 10, 1949, p. 4.

30. Étienne Fajon, *Cominform Bulletin,* January 6, 1950, p. 2.

31. *Cominform Bulletin,* February 10, 1950, p. 2. It was Servin's ironic fate, exactly eleven years later, to be expelled from the politburo on charges of "opportunism," along with Laurent Casanova.

32. January 20, 1950, p. 1.

33. *Cominform Bulletin,* February 3, 1950, p. 1.

34. For example, steel production dropped from 772,000 tons in January to 504,000 tons in March. Dorothy M. Pickles, *French Politics* (London, 1953), p. 124.

35. Victor Michaut, "French People Rebuff Reaction," *Cominform Bulletin,* March 31, 1950, p. 3.

36. "Za mir, za khleb, za svobodu" (For Peace, for Bread, for Freedom) *Pravda,* February 27, 1950, p. 4.

37. "O zadachakh izuchenya istorii stalinskoi vneshnei politiki sovetskovo soyuza" (On the Tasks of Studying the History of the Stalinist Foreign Policy of the Soviet Union), *Voprosy istorii,* no. 4 (April 1950), pp. 3–11.

38. *Cominform Bulletin,* November 29, 1949, p. 1.

39. *Cominform Bulletin,* December 30, 1949, p. 2.

40. The *Cominform Bulletin* had begun in February a campaign to intensify the militant aspect of the Peace Movement on a world scale. "The struggle of the popular masses for peace is rising to a new, higher stage, turning into the phase of concrete patriotic actions against war . . . War cannot be prevented by pacifist invocations. Concrete actions alone distinguish the genuine supporters of peace from the politicians who indulge in pacifist phrasemongering" (February 10, 1950, p. 1). "For the supporters of peace, practical action is the main method of struggle against the policy of unleashing war" (February 3, 1950, p. 1).

41. *Cominform Bulletin,* March 24, 1950, p. 1.

42. Bulganin's anniversary speech, November 6, 1950, *Cominform Bulletin,* November 10, 1950, p. 2.

43. Interview with Pierre Hervé.

44. Pak Hen En, Deputy Chairman, Central Committee, Workers' Party of South Korea, "Heroic Struggle of the People of South Korea for Unity and Independence of the Country," *Cominform Bulletin,* February 24, 1950, pp. 3–4.

45. Among many others, Harry Pollitt, the British Communist, in *Cominform Bulletin,* November 3, 1950. Also, this was a consistent response in the course of interviews by the author with Peace Movement officials in Paris during the summer of 1954.

46. *Cominform Bulletin,* March 31, 1950, p. 1.

47. Georges Cogniot, *Cominform Bulletin,* December 15, 1948, p. 2.

48. Victor Michaut, *Cahiers du communisme,* January 1949, pp. 56–58.

49. Published as brochure by the party; excerpts in *L'Humanité,* April 3, 1950, pp. 2–4; *Cominform Bulletin,* April 7, 1950, p. 2; *Cahiers du communisme,* May 1950, pp. 19–36.

50. *L'Humanité,* April 7, 1950, p. 2.

51. *France nouvelle,* April 1, 1950 (47-page supplement).

VI. SOVIET POLICY DURING THE KOREAN WAR: FIRST PHASE

1. A study of the period lists the following five major interpretations of Soviet motivations advanced by American officials or in responsible American press accounts: the "diversionary move," the "soft-spot probing," the "testing," the "demonstration," and "Soviet Far East strategy." Alexander L. George, "American Policy-Making and the North Korean Aggression," *World Politics*, VII (January 1955), 209–232.

2. James Reston, *New York Times*, June 27, 1960, quoted in George, p. 210.

3. This analysis benefits greatly from consultation of an unpublished manuscript by Alice Langley Hsieh, entitled: "The Strategy and Tactics of Communist China's Foreign Policy Toward Japan," written in September 1956 for the RAND Corporation, Santa Monica, California. It is also based upon material in Allen S. Whiting, *China Crosses the Yalu* (New York, 1960).

4. Whiting, pp. 42–46; Hsieh, pp. 36–38.

5. Whiting, p. 43.

6. Richard P. Stebbins, ed., *The United States in World Affairs, 1949* (New York, 1950), pp. 455–456: "In Washington in September [1949] Acheson and Bevin had agreed that a peace treaty with Japan was urgently necessary. Both governments were known to have the legal and other problems under study, and Japanese spokesmen seemed to expect some kind of decision by early 1950. There being no evidence of a prospective meeting of minds with the USSR, the world was left to conclude that a separate peace was actively under consideration."

7. Alice Hsieh, on pp. 35–36 of the manuscript cited, quotes an official Chinese news-agency editorial describing the treaty as "a great blow to the American imperialists' plot to undermine the peace of the Far East."

8. Hsieh, pp. 44–45; Whiting, pp. 37–38.

9. Speeches by General Douglas MacArthur in 1949 and Secretary of State Dean G. Acheson in January 1950 (Whiting, p. 39). Acheson added that other areas in the Pacific were under the protection of the entire world in accordance with the Charter of the United Nations.

10. George, pp. 229–230: "If we assume that the Soviets moved into South Korea under the impression that the United States had given up this area and, further, that the Soviets were surprised by the American decision to intervene, then the American policy reversal on Formosa might well have seemed to the Politburo evidence of a calculated plan to invite the North Korean attack in order to use it as a justification for putting into effect a far more vigorous Far Eastern policy. Such a Politburo image of devious American policy calculations — moreover, one possibly accompanied by expectations of further 'aggressive' steps by the United States in the Far East — would have led Soviet leaders to view their interests in the Korean War in

a much broader framework than they had when they ordered the North Koreans to attack. The stakes must have been seen now to be much larger than merely the question of control of South Korea . . . The initial policy of advance into a peripheral power vacuum may have been speedily transformed into a major defensive effort to oppose what were regarded as American plans for expansion in the Far East."

11. U. S. Department of Defense, Appropriation Acts for Fiscal Year 1951 (OSD Comptroller, EISED-059, August 17, 1954); for Fiscal Year 1952 (OSD Comptroller, EISED-057, June 21, 1954).

12. *New York Times,* August 8, 1950, p. 14.

13. Richard P. Stebbins, ed., *The United States in World Affairs, 1950* (New York, 1951), pp. 260–265.

14. Speech by Walter Ulbricht, secretary-general of the Socialist Unity Party, August 3, 1950 (*New York Times,* August 5, 1950, p. 4). A statement by Deputy Foreign Minister Gromyko on July 4, 1950, pointedly argued that the right of divided states to unify themselves, in Korea as in the cases of the civil wars in the Soviet Union and the United States, was solely a matter of domestic jurisdiction, and did not justify intervention (RIIA, *Documents on International Affairs, 1949–1950,* p. 654).

15. *Documents on International Affairs, 1949–1950,* p. 331.

16. H.G.L., "The European Defense Community," *The World Today,* VIII (June 1952), 236–248.

17. RIIA, *Survey, 1951,* p. 64.

18. Text of the communiqué in *New York Times,* October 22, 1950, pp. 25–26.

19. Department of State, *Bulletin,* November 6, 1950, pp. 728–729.

20. Department of State, *Bulletin,* July 3, 1950, p. 5.

21. *Documents on International Affairs, 1949–1950,* pp. 648–655.

22. This point is drawn from Whiting, pp. 72–91, where it is developed more completely.

23. Whiting, p. 59.

24. Whiting, p. 76. Alexander George, pp. 229–231, comments on the interesting point that United States attribution of responsibility to the Soviet Union was restrained by the consideration that Soviet policy makers should be given an opportunity to withdraw the attack without losing face. He refers to differences in the literature on the question of whether the Soviet leadership is thought to be susceptible to considerations of prestige where vital interests are involved.

25. Leland M. Goodrich, *Korea: A Study of U. S. Policy in the United Nations* (New York, 1956), pp. 128–133.

26. *New York Times,* October 22, 1950, p. E-1.

27. *Pravda,* November 7, 1950, pp. 2–4.

28. August 20, 1950.

29. RIIA, *Survey, 1950,* p. 60.

30. *Cominform Bulletin,* November 24, 1950, p. 1.
31. *Cominform Bulletin,* November 2, 1951, p. 1.

VII. SOVIET POLICY DURING THE KOREAN WAR: SECOND AND THIRD PHASES

1. Whiting, *China Crosses the Yalu,* pp. 152–160.
2. Whiting, pp. 95–97.
3. Whiting, pp. 160–162.
4. Stebbins, *United States in World Affairs, 1950,* p. 437.
5. Text in *New York Times,* December 21, 1950, p. 22.
6. *New York Times,* March 9, 1951.
7. The *Cominform Bulletin,* December 8, 1950, devoted most of its front page to reactions from various capitals to the President's press-conference statement, under the headline: "Peoples of the World Protest Against New War Hysteria in U.S.A." *Pravda,* in a leading article on December 3, 1950, asked: "Who but the insane can after this believe in the peaceful intentions of Truman and his friends?"
8. The politburo of the French Communist Party expressed the conviction that the dismissal of General MacArthur resulted from the efforts of the Peace Movement (*L'Humanité,* April 14, 1951). A number of leading figures in the Peace Movement in France expressed the same belief, in interviews with me in the summer of 1954. This exaggerated estimate of the influence of the Peace Movement upon the American government appeared responsible for much of the fervor with which non-Communists joined in the movement's signature-collecting campaigns and demonstrations.
9. *Military Situation in the Far East,* Hearings before the Senate Armed Services and Foreign Relations Committees, 82nd Congress, 1st sess. May 3-August 17, 1951 (Washington, 1951), parts I–V, 3691 pages.
10. *Pravda,* December 23, 1950, p. 4, carried the full text of Hoover's speech, with some changes which might have been the result of hasty translation. *Pravda,* December 24, 1950, p. 4, in an article discussing the American "crisis of policy" sought to explain to its readers how it happened that Hoover, who had previously been characterized as a reactionary figure, was now the advocate of peace against the policies of the Administration. The subsequent debate was carefully followed in the Soviet press. The year-end editorial of the *Cominform Bulletin* declared: "The camp of imperialism, the camp of war [is] rent by insoluble contradictions . . ." (December 29, 1950, p. 1). *Pravda,* January 8, 1951, p. 4, carried lengthy excerpts from the speech by Senator Taft. As late as February 2, 1952, *Pravda* still devoted nearly one quarter of its space to another speech by Hoover, proposing that the United States withdraw to a hemispheric defense. Salisbury, p. 242.
11. Stebbins, *United States in World Affairs, 1950,* p. 424.
12. RIIA, *Survey, 1951,* p. 453.
13. *Pravda,* October 26, 1950; also Whiting, pp. 143–146.
14. *Pravda,* January 22, 1951, p. 2.

15. Stebbins, *United States in World Affairs, 1951*, p. 131.

16. Stalin was apparently making a distinction between immediate postwar reductions in the number of men under arms and subsequent increases, as well as other military expenditures. In his speech before the Supreme Soviet on January 14, 1960 (*Pravda*, January 15, 1960), Khrushchev asserted that the Soviet armed forces had been reduced from 11,365,000 in May 1945 to 2,874,000 in 1948. According to conservative Western economic calculations, the total had climbed back to approximately 4,900,000 by the time of the Stalin interview in 1951 (Abram Bergson, *The Real National Income of Soviet Russia Since 1928*, Cambridge, Mass., 1961, p. 364). Bergson estimates Soviet defense expenditures, in current rubles, at 64.3 billion in 1948 and 91.9 billion in 1951.

17. RIIA, *Documents, 1951*, p. 304.

18. February 23, 1951, p. 2.

19. In October 1950, Maurice Thorez, the idolized leader of the party, had been stricken with a cerebral hemorrhage and spent the next three years in the Soviet Union recuperating. In the interval, the party was preoccupied with intense infighting among the second tier of leaders for positions of command.

20. *L'Humanité*, February 15, 1951.

21. *Cominform Bulletin*, February 23, 1951, p. 2.

22. *L'Humanité*, March 19, 1951.

23. RIIA, *Documents, 1951*, pp. 248–251. U. S. note of January 23, 1951, *ibid.*, pp. 251–252; Soviet note of February 5, *ibid.*, pp. 253–255; U. S. reply of February 19, *ibid.*, pp. 255–257; final Soviet acceptance of March 1, *ibid.*, p. 257.

24. An excellent summary of the proceedings may be found in RIIA, *Survey, 1951*, pp. 130–142.

25. RIIA, *Survey, 1951*, pp. 105–110.

26. An intended statement by Truman to the Chinese Communists, inviting a cease-fire and offering to stop at the thirty-eighth parallel and to settle outstanding issues by negotiation, was prevented by an unauthorized declaration by General MacArthur on March 24, which called for a cease-fire but implied a threat to broaden the war against China. The incident was a contributing factor in the relief of MacArthur on April 11. Stebbins, *United States in World Affairs, 1951*, pp. 93–94.

27. By mid-June, it was estimated that total Communist losses exceeded 1,162,500 killed, wounded, or captured. *New York Times*, June 23, 1951.

28. RIIA, *Survey, 1951*, p. 455.

29. RIIA, *Survey, 1951*, p. 25.

30. Stebbins, *United States in World Affairs, 1951*, pp. 31–32.

31. Warner R. Schilling, "The H-Bomb Decision," *Political Science Quarterly*, LXXVI (March 1961), 42.

32. For example, see speech by Dean Rusk, then Assistant Secretary of

State for Far Eastern Affairs, on "Chinese-American Friendship," in New York on May 18, 1951, affirming American support for Nationalist China. *Department of State Bulletin*, XXIV (May 28, 1951), 846–848. See also Stebbins, *United States in World Affairs, 1951*, pp. 114–124.

33. RIIA, *Documents, 1951*, p. 633.

34. A month earlier, on May 20, the Soviet press and radio had given wide currency to a resolution tabled by Senator Edwin C. Johnson proposing a cease-fire along the thirty-eighth parallel. Both the Soviet Union and the United States formally denied that they intended to take any initiative in the matter at that time. RIIA, *Survey, 1951*, p. 439.

35. RIIA, *Documents, 1951*, p. 633–634.

VIII. THE DIPLOMACY OF COEXISTENCE, 1951–1952

1. RIIA, *Documents, 1952*, pp. 41–46.

2. RIIA, *Survey, 1952*, pp. 4, 13.

3. John T. Marcus, *Neutralism and Nationalism in France* (New York, 1958), pp. 85–128.

4. *Collier's,* October 27, 1951.

5. Alexander Chakovsky, in *Trud,* November 16, 1951.

6. Joseph Clark, in *Literaturnaya gazeta,* November 15, 1951.

7. Speech of July 21, 1951, in Warsaw. *Pravda,* July 22, 1951, p. 2.

8. *Pravda,* November 7, 1951, pp. 2–4.

9. *Pravda,* December 3, 1951.

10. A. Belyakov, "Pod znamenem borbi za mir" (Under the Banner of the Struggle for Peace), *Bolshevik,* no. 3 (February 1952), pp. 46–54.

11. For example, V. Cheprakov, "Bankrotstvo burzhuanoi ekonomicheskoi nauki" (The Bankruptcy of Bourgeois Economics), in *Literaturnaya gazeta,* June 10, 1952, p. 2.

12. I. Tikhonov, "Ob obshchem krize kapitalizma" (On the General Crisis of Capitalism), *Pravda,* June 17, 1952, pp. 2–3.

13. August 5, 1951, p. 1.

14. Salisbury, *Moscow Journal,* pp. 208–209.

15. RIIA, *Documents, 1951,* pp. 311–317.

16. Salisbury, p. 211.

17. *Pravda,* October 6, 1951.

18. *Pravda,* April 2, 1952.

19. RIIA, *Documents, 1951,* pp. 318–320.

20. RIIA, *Documents, 1952,* pp. 270–273.

21. *Pravda,* April 6, 1952, p. 3.

22. RIIA, *Survey, 1952,* pp. 180–182.

23. Hsieh manuscript, pp. 139–140.

24. Admiral C. Turner Joy, *How Communists Negotiate* (New York, 1955); William H. Vatcher, Jr., *Panmunjom: The Story of the Korean Military Armistice Negotiations* (New York, 1958).

25. Vatcher, pp. 116–117.

26. Joy, pp. 146–153.

27. RIIA, *Survey, 1952*, pp. 187–188.

28. RIIA, *Survey, 1952*, pp. 331–333.

29. The *Cominform Bulletin*, November 21, 1952, p. 3, in a post-mortem of the American election, interpreted this factor in the following way: "Stevenson, the Democratic candidate for the Presidency, and Truman, who actively campaigned for him, advocated continuation of the U. S. aggression in Korea even at the height of the election campaign, and it was this in the main that doomed them to defeat. Eisenhower, as is known, also opened his campaign in extremely bellicose tones. However, upon realizing that the rabid aggressive speeches of the General were meeting with an exceptionally cold response both in the U.S.A. and abroad, and that in the final analysis this might spell defeat for their candidate, the bosses of the Republican Party hastily changed their tune and thereafter Eisenhower's tone underwent an immediate change. Mindful of the mood of the electorate, Eisenhower now appeared in the guise of champion of a peaceful settlement of the Korean problem . . .

"And a week before the voting Eisenhower declared in a speech that, if elected, he would immediately travel to Korea in order to study the question on the spot as to how 'speedily and honorably' to end the war in Korea. The U. S. newspapers frankly evaluated this declaration as a demagogic move, as a tactical maneuver designed to win votes.

"And the maneuver proved successful."

30. June 13, 1952.

31. An article in the leading Soviet theoretical journal, nominally reviewing Kennan's book, *American Diplomacy, 1900–1950*, which had been published the year before, contained this typical condemnation: "Mr. Kennan's theoretical and historical exercises are a brazen gospel of aggression and the use of force by American imperialism, which is bent on achieving world domination." V. Mikhailov, "Raznuzdannaya propoved agressii i nasilia" (All-Out Gospel of Aggression and the Use of Force), *Kommunist*, no. 22 (December 1952), pp. 118–123.

32. *L'Année politique, 1952*, pp. 355–356.

33. RIIA, *Documents, 1952*, pp. 85–88.

34. March 21, 1952, p. 4. In its roundup of world reaction, the *Cominform Bulletin* included a one-sentence report by Pierre Courtade in *L'Humanité* which referred to the Soviet note only as being "enormously significant."

35. Note dated April 9, 1952. RIIA, *Documents, 1952*, pp. 91–94.

36. RIIA, *Documents, 1952*, pp. 100–105.

37. *L'Année politique, 1952*, p. 343.

38. Note of July 10, 1952. RIIA, *Documents, 1952*, pp. 175–177.

39. RIIA, *Documents, 1952*, pp. 186–192.

40. Note of September 23, 1952. RIIA, *Documents, 1952*, pp. 195–197.

41. Walter Z. Laqueur, "Thoughts at the Wall," *Encounter,* XIX (August 1962), 66.

42. Melvin Croan, "Reality and Illusion in Soviet-German Relations," *Survey,* no. 44–45 (October 1962), pp. 12–28 (special issue, "Russia and Germany"). Evelyn Anderson, "East Germany," *ibid.,* no. 42 (June 1962), p. 97.

43. Khrushchev, speech before the closed session of the Twentieth Congress, February 24–25, 1956: "All those who interested themselves even a little in the national situation saw the difficult situation in agriculture, but Stalin never even noted it." *The Anti-Stalin Campaign,* p. 77.

44. Khrushchev, speech to the Central Committee, September 3, 1953, in *Pravda,* September 15, 1953; Khrushchev, speech to the Central Committee, December 15, 1958, in *Pravda,* December 16, 1958. In the latter speech, Khrushchev accused Malenkov of having exaggerated the grain output of 1952 by approximately 40 percent, through statistical falsifications.

45. Khrushchev, in his speech before the closed session of the Twentieth Congress, is quoted as saying, ironically: "If Stalin said anything, it meant it was so — after all, he was a genius . . ." In another place occurs this enigmatic sentence: "During Stalin's leadership our peaceful relations with other nations were often threatened, because one-man decisions could cause, and often did cause, great complications." Dedijer (p. 320) and Djilas (p. 181) also give an instance in which Stalin is reported to have rejected arbitrarily and angrily the information that the Netherlands was a constituent element in Benelux.

46. RIIA, *Survey, 1952,* p. 148. In his secret speech at the Twentieth Congress, Khrushchev referred to "manifestations of local bourgeois nationalism in Georgia as in several other republics." He acknowledged that a number of party and government workers in Georgia had been arrested in late 1951 and early 1952 for complicity in a nationalist organization, but he claimed that these charges were based on falsified documents for which Stalin was responsible. *The Anti-Stalin Campaign,* p. 60.

47. Conquest, pp. 172, 438–439.

48. Imre Nagy, *On Communism* (New York, 1957), p. 38.

49. Brzezinski, *The Soviet Bloc,* p. 142.

50. Conquest, pp. 154, 173–174.

51. RIIA, *Survey, 1952,* pp. 353–354.

52. RIIA, *Survey, 1952,* p. 354.

53. Howard L. Boorman, "The Sino-Soviet Alliance: The Political Impact," in *Moscow-Peking Axis,* by Howard L. Boorman, Alexander Eckstein, Philip E. Mosely, and Benjamin Schwartz (New York, 1957), p. 11.

54. Hsieh manuscript, pp. 116–117.

55. Kramish, pp. 124–127.

56. Asher Lee, *The Soviet Air Force* (New York, 1962), pp. 118, 137.

57. Lee, pp. 136, 140, 150–151.

IX. THE USE OF THE PEACE MOVEMENT AND THE FRENCH
COMMUNIST PARTY, 1951–1952

1. *Cominform Bulletin,* July 27, 1951, p. 1.
2. Report printed as supplement to *Cominform Bulletin,* August 3, 1951.
3. RIIA, *Documents, 1951,* pp. 306–307.
4. *Cominform Bulletin,* November 9, 1951, p. 3.
5. *Cominform Bulletin,* November 30, 1951, p. 2.
6. *Cominform Bulletin,* May 25, 1951, p. 2.
7. "Program of National Independence, Social Progress, Democracy, and Peace," *Cahiers du communisme,* June 1951, pp. 636–639.
8. *Cominform Bulletin,* April 20, 1951, p. 1.
9. *Cominform Bulletin,* June 15, 1951, p. 1.
10. *L'Année politique, 1951,* pp. 154, 198.
11. *Cominform Bulletin,* August 24, 1951, p. 1.
12. *L'Humanité,* September 8, 1951, p. 1.
13. *Cahiers du communisme,* October 1951, p. 1137.
14. Étienne Fajon, *L'Humanité,* September 10, 1951, p. 3.
15. *L'Humanité,* September 11, 1951, p. 1.
16. *L'Année politique, 1951,* p. 253.
17. *L'Humanité,* October 8, 1951.
18. Resolution of Central Committee, October 18, 1951, *L'Humanité,* October 19, 1951.
19. "Historic Example of October Revolution and Middle Strata," *Cominform Bulletin,* November 2, 1951, p. 3.
20. *Izvestiya,* January 12, 1952, p. 4.
21. *L'Humanité,* February 13, 1952, p. 1.
22. *L'Humanité,* February 4, 1952.
23. *L'Humanité,* February 15, 1952.
24. Two weeks earlier, with the approval of the politburo of the French party, Lecoeur had despatched a letter to secretaries and treasurers of local party cells, ordering them to designate one of the most conscientious members of each cell as a "political instructor" to improve the attendance and the general political level of the cell's activity. These instructors, said Lecoeur, were to "meet members at home and persuade them politely . . . The Party is not just a sect of 'les durs, les purs, les sûrs,' but a large organization with political influence" (*L'Humanité,* January 31, 1952; *Cahiers du communisme,* February 1952, pp. 188–192). This network of political instructors, with a separate chain of communication to the top, came to be regarded by some leaders as an imitation of Stalin's use of the Orgburo to consolidate power within the Soviet party, and it was to be cited as justifying Lecoeur's expulsion from the party two years later. Reviving the old issue between Lenin and Martov in 1902, Lecoeur's critics charged him with taking an anti-Leninist position by failing to insist that persons could not be members merely by

adhering to the party, nor even by attending meetings, but only by committing themselves to work actively for it.

25. *Cahiers du communisme,* February 1952, pp. 121–125.

26. *L'Humanité,* March 12, 1952, pp. 1, 5.

27. *Le Populaire,* March 13, 1952.

28. "In May 1952, *Action* ceased to appear, officially because of its financial difficulties. It is true that its own resources had never been sufficient and that it had always been supported by the Party; but, in fact, the latter did not continue its support because of the attitude of certain members of the Permanent Commission (Yves Farge in particular), in the face of the Soviet note on the unification of Germany. Among the upper levels of the Party, it was generally thought that the disappearance of *Action* was due to the 'erroneous' policy which the journal had a tendency to follow." Alain Brayance, *Anatomie du parti communiste français* (Paris, 1952), p. 149.

29. See below, note 36.

30. The article, entitled "The Tasks of the Party Two Years After the XII Congress: To Organize and Direct the United Action of the Masses, To Impose a Policy of Peace and National Independence," received an unusual dissemination. It was first published in *France nouvelle,* no. 333 (May 3, 1952), pp. 6–8, and also published as the lead article in *Cahiers du communisme,* May 1952, pp. 453–468.

31. Jacques Fauvet in *Le Monde,* May 30, 1952; "La Nouvelle orientation du parti communiste," Unsigned [Gilles Martinet (?)] in *L'Observateur,* no. 106 (May 22, 1952), pp. 10–11. *L'Observateur,* a left-wing journal with excellent contacts within the party, explained this turn in the party line as a result of "the sagging of influence of the Communist Party . . . This sagging had probably been related to the recent efforts at 'broadening,' which have not produced the results anticipated, but, on the contrary, have contributed to the political 'disarming' of the militants as well as sympathizers. It is significant in this connection that the disappearance of *Action* was accompanied in certain Communist circles by uncomplimentary commentaries toward the orientation taken by that weekly in recent months. Lately, the militant workers (who had been keeping in the background behind the intellectuals and the 'personalities'), have been participating in a much more active manner in the Peace Movement. These directives appear to us to be equally related to certain aspects of the international situation, and above all, to the evolution of the German problem. Under present conditions, the fight conducted by the Communists against the rearmament of West Germany, the development of the European army, and the installation of American bases tends to bring out again the most direct and most concrete forms of action." See also articles by Gilles Martinet in *L'Observateur,* no. 109 (June 12, 1952), pp. 7–9; no. 111 (June 26, 1952), pp. 7–8.

32. Duclos quickly corrected his public position on the class issue following the politburo discussions of the Billoux message. In an article significantly

entitled, "Two Worlds — Two Policies," in the *Cominform Bulletin,* April 25, 1952, p. 2, he completely reversed the line he had taken the previous November: "The bourgeoisie, acting in its class interests, commits cynical betrayal, while the working class acts as the only class representing and defending the interests of the nation, rallying around itself all the elements of the population who do not want to be accomplices in betrayal." In a speech at the close of a four-month central school for cadres of the French Communist Party, on May 10, 1952, Duclos hammered away at the old Zhdanov theme of the division of the world into two camps and the treason of the French bourgeoisie for its alignment with the Western alliance (National Assembly, *Journal officiel,* no. 4415 [October 21, 1952], supplement, p. 99).

33. Duclos notebook, pp. 1, 2, 135.

34. *L'Humanité,* May 8, 1952–May 26, 1952.

35. Auguste Lecoeur, *L'Autocritique attendue* (St. Cloud 1955), p. 38.

36. *Le Monde,* May 31, 1952. Duclos' notebook was "unofficially" made public in July through an American news agency. An annotated selection of items from the notebook, containing pages photographically reproduced from the original, was published, presumably by an anti-Communist organization, under the title: *La Signification politique du cahier de Jacques Duclos* [Paris], July 1952. Extracts from the notebook were also published in the National Assembly's *Journal officiel,* October 21, 1952, supplement (138 pp.).

37. Evidence of the demoralization of the party during this period is from hostile sources but is reasonably circumstantial. The socialist paper, *Le Populaire,* May 30, 1952, referred to "a profound disarray paralyzing the CP of France." Marty, in his book published after his exclusion from the party, confirms this by implication (*L'Affaire Marty,* Paris 1955, p. 32). A detailed report on the French Communist Party during this and the following period by an organization opposed to the Communists is contained in *Est & Ouest,* no. 168 (February 16–28, 1957), pp. 63–81. This bulletin is published by Association d'Études et d'Information Politiques Internationales, Paris.

38. Marty, p. 32.

39. Lorwin, pp. 140–141.

40. *Pravda,* June 9, 1952, p. 1 editorial. In the following week, *Pravda* and *Izvestiya* carried more than two dozen articles on the situation of the French Party.

41. *L'Année politique,* 1952, p. 76.

42. *Journal officiel,* October 21, 1952, supplement.

43. "Concerning the Turning Point," *L'Humanité,* June 6, 1952, p. 1.

44. "The Factory and the Street," *L'Humanité,* June 11, 1952, p. 1. Italics in the original.

45. *Cominform Bulletin,* editorial, June 13, 1952, p. 1.

46. *L'Humanité,* June 19, 1952, pp. 4–5.

47. Pen-name of Hubert Beuve-Méry, editor of *Le Monde,* who, both as writer and editor, was an important influence in the development of French

neutralism. The article by Courtade which Fajon had in mind may have been one entitled, "It Is the War Party That Must Be 'Neutralized,'" in *L'Humanité*, February 13, 1950, which said that the neutralists, for all their differences with American imperialism, nevertheless were to be regarded as part of the "war camp."

48. *Cahiers du communisme*, August 1952, p. 686.

49. For example, a letter addressed to the president of the republic protesting against the conspiracy charges as a "crude fable," signed by Jean-Marie Domenach, editor-in-chief of the Catholic left-wing magazine, *Esprit*, and twenty-nine other prominent non-Communists of the left. *L'Humanité*, June 21, 1952, p. 4.

50. *L'Humanité*, July 3, 1952, p. 1.

51. *Cominform Bulletin*, July 4, 1952, p. 1 editorial.

52. *Cominform Bulletin*, July 4, 1952. Incidentally, this issue of the *Bulletin* taken as a whole provides a striking documentation of the right-wing cast of the Cominform's inclination in this period. It contains, for example, a lengthy extract from a report by Palmiro Togliatti to the central Committee of the Italian Communist Party on June 21, defining and justifying a broad strategy in prevailing circumstances. In an implied reference to the experience of the French party with the Ridgway riot, Togliatti warned against working-class parties being provoked into "premature clashes and conflicts" and thus precipitating "a regeneration of reaction." Togliatti's definition of a broad "strategy of struggle for peace" provided an ideological justification for the necessity of collaboration with elements of the bourgeoisie which was to become an important document in the subsequent discussions within the Communist parties of the West.

53. *France nouvelle*, July 5, 1952, pp. 6–7.

54. Nos. 7–8, pp. 675–686. No issue of the *Cahiers du communisme* appeared in July.

55. Hsieh manuscript, pp. 145–149, 183–184.

56. It may be significant in this connection that the same August issue of the *Cahiers du communisme* which carried the Billoux article on the formation of a National United Front also devoted forty pages to a translation of Mao Tse-tung's essay, "On Contradiction."

57. The full text is believed to have been published as a brochure by the party under the title, *Pour un puissant Front National Uni*, which is unfortunately unavailable. Two pages of extracts, with excisions indicated and summarized, were published in *L'Humanité*, September 4, 1952, pp. 4–5. A full page of extracts was published in *Cominform Bulletin*, September 12, 1952, p. 3. Brief extracts were also published in *Cahiers du communisme*, September 1952, pp. 819–824, under the title, "L'Unité d'action de la class ouvrière, ciment de l'unité nationale." Quotations used here are largely from the *Cominform Bulletin*, with additions from the other sources.

58. "Communiqué of the Secretariat of the French Communist Party,"

September 16, 1952, *L'Humanité,* September 17, 1952.

59. Report of the politburo presented to the Central Committee by Léon Mauvais, September 3 and 4, 1952, *France nouvelle,* September 27, 1952, pp. 5–8. "Les problèmes de la politique du parti et l'activité fractionnelle des Camarades André Marty et Charles Tillon," document of the politburo, October 3, 1952, *Cahiers du communisme,* October 1952, pp. 936–955; *France nouvelle,* October 4, 1952, pp. 8–11; *L'Humanité,* December 8 and 9, 1952.

60. Auguste Lecoeur, who was expelled from the party two years later, in his book said that Jeannette Vermeersch, wife of Thorez, was responsible for the elimination of Tillon, as a result of a discussion between the two over an aspect of the contribution of women during the war. Tillon is reported as saying: "What do you know about it, you weren't there!" Vermeersch, sensitive over having been in Moscow during the war, like Thorez, resented this and used her influence, which was considerable, against him (*L'Auto-critique attendue,* Paris, 1955, pp. 17–18). Whether or not this was an important factor in the case, it is striking what venomous tensions among the party leaders are revealed in the books of Marty and Lecoeur. This includes their attitude toward each other. In an interview with me in 1959, Lecoeur placed great emphasis upon Marty's personal boorishness as a factor in his unpopularity within the party and in his downfall. Marty died on November 22, 1956, in a hospital near Toulouse.

61. These charges presumably referred to Marty's long-term connection with the MGB, the Soviet police apparatus. At the time of Marty's expulsion, a mimeographed copy of an alleged letter from Marty to Lavrenti Beria, chief of the Soviet police, circulated privately in party channels in Paris, to add substance to the party's charges. The expulsion of Marty coincided with the temporary decline of Beria, and with the trial of Slansky and Geminder in Prague, which appeared to be part of a drive against Beria's international police apparatus.

62. Marty, *L'Affaire Marty* (Paris, 1955).

63. In February and May 1952, another former prominent leader of the resistance, Georges Guingouin, former mayor of Limoges, once known as the "prefect of the Maquis of Limosin," had also come under attack by the party in similar circumstances.

64. Among other charges, Marty and Tillon were accused by the Central Committee of having plotted to seize power in France in 1944. In the course of the indictment, Thorez and the Central Committee found it necessary once again to explain and justify the nonrevolutionary policy of the postwar period, on the grounds that an attempt to seize power in France would have aroused the United States against the Soviet Union. *L'Humanité,* September 17 and October 4, 1952; Rieber, pp. 151–155.

65. Marty, pp. 258–259.

66. Marty, pp. 172–173.

67. Marty, p. 187.

68. Marty, p. 260.

69. I am indebted to Pierre Hervé for his suggestive comments on this point in the course of an interview in 1959.

70. Jean-Marie Domenach, "Tillon-Marty et le 'Front National Uni,'" *L'Esprit,* November 1952, pp. 731–734.

### X. THE NINETEENTH PARTY CONGRESS

1. *Pravda,* August 20, 1952, p. 1.

2. "Ekonomicheskie problemy sotsializma v SSSR," *Bolshevik,* dated September 1952 (but distributed October 2), pp. 1–50. Available in English as supplement to *Current Digest of the Soviet Press,* October 18, 1952, and in a pamphlet under same title published by International Publishers, New York, 1952, 71 pp.

3. I am indebted to Donald S. Zagoria for his detailed analysis of this correspondence, which he generously shared with me.

4. See Chapter 2 above.

5. See Alec Nove, "Recent Developments in Economic Ideas," in *Survey* (London) no. 21–22 (November-December 1957), pp. 19–26; Alfred Zauberman, "The Revisionism in Soviet Economics," in Leopold Labedz, ed., *Revisionism* (London, 1962), pp. 268–280; Conquest, pp. 95–111.

6. *Voprosy ekonomiki,* no. 12 (December 1952; published in January 1953), pp. 102–116.

7. The principal proceedings of the Nineteenth Congress, including these three documents, are conveniently available in English in Leo Gruliow, ed., *Current Soviet Policies* (New York, 1953).

8. Stalin, *Economic Problems of Socialism in the U.S.S.R.* (New York, 1952), p. 28.

9. Stalin, *Economic Problems,* pp. 26, 45.

10. Malenkov, Report of Central Committee, *Current Soviet Policies,* p. 101.

11. Stalin, *Economic Problems,* p. 27.

12. Here he dated his doctrine of "temporary stabilization of capitalism" only to "before the Second World War."

13. Malenkov, Report, p. 101.

14. Stalin, *Economic Problems,* p. 29.

15. Report, p. 106. Three years later, Malenkov was to be criticized for revising this formulation to read that a third world war would mean the end of civilization.

16. Report, p. 104.

17. Stalin, *Economic Problems,* pp. 27–28. Italics added.

18. "The inevitability of wars between capitalist countries remains in force." *Economic Problems,* p. 30.

19. "The contradictions now rending the imperialist camp may lead to a war of one capitalist state against another." Report, p. 105.

20. Malenkov, Report, p. 105.

21. This prophecy was to produce an unexpected backfire among foreign Communists: both Togliatti (*Cominform Bulletin,* November 28, 1952) and Billoux (*Cominform Bulletin,* December 26, 1952) gave evidence of having to argue with comrades who asked the logical question: since war among the capitalist states is inevitable and will result in the end of capitalism, why fight for peace?

22. Malenkov, Report, pp. 105–106.

23. *Economic Problems,* p. 30. Italics in the original.

24. Report, p. 104.

25. *Current Soviet Policies,* p. 236.

26. Report, p. 103.

27. Speech on October 10, 1952, *Cominform Bulletin,* October 17, 1952, pp. 5–6.

28. Malenkov, Report, p. 104.

29. Alexander N. Poskrebyshev, then chief of Stalin's secretariat, *Current Soviet Policies,* p. 214; also Mikhail G. Pervukhin, in his speech on the anniversary of the revolution two weeks later, *Pravda,* November 7, 1952, pp. 2–4.

30. This strategy bears some resemblance to one described as "Neo-Maoist" by John H. Kautsky, in *Moscow and the Communist Party of India* (New York, 1956), pp. 8–14.

31. In his closing speech at the congress, Stalin paid tribute to Thorez and Togliatti for their declarations that their workers would not fight against the Soviet Union. This was the kind of support needed by the Soviet Union from its fraternal parties, he said (*Current Soviet Policies,* p. 235). The point was emphasized again by Pervukhin in his speech on the anniversary of the revolution, cited in note 29.

### XI. THE EVOLUTION OF SOVIET POLICY

1. I. F. Ivashin, "The Periodization of the History of Soviet Foreign Policy," *International Affairs* (Moscow), no. 7 (July 1958), pp. 59–63.

2. Ivashin, p. 62.

3. The editors of *International Affairs,* in an interview with me in 1959, indicated that the controversy had evoked more letters from its readers than any issue discussed in the magazine up to that time. Other articles on the subject may be found in *International Affairs,* no. 2 (February 1958), pp. 63–70; no. 5 (May 1958), pp. 71–75; and no. 7 (July 1958), p. 64.

4. S. Yeshin, "Periodization Should Be Soundly Based," *International Affairs,* no. 7 (July 1958), p. 64.

5. V. M. Khvostov, "A Summing Up of the Discussion Concerning the Periodization of the History of Soviet Foreign Policy," *International Affairs,* no. 8 (August 1958), pp. 67–71.

6. Mikhail E. Airapetyan and Grigori A. Deborin, *Etapi vneshnei politiki*

*SSR* (Stages in the Foreign Policy of the USSR; Moscow, 1961), p. 369. Airapetyan was the author of the article in the February issue of *International Affairs* which started the discussion.

7. Airapetyan and Deborin, p. 396.

8. "The difficulties of periodization have been and remain in the fact that we have to take into account the laws of internal Soviet development as well as the laws governing international development, since Soviet foreign policy has always been implemented against the background of a definite international situation. That is just what we wish to show in our curriculum and concise study aid which . . . neither identify foreign and domestic policy nor divorce them." Ivashin, p. 60.

9. *The Anti-Stalin Campaign*, p. 84.

10. In the Kiev Case, a local official, H. A. Khain and two others, all Jews, were sentenced to death by military tribunal in Kiev in November 1952 for "counter-revolutionary wrecking in the provinces of trade and goods turn-over," and two more were imprisoned for twenty-five years. The case had reverberations within the party as the charges widened of complicity with or lack of vigilance in regard to the "Khain gang." Conquest, *Power and Policy in the USSR,* p. 172.

11. George F. Kennan, *Russia and the West Under Lenin and Stalin* (Boston, 1961), p. 386.

12. Conquest, pp. 170–172.

13. The Italian Communist journalist, Giuseppe Boffa, writes: "There were some who blamed the 'system' for the errors committed during the time of the 'cult.' Answering one such critic a Soviet journalist said: 'It was the system that actually saved us.' He was right. The Socialist regime had made possible the impetuous progress of the USSR, and this progress, which became incompatible with the despotic aspects of Stalin's regime, created the forces which stopped that despotism." *Inside the Khrushchev Era*, p. 84.

14. Mikhail G. Pervukhin, speech on the anniversary of the revolution, *Pravda*, November 7, 1952, pp. 2–4; D. I. Chesnokov, in *Kommunist*, January 1953, pp. 14–34.

15. *Pravda,* December 26, 1952, p. 1.

16. Interview with Saiffudin Kitchlu, February 14, 1953, reported in Salisbury, *Moscow Journal*, pp. 331–332.

17. Pierre Fougeyrollas, "France," in *Survey*, no. 42 (June 1962: special issue on "Polycentrism"), pp. 121–122.

18. "Ob imperialisticheskoe 'integratsii' v zapadnoi evrope ('Obshchii Rynok'): Tezisy" (On the Imperialistic "Integration" in Western Europe ["Common Market"]: Theses), *Pravda*, August 26, 1962, pp. 3–4.

19. *International Affairs* (Moscow), no. 10 (October 1962), pp. 93–98, abridged preface to forthcoming first volume of a projected three-volume series, International Relations after the Second World War, to be published

by the Institute of World Economy and International Relations, USSR Academy of Sciences.

20. *Pravda,* September 29, 1951.

21. For example, the theses cited in note 18.

22. Lee, *The Soviet Air Force,* p. 195.

# INDEX